Reflections of a Police Psychologist

Second Edition

Reflections of a Police Psychologist

Jack A. Digliani, PhD, EdD

To order additional copies of this book, contact:
Xlibris
1-888-795-4274
www.Xlibris.com
Orders@Xlibris.com
582791

Contents

Acknowledgements

I would like to thank my colleagues and those police officers, deputy sheriffs, state troopers, park rangers, and other law enforcement officers who have contributed to this book by sharing their thoughts, feelings, and experiences.

I am grateful to Bruce Glasscock, the Fort Collins Police Services (FCPS) Chief of Police from 1984 to 1990. It was under his administration that the FCPS Traumatic Incident Debriefing Team and the FCPS Office of Human Services were created. Thank you to Howard "Bud" Reed, Sherri Wagner, and Dave Wilson, the FCPS police officers who joined me in comprising the first FCPS Traumatic Incident Debriefing (Peer Support) Team.

I would like to especially thank Lorie, my wife of many years for her unwavering support, faith, and love. Now and forever.

To law enforcement officers for their service and sacrifice.

Author photo by Mike Halloran.

Foreword

The streets are protected each and every day by cops who feel, cops who love, cops who need and want—just like you. They are sometimes single, sometimes married, sometimes moms and dads. All have bills to pay, yards to mow and a life away from the job. Yet even off duty, they carry the emotional baggage and mental strain of what they sometimes have to do to stay alive and make it home. Occasionally, the bucket in their mind reserved for miserable memories and pictures gets full and threatens to overflow. When that happens, there is no one more valuable—more indispensible—than a competent police psychologist. He or she can literally save the life of a hero worth saving. A gallant soldier we pay to protect our community.

Dr. Jack—Jack Digliani—does this like few others. He knows, like few police psychologists can, because before he was a shrink, he was a cop. While attending university to become a leading expert in this highly specialized field of psychology, he worked as a police officer in Wyoming and Colorado, learning first-hand the trials and tribulations with which he would one day be called upon to help his brothers and sisters—the men and women still on the street.

Those who first come to him as his patients ultimately discover that Dr. Jack is a peer, a friend, a brother, and a trusted confidant. I did. I still do.

Trooper Jim Geeting, Wyoming Highway Patrol, Retired
Author of *The Badge: Thoughts from a State Trooper*

Author's Notes

I have chosen to write in a style that I feel is conducive to easier reading. For the most part, I have taken the liberty of using the masculine pronoun in sentences that require a pronoun. This permits the avoidance of the more descriptive yet more cumbersome phrases *he or she, himself or herself,* and so forth. I regret that the English language does not have a single pronoun that is inclusive of both genders. Rest assured that unless otherwise specified, the information applies equally well and is intended to include men and women. I hope that this style of writing, selected only for ease of reading, is viewed as nothing more than convention by female readers. Certainly, it is so intended.

The use of the terms *officer* and *police officer* are intended to include civilian police department employees, deputy sheriffs, state troopers, park rangers, and other law enforcement or peace officers at all levels of government.

Although many issues and concepts are presented and discussed in terms of police officers and policing, most are equally applicable to those outside of police work.

The Second Edition (2015) includes the changes made in the earlier Revised Edition (2010). Both editions include references to the Colorado Revised Statutes (C.R.S.). State statutes are dynamic and always subject to change. Readers should consult the C.R.S. to confirm pertinent statute designations and text before implementing any statute-based programs or actions.

The various chapters of this book may be read independently of one another. References to other chapters are indicated when appropriate.

The ideas and opinions expressed are the result of many years of personal experiences as a husband, deputy sheriff, police officer, detective, mental health associate, and police psychologist.

For additional information visit *www.jackdigliani.com*

Introduction

Police Psychology

H ow is police psychology different from general psychology? Police psychology differs from general psychology in that the major areas of interest in police psychology are those that are inclusive to the profession of policing. These areas include psychological assessment of police candidates, fitness for duty evaluations, job stress management, critical incident protocol development, supervision of peer support teams, trauma therapy, officer and family counseling, specialized police training, and police career development. Because the fundamental principles of psychology apply as well to the profession of policing as they do any occupation, it makes sense to think of police psychology as the study and application of fundamental psychological principles as they relate to the profession of policing.

A psychologist that works in the area of police psychology is called a *police psychologist*. Currently there is not a legal definition or title protection for the use of this designation, although use of the title "psychologist" is regulated in Colorado and all other states.

Police psychologists are professionally associated through a number of organizations, including the International Association of Chiefs of Police (IACP) and the American Psychological Association (APA). The APA recognizes police psychology as a specialty within the field of psychology in Division 18, *Psychologists in Public Service, Section: Police and Public Safety* (n.d., para.,1).

Police psychology differs from criminal psychology. As a police psychologist, I have encountered persons who have asked me what it is like working with criminal offenders. My reply is usually the same: "I work with police officers. Criminal psychologists work with offenders." Professionally, there is no prohibition against a psychologist working with police officers and criminal offenders as long as established ethical standards of conduct and statutory requirements are maintained. However, my practice has always been limited to police officers, police employees, and their families. This is the true realm of police psychologists.

Law Enforcement and Policing

It is more accurate to use the term *policing* than it is to use the term *law enforcement* because modern police officers do much more than enforce the law. Although law enforcement is a major responsibility of police officers, police officers serve their communities in a variety of additional ways. Police officers function as peacekeepers, negotiators, teachers, role models, advisors, individual and family counselors, security consultants, community representatives, problem solvers—the list goes on and on. One thing is certain, policing in America today has become a multifaceted profession which brings with it an increased demand for the acquisition of special knowledge and unique skills.

Most people would agree that policing looks quite different today than it has in the past. The advances in policing technology over the last several decades were not likely foreseeable by police officers of the 1940s and 1950s. Some of the more obvious changes in policing include the use of ballistic vests (policing in America years ago was regularly conducted without such protection), miniature communication and recording devices, dashboard and personal cameras, high-capacity semiautomatic pistol magazines (many police departments previously prohibited the carrying of semiautomatic handguns citing their unreliability), global positioning and navigation devices, and computers mounted inside police vehicles.

The development of policing technology has not been limited to that mentioned. Research into the realm of alternative weaponry has produced an array of less-lethal technologies, including rubber baton weapons, beanbag rounds, chemical weapons, and electrical stun devices. Additionally, scientific advances now allow police officers to solve cases based on DNA evidence and the results of increasingly sophisticated laboratory procedures.

Training and tactics have also evolved. Patrol officers can now summon specially trained police officers or units to address particular situations. Police officers with advanced training in crisis intervention now assist other officers dealing with persons who are seriously mentally ill, as well as help other officers when dealing with families in crisis. Police hostage and crisis negotiators regularly work with Special Weapons and Tactics (SWAT) units to resolve difficult and dangerous situations. Even the on-scene assistance of police psychologists during SWAT operations has become more common. This is very different from the days when "beat" cops were expected to handle any situation that might arise, no matter how dangerous or complex.

There is inherent risk in policing. Due to differences in political views, personal values, patterns of thoughts and beliefs, and the ultimately unpredictable nature of human beings, this risk will never be zero. Police agencies counterbalance the risk inherent in policing by applying the three T's of policing—Training, Tactics, and Technology.

Dangerous Environments, Police Officers, and the Community

It is a sad commentary that American communities must be considered dangerous environments; however, this is a fact for police officers. For a glimpse into the police world, think about a job where every one of your clients must continually be evaluated for the risk that they pose to your safety. This is not to say that everyone represents a risk, but only that they must be continually evaluated. This is true even in "safe" neighborhoods. Many police officers have been killed or injured in safe neighborhoods by "good" people. This is the reality of policing.

New officers must adapt to a work environment where there is danger. Sometimes the danger is known. Other times, the danger is unknown. Confronting an armed bank robber represents a known danger. Stopping a vehicle with several occupants represents a possible unknown danger. In all cases, officers rely upon their observations and assessment of actual or potential danger to determine the appropriate course of action.

Remaining mindful that even initially cooperative persons may become violent is a component every police officer's reality. It does not matter if the person is young or elderly, male or female, verbal or silent, attractive or homely, intoxicated or sober, all can become a threat. This compels police officers to live in an occupational world of *assumption of possible threat*. It is much different than most other workers, who live in an occupational world of *assumption of safety*.

The truth of the matter is that American society accepts a degree of risk for its police officers. This is expressed in social acceptances of what constitutes appropriate police behavior. Consider the case of an escaping bank robber who shot a bank employee during the robbery. Once the police locate and stop the getaway vehicle, no one would object to police officers taking a guns-drawn approach. In police terminology this is called a *felony* or *high-risk* stop. In such vehicle contacts, police officers take cover positions, prepare themselves to use deadly force, and order the suspect out of the car. In this bank robbery scenario, engaging the high-risk car-stop procedure is the best that police officers can do to protect themselves and the public. (Note: for those unfamiliar with police terminology, *cover* differs from *concealment* in that objects of cover will likely stop a bullet while objects of concealment will only keep officers from being seen.)

Now think of police officers taking a similar approach with *all* vehicle contacts. Keep in mind that all vehicle stops may represent an *unknown* danger to officers. Because officers cannot know the unknown, it would be safer for them to routinely utilize high-risk procedures. But is this policing strategy too aggressive? Maybe not, when you consider that several police officers are killed and many more are injured each year by the driver or a passenger of a vehicle that has been stopped for reasons no more serious than a traffic infraction. However, there is a problem.

The problem with this kind of universal, defensive police behavior, albeit safer for officers, is that it is unacceptable to the vast majority of citizens. In fact, it is unacceptable to the vast majority of police officers. High-risk defensive tactics are used by police only upon justifying cause. During vehicle stops, even though there may be an actual danger, without such knowledge or other indications of threat, officers will approach the vehicle and greet the driver. Although this places officers at greater risk, (officers are without cover, can easily be watched, and can be surprised by the unanticipated actions of vehicle occupants), it is an accepted risk. There is not a community or police agency in America that would endorse the high-risk vehicle stop procedure as a common practice. In law, policy directives, and in social acceptances, police officers are expected to assess risk and act accordingly. If their assessment is incorrect or if there is unknown malicious intent, officers suffer the consequences.

In America, police authority and options for police action are intentionally limited. The limits of police authority are known and acknowledged by police officers. In order to protect the constitutional liberties of citizens and to better serve the community, police officers willingly accept the increased personal risk associated with policing a free society.

The degree of risk that America accepts for its police officers varies. It varies over time, individually and among groups, and with perceived social realities. The accepted risk for police officers involves the balance of individual rights with the safety of officers. Most citizens and police officers support a reasonable individual-rights/safety-of-officers balance.

Police officer risk is increased by a small percentage of persons that maintain anti-police sentiments. Of these, some voice their opinions peacefully. Others express themselves through violence. Those willing to act out violently represent a significant risk to police officers, including the risk of assassination. This is the current risk status of policing in America.

Chapter 1

The Transition

Transitioning from civilian to police officer is a complex process, one which requires significant effort and a change in mindset. To make sense of this, you have to think about what it means to learn a new job. When individuals attempt to learn a new job, they must gain knowledge specific to the occupation and acquire relevant skills. This combination of job knowledge and behavioral abilities is sometimes referred to as a skill set. The skill set necessary for a police officer is characterized by the well known police expression, *serve and protect*.

Serving and protecting in modern society requires a wide range of knowledge and behavioral skill. Police officers must have knowledge of the law, understand discretion, be able to perform life-saving first aid, know how to direct traffic, evaluate child welfare, investigate crimes, assist the mentally ill, operate emergency vehicles, know how and when to protect themselves with appropriate force, make arrests and control violent suspects—well, you get the idea. To begin the process of acquiring the knowledge and skill necessary to become a police officer, police candidates are required to attend training academies.

New officers who have successfully completed their training academy advance to field training (chapter 2). Some officers who have done well in academy training struggle in field training. In fact, not every officer that has successfully completed academy training successfully completes field training. These officers leave field training for a number of reasons. Some officers leave voluntarily. They discover that policing is other than what was anticipated and decide to resign. Other officers are terminated. Termination occurs when new officers consistently fail to meet minimal acceptable standards of performance in at least one critical area of their field training program.

Accidental and Intentional Injury

All work environments produce some risk of accidental injury or death. High-risk work environments for accidental injury or death include underground mining, firefighting, roadwork, and commercial fishing. Policing differs from these work environments in at least one significant aspect: in addition to the probability of accidental injury or death, police officers also confront an increased risk of *intentional* injury or death. This is because there are persons that, at least at times, seek to kill or otherwise injure police officers. New officers must come to understand this feature of policing and of human behavior.

The problem for officers is that most of the time they cannot be certain beforehand whether any particular person at any particular time has the intent to injure or kill. In response to this inability to ascertain threat before it is presented, police officers are trained to routinely engage officer safety strategies. These strategies are designed to increase the margin of safety for police officers. They enhance the probability that officers will be able to mount some defense in the event of an attack. Fortunately for the police, most people respect the law and would not attempt to injure or kill police officers.

The possibility of intentional injury or death is not unique to policing. Another occupation characterized by an intentional injury or death risk is combat military.

Confrontation

Confrontation is an unavoidable stressor of policing. New officers must have or must develop a means of coping with confrontation. Even when the police are requested to assist in particular situations, there is often at least one person who does not want officers present. Some confrontations are mild and consist of verbal discussion or nonverbal posturing. Others are critical and may involve officers fighting for their lives. Like everyone else, police officers have a right to protect and defend themselves. Unlike others, police officers also have a duty to protect and defend others. This is true even if it means that officers must place themselves in jeopardy. There are consequences for officers that fail to meet this duty, including departmental discipline, employment termination, and civil lawsuits. This is different from most other occupations.

Confrontation on a daily basis is one of the unique aspects of policing. Remaining aware of potential confrontation and potential threat is the mindset required of police officers. Officers compromise this mindset at their own risk.

Beyond Mindset

In addition to the development of the appropriate mindset, new officers must address three other primary challenges: (1) geography, (2) report writing, and (3) the application of authority.

Geography. Some new officers have lived for years in their jurisdiction before they were hired. Others moved to the jurisdiction because they were hired. In either case, officers must learn the jurisdiction geography. Officers that have lived in the jurisdiction have some background knowledge of the streets, alleys, businesses, and so forth. Officers new to the jurisdiction must learn it from scratch.

There are many ways to learn the layout of a jurisdiction. All require effort. If you are a visual person, you can study maps and perhaps mentally retrieve or "see" the map in your imagination when needed. If you are more of an experiential person, there is no substitute for walking or driving the area. Verbal learners will want to be read directions or read about various locations. Most of us can take advantage of all these learning strategies.

For officers that have grown up in the jurisdiction, this fact alone does not guarantee jurisdiction familiarity. Being familiar with the city in which you grew up does not always translate into knowing the city in the way police officers need to know it. Fortunately, the learning of jurisdiction geography is positively correlated with experience and exposure.

Report writing. New officers must be able to document their observations and actions. Good writing skills are necessary but insufficient for good report writing. Police report writing must be complete, concise, accurate, and objective. Learning to structure these features into a report can be challenging, even for good writers.

Another difficulty involves how the report is generated. Many agencies require that officers dictate their reports. Some officers are good report writers, but poor report dictators. These officers experience *mic fright*, a normally temporary condition characterized by a loss of thought cohesiveness and mind-blank. Mic fright is a type of performance anxiety. It usually subsides or disappears after a period of practice. To manage mic fright, some officers write their reports and read them into the recorder. Unfortunately, this defeats the primary purpose of dictating reports...saving time. Some agencies require that officers type reports. Years ago, officers were not required to have typing skills. Today it is an essential skill. It is another example of how policing has evolved.

Application of authority. New officers must have or develop a conception of how to utilize police authority. They must avoid becoming "badge heavy" (exercising police authority in a heavy-handed manner) while also avoiding a failure to exercise sufficient authority when needed. As part of this balance, new officers must learn *police discretion.* Police discretion is the long-accepted practice of officers exercising individual judgment. If you have ever been stopped by a police officer for a traffic violation and released without receiving a citation, you can thank police discretion. Learning how to appropriately apply police authority for the good of the community and to meet the mission of the police agency is a primary challenge for new officers.

Officer Reputation

New officers will earn a reputation. It is inevitable. They will earn a reputation with their trainers, coworkers, supervisors, dispatchers, and citizens. The question becomes, "Being that developing a reputation is inevitable, why not earn a good one?" New officers should make an effort to develop a good reputation. However, a good reputation should not be pursued directly; it should be pursued through performance. Good reputations develop from good performance. Another way of saying this is, "Don't tell them how good you are, show them how good you are." For new officers, this means working diligently to learn and perform the job.

To succeed, officers must maintain their part of the employment bargain. The officer's side of the bargain is performance. The department's side of the bargain is appropriate training, adequate equipment, competent supervision, and fair compensation. Simply stated, the employment bargain is agency support for officer performance. Officer performance expectations are expressed in the police officer job description, departmental mission and values statements, departmental policies and procedures, supervisory expectations, and the law. When officers fail to meet their part of the bargain, their reputations suffer. The same is true for police agencies. The agency must support its officers and meet its part of the bargain. (Note: the general concept of compensation for performance should not be confused with the various specific pay-for-performance salary systems used by some police departments. Pay-for-performance salary systems tie performance ratings to rate of pay. This is different from the philosophy of compensation for performance.)

If a poor reputation is developed, it can be changed, but only slowly. To improve a poor work reputation, consistently good work is needed. However, changing a poor work reputation is more difficult than establishing a good one from the beginning. When it comes to reputation, new officers should endeavor to start strong, stay strong, and finish strong. This is easily accomplished by performing conscientiously and maintaining a positive work ethic.

For officers, one of the most clearly seen features of a positive work ethic is responding to calls. New officers should remember throughout their careers: *any call, anytime, anywhere*. Complaining that dispatch is assigning calls too close to the end of shift, out of an assigned district, or beneath some perceived skill level is indicative of a poor work ethic and a sure way to create a poor reputation. Trust your dispatch; take any call without complaint. Keep your part of the bargain. Every call reinforces your work ethic and contributes to your experience. After five years on the job, you want to have five years of experience, not one year of experience five times.

Like new officers, veteran officers can enhance or maintain their work reputation by following the *any call, anytime, anywhere* work ethic.

Police Truthfulness

Always tell the truth. As a new officer it may be tempting to misrepresent an action or observation in an attempt to protect yourself from getting into trouble, to accomplish some goal, or to be seen as "one of the boys." Don't do it. Lying undermines the very foundation of police professionalism. It will destroy your credibility, undermine your reputation, and lead to several other major difficulties. If you make a mistake, bring it to the attention of supervisors. If a citizen files a complaint about your behavior, be honest when describing your actions during internal inquiry. Many officers have been terminated for being untruthful in circumstances wherein their actual behavior would have resulted in no or lesser consequences. Stay true to this most important of police values: *always tell the truth*.

Police Action

New (and veteran) officers should act as if they are being recorded. This idea helps officers to moderate their behavior and maintain a high level of professionalism. In today's world, acting as if you are being recorded is an excellent idea. After all, there is a considerable probability that it is true!

In one case, a police agency received a complaint about the verbal behavior of an officer during a vehicle contact. After the complaint was filed, the complainant produced a recording of the exchange. Although the complainant was the driver of the vehicle, the recording was made by a back seat passenger using a cell phone. At the time, neither the driver nor the officer knew that they were being recorded. The recording demonstrated the intensity of the officer's communication, as well as the numerous threats, insults, and expletives. Upon internal investigation interview, the officer explained that he was just "chewing out" the group of young men to help "keep them straight." The department found the recording telling and the officer's explanation lacking. His employment was terminated following completion of the investigation.

This represents one of many times that officers have been undone by recordings made by citizen observers, store surveillance cameras, residential security cameras, and cell phone recorders. Interestingly, the bad behavior of some police officers has been confirmed by their own in-car cameras. Evidently, even knowing that one's actions are being recorded is not enough to contain the inappropriate behavior of some officers.

The idea of acting as if being recorded is related to the notion of integrity. This is well expressed in U.S. Air Force Doctrine Document 1-1, *Leadership and Force Development*. In this document, integrity is defined as "the willingness to do what is right even when no one is looking" (Dobbins, 2008, 1). This is the other side of the "acting as if being recorded" coin. Whether being recorded or no one is looking, new officers should endeavor to act at all times within the finest traditions of policing. Such a commitment reflects not only the highest level of police professionalism, it is also the best defense for officers falsely accused of wrongdoing.

Psychology of Earning and Psychology of Entitlement

New officers must keep in mind that what can be accomplished is often related to the effort expended. A good way to remember this is what you can achieve is related to how hard you are willing to work. This idea is part of the psychology of earning.

The psychology of earning is different from the psychology of entitlement. In the psychology of entitlement, persons believe that good things should happen to them solely because they somehow inherently deserve it (this is different from the legal notion of entitlement).

When learning to become a police officer and in other areas of your life, avoid the psychology of entitlement. If you are pursuing a goal, apply effort to increase the probability of success. Make short-term sacrifices for long-term gains (like studying when you would prefer to go out with friends). Your efforts will almost always be rewarded. In any event, if you work hard and fail, you will know that you gave your best. This is the most that you can ask of yourself.

Work and Luck

What about work and luck? Are some people just luckier than others? Maybe so, but as the saying goes: *the harder you work, the luckier you'll get.*

Chapter 2

Field Training and PATROL

N ew police officers have always learned the job from veteran police officers. Years ago, the best a new officer could expect was to find a veteran officer who would "break him in." With this method of training, bad as well as good work habits were passed down from police veteran to police rookie. Too many times this included learning how to avoid supervisors, how to take advantage of the system, and where to find free coffee.

If a new officer did not have a veteran officer to assist him in learning the job, the officer had to learn by observation, personal effort, and trial and error. As you might expect, the quality of police officers produced by this type of initiation into policing was quite variable. The skills of new officers ranged from acceptable to nearly incompetent. Today, things are much different. There are established standards of knowledge and performance for new police officers. Most new police officers are extensively trained, and accepting free coffee will get police officers fired in many jurisdictions.

The training sequence for most new police officers includes completing (1) a basic police academy, (2) a police department pre-service skills academy, and (3) a field training and evaluation program.

Basic Police Academy and Pre-service Skills Academy

There are differences among the training academies of various jurisdictions; however, the core curriculum of most basic police academies is similar.

Basic police academies can vary widely in their orientation. Some academies resemble military boot camp, while others look and feel more like college environments. In fact, in some states basic police academy training is conducted through local community colleges.

The length of basic police academies also varies. Police academies can range anywhere from less than ten weeks to over twenty-four weeks.

If police agencies conduct their own academies, the basic and pre-service skills academy are often combined. For police agencies that rely on outside basic academy training, the pre-service skills academy is normally conducted in-house as an independent training component following the completion of the basic academy.

Field Training

Police field training is different from its predecessor, *on-the-job training* (OJT). Although OJT programs involved new officers working with veteran officers, OJT was normally haphazard in its approach. It provided new officers with some supervised exposure to policing, but did little more. OJT was normally time limited (an officer would ride with various officers for days or weeks) and much depended on the willingness of veteran officers to train. The quality of OJT varied widely among police agencies. Similar to the "breaking in" method of police training, just how well-trained new officers were following the completion of OJT was anybody's guess.

In contrast, field training is formally structured, has specified goals, processes new officer experiences in a number of ways, and includes standards of performance and evaluation. Field training programs were developed when it was recognized that (1) OJT programs were lacking and (2) academy training was necessary but not sufficient to best develop the knowledge, skills, and emotional stability necessary to become a modern-day police officer.

Modern field training programs are designed to build upon the classroom and training exercises of the academy. These programs are known by various names such as Field Training Officer, Field Training and Evaluation, Patrol Training Officer, and Recruit Training and Field Evaluation. All involve the field training of new officers by pairing them with veteran officers.

Field training has improved significantly over the past decades. There are two primary police field training programs in use today: the Field Training Officer Program (FTOP) and the Patrol Training Officer Program (PTOP). The Field Training Officer Program was created in the late 1960s. For many years it served as the standard for police field training. The Patrol Training Officer Program was developed in the early 2000s. It is the result of U.S. Department of Justice funded research to develop a new and comprehensive police field training program. The Field Training Officer Program differs from the Patrol Training Officer Program in philosophical orientation and process. Despite their differences, both utilize training phases: Phase I, II, III, and IV for the Field

Training Officer Program and, Orientation Phase, Integration Phase, Phase A, Phase B, Midterm Evaluation Phase, Phase C, Phase D, and Final Evaluation Phase for the Patrol Training Officer Program. Although the discussion below is presented in terms of the more traditional FTOP, most elements are equally applicable for field training officers of the PTOP.

Field Training Officer

A field training officer is a veteran officer who has received specific training in how to train and evaluate new officers. A field training officer is called an *FTO* in the FTOP, and a *PTO* in the PTOP.

FTO and Phase Training

The core of FTOP phase training involves field exposure and evaluation in at least four phases. In a four phase FTOP training program, each of the first three phases lasts about four weeks. The fourth phase is usually two weeks. The new officer is paired with different FTOs in each of the first three phases. In the fourth phase, the first phase FTO returns to complete a final evaluation of the new officer's performance. The reason for different FTOs in the first three phases of field training is so that new officers are exposed to the working or policing style of various veterans.

As a new officer moves through field training, the responsibility for decision making, police discretion, work management, time management, enforcement activities, and general policing, changes. To better understand this, consider veteran officers working solo. Veteran officers are responsible for patrolling their assigned districts, responding to calls for service, self-initiated activities, and so on. When not on an assigned call, officers can choose to enforce traffic laws, execute warrants, contact business owners, or perform a myriad of other police related duties. This is possible because police officers work autonomously. They are responsible for deciding how their assigned district will be policed on any given day. This responsibility can be thought of as being in *car command*. In other words, police officers are for the most part, in command of how they police their assigned district.

In field training programs, when the FTO is in car command, the FTO has primary responsibility for the policing activities of the unit. In Phase I, the FTO starts in car command. During this period, the FTO is functioning as a model for the new officer. As Phase I progresses, and as deemed appropriate by the FTO, the new officer incrementally assumes greater responsibility for car command. The general process of moving car command from the FTO to the new officer continues throughout field training. By the end of Phase III, the new officer assumes nearly all the responsibilities of car command. This helps to prepare the new officer for Phase IV. (In reality, the FTO is always in car command. This is because the new officer is subordinate to the FTO. However, the gradual transfer of this responsibility is part of the field training process.)

As mentioned, Phase IV reunites the new officer with the Phase I FTO. This phase is sometimes called *checkout*. To deemphasize the role of the FTO during checkout, the FTO wears civilian clothes. Throughout checkout, new officers are not permitted to use the FTO as a resource. The primary role of the checkout FTO is the evaluation of the new officer's semi-solo performance. As expected, the checkout FTO will engage in any action necessary in emergency situations.

To successfully complete checkout, new officers must consistently meet minimum acceptable standards of performance. If they fail to accomplish this, they are not advanced to independent assignment. Depending upon actual circumstances, new officers that fail to complete Phase IV may be required to complete remedial training and reevaluation, or may be terminated from the program.

Psychologist and Training/Recruit Officer Liaison—PATROL

Learning a new job is stressful. In 1990, after considering the stressors inherent in learning how to become a police officer, I developed the *Psychologist and Training/Recruit Officer Liaison* (PATROL) program. The PATROL program is proactive and brings the police psychologist and new officers together very early in the training process. It is comprised of a group orientation and training presentation within the pre-service skills academy, and individual meetings at least once during each of the first three FTOP training phases. Spouses are encouraged to participate.

The PATROL program is easily adapted to the PTOP training phases. The meetings between the psychologist and new officers would be scheduled for the Orientation Phase and all or some combination of Phases A, B, C, and D.

The PATROL program is founded upon four principles: (1) that counseling can be supportive and proactive, (2) that early exposure of new officers to the police psychologist increases the probability that officers will seek counseling when it is likely to help, (3), that problematic behavior can be targeted for change from a multidimensional perspective, and (4) that the training experience of new officers is enhanced by meetings with the police psychologist. Below is a descriptive outline of the PATROL program.

Orientation and Training. During orientation and training many issues are discussed. Topics include career choice, adult learning, stress and anxiety management, family dynamics and issues, being new to the community, departmental policy, FTO program, critical incidents, PATROL, and services of the peer support team and police psychologist.

Meeting during FTO Phase I. Information discussed during phase meetings is confidential. Reconciling the reality of police work with expectation is the primary focus of the Phase I session. Within this framework, officer observations are processed, officer safety is discussed, stressor and anxiety management strategies are assessed, application of skills is encouraged, and features of reputation and work ethic are explored. Family issues are assessed. Specific problematic issues are identified and addressed.

Meeting during FTO Phase II. Issues surrounding the Phase II session frequently involve motivation and persistence. Some new officers report that field training is more rigorous or stressful than anticipated. Officers with prior experience sometimes struggle with being in training again. The psychologist works to enhance motivation by pointing out successes, commenting on the growing sense of competence, discussing alternative learning and stressor management strategies, identifying problem areas, and designing specific interventions. Emphasis is placed upon the assumption of responsibility, officer discretion, and the appropriate application of authority.

Meeting during FTO Phase III. The Phase III session centers on rehearsal for Phase IV. In addition to stressor management and job skill enhancement, officers are encouraged to scan their knowledge and skill level for areas in which they need improvement. They remediate these areas or bring them to the attention of the FTO for assistance. The FTO then works to provide the new officer with the appropriate review, practice, exposure, or experience. In preparation for Phase IV, new officers implement the three Rs: *Review, Rehearse, Repeat.*

Phase IV. Checkout. Upon successful completion of Phase III, the new officer is advanced to Phase IV. As the focus of this phase is independent behavior, Phase IV meetings are optional. Phase IV appointments may be requested by the new officer, by the officer's FTO, or recommended by the police psychologist. Upon successful completion of Phase IV, field training is completed.

<h2 align="center">PATROL Program Features</h2>

The PATROL program is flexible and may be adjusted to meet individual needs. For instance:

1. More than one session per phase may be requested by the new officer or FTO.
2. Family members of new officers may initiate independent counseling programs.
3. The FTO may attend any or all (or portions) of the sessions if requested by the new officer.
4. The psychologist may share information with FTOs and supervisors upon request (with waiver of confidentiality). This permits a team approach for performance improvement.
5. The FTO and new officer may arrange joint sessions with the police psychologist to address a specific performance issue.
6. The new officer may initiate a comprehensive counseling program. Such programs can involve other significant persons and extend beyond FTOP training.
7. If the new officer is failing to progress as expected, counseling can be integrated into a remedial plan. Such plans may involve family members of new officers.
8. If the new officer fails to succeed in the FTO program, counseling may assist the officer and/or FTOs in processing the officer's resignation or termination.

The PATROL program was new in 1990 and was considered experimental. No one knew how FTOs or new officers would respond to working with the department "shrink" as part of police training. PATROL was first initiated within the Fort Collins Police Services in 1990, followed shortly thereafter by its introduction into the Loveland Police Department.

One of the most controversial aspects of PATROL was the confidential nature of the phase meetings. This feature meant that new officers and the psychologist could discuss the behaviors of the FTO, training styles, personal relationship of the FTO/new officer, and so on, without any of this information being available to the FTO. To their credit, the FTOs of both agencies immediately endorsed and supported PATROL. It was quickly recognized that the FTO, the new officer, and the police psychologist shared the same goal—the success of the new officer. The FTOs were willing to try something new in the hope that it might enhance the training experience of new officers.

The PATROL program has proven its efficacy and is no longer experimental. The feedback received from new officers and trainers alike has been overwhelmingly positive for well over two decades. Due to the success of the PATROL program for police officers, similar programs were developed for jail deputies and corrections officers, emergency services dispatchers (Communications Training Support Program) and police records personnel (Records Training Support Program).

One of the most significant ancillary benefits of PATROL has been the reduction of perceived stigma associated with visiting the psychologist. Through PATROL, new officers become acquainted with the psychologist early in their careers. They work with the psychologist through the skills academy and field training. They sit in the psychologist's office and get to know the psychologist as a person. They learn first-hand what they can accomplish together. In essence, the mystique of the psychologist's office is diminished. This helps to establish and maintain a positive relationship between the psychologist and new officers. Officers come to see that meeting with the psychologist is just another venue for addressing relevant issues. Stigma reduction has been a highly desirable secondary benefit of PATROL.

As a preemptive counseling program, PATROL is designed to assist new officers prior to the development of psychological and performance difficulties. Veteran police officers can also benefit from preemptive counseling. This is especially true for those officers in highly stressful assignments such as SWAT, crisis negotiation, homicide and assault investigation, and the investigation of crimes involving child victimization and exploitation.

PATROL Information

Over the years, the information gathered from the officers participating in the PATROL program has led to several relevant insights into police field training. For the most part, new officers speak highly of their FTOs and the field training program. This is a testament to the efforts, professionalism, and conscientiousness of the field training officers. However, several FTO pitfalls have been identified. FTOs should remain mindful of the pitfalls and work to avoid them.

FTO Pitfalls

The majority of new officer PATROL comments have centered on the issue of FTOs not training enough. This is pitfall #1.

Pitfall #1 is assuming that the new officer is learning without an FTO effort to train. This FTO training strategy relies heavily upon modeling. Although modeling is one of the most effective adult learning strategies, high-functioning FTOs engage in active training, using all methods of adult learning. Lacking active training, some new officers have reported that their FTO did not train at all. To avoid pitfall #1, *remember to keep the* "T" *in* FTO.

Pitfall #2 is moving from training to evaluation too soon. New officers in field training need to be trained before they can be evaluated. Assessing the amount of training any new officer requires in specific areas is a primary responsibility of the FTO. Many new officers have reported that they thought their FTOs relied too heavily on academy training and did not provide adequate field training in evaluated areas. Moving from training to evaluation too soon is possible in FTO programs because FTOs have training and evaluation responsibilities. The Patrol Training Officer program has addressed this issue by separating training and evaluation phases. PTO's either train or evaluate. Supporters of the PTO program view this as a significant improvement in police officer field training.

Pitfall #3 is *reverse bias* and is related to pitfalls #1 and #2. Reverse bias involves officers who are new to a department but come with prior policing experience. It is relatively easy for an FTO to rely on a new officer's prior policing experience. In some cases, these new officers have more overall experience than their FTO. No matter. FTOs must train as they would any new officer. Any advantage held by experienced officers will show itself as they progress through the program. *A word of caution*: having prior policing experience does not always translate into having an advantage in a new police department. Prior knowledge can conflict with new information. Prior skills can interfere with learning new techniques. For example, a new officer that is well-skilled in arrest and control style A may have a difficult time learning arrest and control style B. This is because the habit-strength of style A must be overcome. This can cause initial confusion and detrimentally influence field performance. In memory theory, when previous information interferes with remembering something new, it is called *proactive interference*. When newer information interferes with remembering something older, it is called *retroactive interference*. FTOs should be able to identify cases of memory interference and address them appropriately. With time, patience, and practice, memory interference will diminish and the desired knowledge or performance will be maintained. In summary, to avoid pitfall #3, train all new officers in all areas. Do not get caught in the trap of assuming that new officers with prior policing experience know how to be police officers in their new department.

Pitfall #4 is inconsistent information. In some FTO programs, FTOs do not meet on a regular basis. This means that they do not share information. The lack of FTO communication increases the probability of inconsistent FTO performance. There is not much that is more confusing to new officers than being told one thing by one FTO and later having that information contradicted by another FTO. This circumstance represents a basic failure in the organization and functioning of the FTO program. Although it is recognized that FTOs have varying policing styles, information that *can* be consistent *should* be consistent. This is also true of information or tactics involving non-FTO department instructors. An actual example will help to illustrate this point: several new officers had recently completed the department skills academy. In the skills academy, department experts taught a specific technique as part of arrest and control. Later, while in the FTO program, a new officer applied the technique learned in the skills academy. It was different than that used by the FTO. The FTO "corrected" the new officer. The new officer informed the FTO that "this is the way we were taught to do it in the skills academy." Upon inquiry, the FTO learned that the technique had changed. The new officer knew it; the FTO did not. The technique used by the FTO had become obsolete and was no longer being used by the department! For FTOs to avoid this pitfall, do not forget that new officers have just completed weeks of academy training. Make certain that your knowledge is consistent with that of the department experts and other FTOs. Keep yourself current.

Pitfall #5 is not enough patience. Many new officers say that in cases where there is no emergency, some FTOs have been too quick to take over due to lack of patience. Having an FTO take over when it is not necessary tends to undermine new officer confidence and impede skill development. To avoid pitfall #5, FTOs should be patient in circumstances that permit it.

Pitfall #6 is intentionally adding to stress levels. An actual example will best explain this pitfall. A new officer reported that his FTO would consistently play the police vehicle music radio at a volume that interfered with hearing the police radio. When the new officer advised the FTO that he could not hear the police radio and requested that the music volume be lowered, the FTO responded that the increased volume was intentional to increase stress. Does this make sense? How does keeping a new officer from hearing the police radio contribute to his training or evaluation? Observing and evaluating a new officer's performance under stressful conditions is part of field training; however, due to the stress inherent in policing, there is little need for an FTO to artificially create stressful situations. And in any event, if the FTO is trying to assess the new officer's ability to manage particular stressors, the new officer's request to lower the music volume is right on. *The best way to deal with the stress caused by a music radio that is too loud is to turn down the volume!*

Pitfall #7 is *nit-picking*. FTOs should always remain mindful that there are usually several ways to accomplish any task. As long as the overall manner in which new officers are performing is acceptable, is it necessary that they perform it exactly as you would? In circumstances where it is appropriate, new officers appreciate the latitude to develop their own style. Avoid undermining new officer confidence by becoming overly focused on minutia.

Pitfall #8 is not enough reinforcement. There are two types of reinforcement identified by officers in PATROL:

1. The first is repetitive reinforcement. As one new officer put it, "I could hear something once and be expected to know it, no reinforcement." The new officer is actually talking about *encoding*. Encoding is the process whereby information is moved from short-term memory to long-term memory. In the case mentioned, the new officer felt that the FTO did little to assist the encoding process. The original information was not repeated, therefore not reinforced. There are several ways to reinforce encoding. Reviewing, repeating, rehearsing, organizing, visualizing, and categorizing are excellent strategies to enhance the encoding process.

2. The second type of reinforcement is associated with reward for something well done. For new officers, positive FTO comments and nonverbal behaviors are greatly valued. Positive verbal feedback such as "Good job" "I liked what you did" and "That was great" goes

a long way to build new officer confidence. Correspondingly, the simple nonverbal reward of a nod, a wink, a thumbs up, and so on from an FTO is highly meaningful to new officers. Most new officers acknowledge that their FTOs provide them with positive verbal and nonverbal feedback. However, many say it is not done often enough. The likely underlying issue here is that many tasks that are seen by the FTO as simple and routine are experienced as a challenge by some new officers. When these officers perform well at a task that was for them challenging, they seek the acknowledgement of their FTO. If there is acknowledgement, the new officer feels encouraged and motivated (reinforced). If acknowledgment is lacking, the new officer comes away with feelings of confusion and uncertainty. This can occur even when the FTO is satisfied with the new officer's performance. Communication is the key. One officer summed things up this way, "My FTO barely talks to me. I don't know what he wants. I get no reinforcement. I'm just trying to survive." Keep in mind that when FTOs are non-communicative, it presents a *blank slate* to new officers. They will project some meaning into FTO silence. The meaning projected is almost always negative. FTOs that are naturally introverted must be especially cautious to avoid this pitfall.

FTOs should consistently try to find something that can be reinforced. Even when new officers have a bad shift, FTOs should think, "Did the officer do *anything* right?" Barring imagined scenarios that are quite unlikely, the answer will always be "yes." This means that following a discussion of performance difficulties, the FTO can close on a positive note. This is *communication for motivation*. Communication for motivation increases the probability of new officer continued effort and success.

Pitfall #9 is inconsistent FTO behavior. When FTOs act significantly different with buddies than with new officers, it leads to very negative perceptions. For FTOs, it is natural to behave somewhat differently with friends and coworkers than with new officers, but to act significantly different is often detrimental. For example, it does little to help new officers when FTOs behave friendly and supportive to friends, only to express *boot camp drill instructor* behavior during field training. Such behavior often appears superficial, intentionally intimidating, and "power tripping" to new officers. None of these perceptions contribute anything positive to the training relationship.

Another form of FTO inconsistency is behaving one way, while instructing new officers to do otherwise. For instance, during a recent PATROL meeting, a new officer reported, "I have a 'do as I say and not as I do' FTO." What message does this FTO behavior send to new officers? The message can range from "I'm an FTO. I don't have to follow the rules" to "This department is bogus. I do what I want." Is this a good way to train new officers? It certainly is not a positive model for desired behavior. To avoid confusing new officers and to remain a positive role model, FTOs *must* model desired behavior. When FTOs engage in *do as I say, not as I do* behavior, they undermine themselves and the entire FTO program. To avoid pitfall #9, act in accordance with policy and procedure and be consistent.

Pitfall #10 is not being ready to work. Most police departments seek as FTOs those officers who have demonstrated consistently good work performance, a positive attitude, and a willingness to work with recruits. Field training officers are smart, perceptive, intuitive, and have a sense of others. This is one thing that new officers and FTOs instantly have in common. Police agencies look to hire persons who are also smart, perceptive, intuitive, and have a sense of others. These qualities are as sought after in new officers as they are in FTOs. Armed with these qualities, FTOs have little difficulty determining when something is not quite right with a new officer. Is it any surprise that new officers can also easily determine when FTOs are not at their finest? Experienced FTOs know that as they are observing and assessing the new officer, the new officer is observing and assessing them. If the FTO is having a bad day, the new officer knows it. If the FTO is not focused, the new officer knows it. If the FTO is not engaging the new officer, the new officer knows it. In the worst of these scenarios, the FTO is burned out, and the new officer knows it. The latter circumstance was clearly expressed by one new officer in PATROL, "My FTO really does not want to be here." This is unfortunate. It is an example of an FTO who has stayed in the program too long. To avoid pitfall #10, FTOs should come to work, ready to work.

Field Training Officers

What kind of police officer should become a field training officer? There are several attributes that characterize high-functioning field training officers.

Aptitude. Functional FTOs have an aptitude for training. They are competent police officers. They enjoy being with others and enjoy sharing their knowledge. They relate well to others and are positive role models. They are patient.

Interest. It is possible to have an aptitude for training but no interest in training. Functional FTOs have a genuine interest in training and in the philosophy and goals of the FTO program.

Commitment. Being an FTO requires more effort than not being an FTO. Functional FTOs consistently apply themselves so that the highest levels of FTO performance are consistently achieved. A commitment check should be performed at least annually. Commitment checks reaffirm your commitment to FTO principles and philosophies. If you became or remain an FTO solely for power or to advance your career, you are an FTO for the wrong reason.

Credibility. FTOs must be credible. Credibility must be part of an FTO's overall reputation. This can only be established by years of honorable policing prior to becoming an FTO.

As an FTO, you accept special-unit responsibility. It is appropriate for the department to expect that you will fully meet the responsibilities associated with the special unit. If the duties of being an FTO become too great for you to manage, you should talk with your program supervisor. There are several options available for overwhelmed or burned out FTOs. These include a training hiatus, learning new coping strategies, and disengagement from the FTO program. No one truly benefits from FTOs who have already given all they can to the FTO program.

Field training officers should maintain a goal of becoming better FTOs. To do anything less stalls FTO development and freezes the status quo. Field training officers should engage in advanced in-service FTO training and meet regularly to discuss their training experiences. By meeting, FTOs share information and learn from one another.

Exemplary FTOs

Field training officers vary in personality and style. While most FTOs are competent and do an excellent job, there are traits and behaviors that characterize exemplary FTOs.

In a recent survey, exemplary FTOs were identified and interviewed. To be considered an exemplary FTO, individual FTOs had to be described as outstanding by FTO program supervisors and *all* of the new officers trained by the FTO. Here are some of the more interesting comments collected from exemplary FTOs:

- "I do not believe that an FTO should ever say, 'I have to find something that you did wrong tonight'."
- No "derogatory language or behaviors."
- No "injection of personal feelings."
- If a trainee and FTO cannot get along, "this is an FTO problem and not a trainee problem."
- "I adjust my personality to give the trainee what he or she needs to succeed."
- "I train the same in each Phase, with respect, however the content changes."
- "I will go back to a prior Phase or Academy and build upon whatever success is there."
- "I will put the trainee into situations where I know they can succeed."
- "Some initial mistakes I do not record on the Daily Observation Report. If the mistake is repeated, then both incidents are documented. This helps to build trust. Then the trainee thinks, maybe he's not here to just hammer me."

Providing Constructive Feedback as an FTO/PTO

Field training officers have a complex role. In both of the major components of field training, training and evaluation, there is a need to provide feedback to new officers. Feedback is information that is designed to assist new officers. Feedback should always be constructive. Constructive feedback is characterized by providing at least something upon which the recipient can build.

Performance feedback is communication from others that helps the receiver to alter behavior to achieve an identified performance standard. There are two primary types of performance feedback: (1) feedback for change and (2) feedback for consistency. Feedback for change involves providing information which assists the recipient to achieve some degree of performance competency. Feedback for consistency assists the recipient to maintain performance competency once it is achieved.

Summary: FTO Constructive Feedback

In general, FTO feedback should be comprised of items of information. The information that comprises feedback tends to be most useful to recipients when it is characterized by the following:

1. Feedback should be non-threatening. Information that represents a personal attack is more likely to initiate defensive responses. Defensive responses tend to shut down the exchange of information, thereby limiting the effectiveness of feedback. For example, "When you raised your voice, the citizen also raised his voice" is much better than "You're a person who doesn't know how to talk to people."
2. Select and prioritize your feedback.
3. Focus on things that can be changed.
4. Remain aware that your non-verbal communication speaks volumes.
5. Talk about the new officer's behavior. Describe your observations (as in number 1). Present information about what the officer might do differently, followed by what you liked.
6. Restrain from injecting your personal feelings for the new officer into your professional relationship. You may like, dislike, or feel neutral about the new officer. Regardless, keep it friendly and professional.
7. Do not forget the old standby, the use of "I" statements. "I observed that . . ."
8. Know when to "go behind" behavior and talk about reasoning. Some behaviors which seem inappropriate may have reasonable explanations. Avoid making premature inferences to mental states. Most new officers will readily tell you about their observations, motives, thoughts, feelings, and intentions. Appropriately confront unreasonable rationalizations.
9. Specific feedback information is superior to general feedback information.
10. Timing is important. Unless duty-bound, provide feedback at appropriate times in appropriate settings. Immediate feedback can be quite effective if you can provide it within this guideline. Non-immediate feedback can be based upon a series of behaviors that were observed over a period of time.
11. To increase the probability that you are understood, summarize your thoughts at various points and at the completion of feedback. In this

way, you can check to see if the message you intended to send was accurately received. In essence, *get feedback on your feedback*. Avoid needless or non-productive repetition. Excessive repetition of information will cause the recipient to tune out.

12. Feedback is most effective when the recipient is motivated by your information. ("Let's try that again. The first part looked great.")
13. The addition of humor in feedback can be used effectively if used appropriately. Do not overdo it. The appropriate use of humor does not include making fun of new officers or belittling them for mistakes.
14. Remember, new officers are still learning the job.
15. Be descriptive in feedback ("I observed..."); be evaluative in evaluations ("Your behavior did not meet the performance standard for...").

Anxiety

It is normal to experience a degree of anxiety when learning a new job. Anxiety is a feeling of apprehensiveness or fear accompanied by a sense of immediate or anticipated danger. The danger does not have to be physical. Any perceived threat to well-being can trigger anxiety.

Anxiety also has physiological components. Everyone is familiar with being so nervous that "I thought my heart was going to jump out of my chest." In addition to a pounding heart, other physiological components of anxiety include sweating, rapid breathing, and muscle tension or weakness.

Anxiety and Performance

Anxiety has a long and interesting relationship to performance. Low levels of anxiety do not create significant performance deficits. High levels of anxiety can bring performance to a standstill. On simple tasks, higher levels of anxiety can be tolerated. As task complexity increases, there is a decrease in the ability to tolerate anxiety without performance degradation.

Assisting new officers to manage performance anxiety should be a primary focus of FTOs. Because anxiety can impede performance, keeping anxiety at manageable levels is imperative. If FTOs assist new officers to manage performance anxiety, especially when new officers first attempt a new task, the true capabilities of new officers are more readily observed.

Anxiety and Perception of Competency

One's perception of competency can affect anxiety. The perception of competency tends to be negatively correlated with the experience of anxiety. This means that as a person's perception of competency increases, the experience of anxiety decreases. To fully understand this, think of a man who has a fear of water. He has a fear of water because he cannot swim. Being a non-swimmer, he likely avoids activities associated with water, such as boating, kayaking, and other water sports. If he is on water or in water, he is uncomfortable. His level of discomfort varies with the actual circumstances. He is more comfortable standing in water up to his waist than he is standing in water up to his chin. In the water, he is *bottom oriented*. He must know where the bottom is to avoid further anxiety or panic. This is because deep water represents a life threatening circumstance for him. This is certainly a reason for anxiety.

One day, he decides to confront his fear of water by enrolling in a swimming class. At the first class session, his perception of his competency in the water is low, so his anxiety is high. However, as he begins water training and progresses in the program, he begins to acquire the skills necessary for swimming. This developing skill set is slowly building his confidence and lessening his water anxiety. It is not a smooth process. He experiences more anxiety in some sessions than others, but overall his water anxiety is gradually diminishing. With more practice, he eventually reaches a point where being in deep water no longer represents an imminent life-threatening event. He has become *surface oriented*. As long as he has some idea of where the surface is, he is ok. If he continues his water training and comes to master the skills of swimming, his anxiety in water will virtually disappear.

So it is for new police officers. As they develop a sense of occupational competency, their on-duty experience of anxiety will diminish.

Anxiety and Breathing

For millennia, controlled intentional breathing has been utilized to manage anxiety. *Relaxation breathing* is the best cost-benefit anxiety reduction technique known. Although there are many types of relaxation breathing, enduring success can be achieved with one of the simplest. It is comprised of the following: (1) inhale deeply through the nose, (2) hold your breath for two seconds, and (3) exhale slowly through the mouth. You can enhance the effectiveness of this breathing technique if, while exhaling, you engage a coping statement. Examples of coping statements are "I can do this," "Relax," and "I can handle this." Coping statements can be said out loud or thought internally. There are several reasons why this technique is effective. Suffice it here to say that it works. Relaxation breathing can help new officers better perform in situations that naturally produce anxiety, such as emergency response driving. Not only can FTOs teach this anxiety reduction technique to new officers, they can also use it themselves. Regardless of the situation, the next time you feel anxious, try this: take a deep nose breath; hold it for two seconds; exhale slowly through your mouth. While exhaling, think "I'm ok, I can handle this." You'll be glad you did.

Other anxiety reduction strategies that may be taught (and used) by FTOs are presented in *Some Things to Remember* (chapter 3).

Field Training Remedial Programs

Police departments have developed various means to assist new officers who fail to progress as expected in field training. A commonly applied remedial intervention involves removing the officer from field training, conducting additional training in the deficit area, and if satisfactorily completed, returning the officer to field training. This remedial sequence is successful in many cases.

To address field training concerns when it is deemed unnecessary to remove the officer from field training, the *Within Phase Observational Period* (WPOP) and the *Within Phase Emphasis Period* (WPEP) can be utilized.

Within Phase Observational Period

The WPOP is best utilized in cases where new officers have previous policing experience. It can help answer questions related to performance anxiety and work consistency. WPOP is designed to provide a respite from the ever-present evaluation of most field training programs. It provides the new officer with a slightly different field training environment. The WPOP is normally engaged in the latter phases of field training and takes place over three work shifts:

First shift: The FTO operates the police vehicle and assumes car command. The daily observation report is waived. The

FTO's primary task is to act as a model. The new officer's primary task is to observe the FTO.

Second shift: The new officer operates the police vehicle and assumes car command. The FTO intervenes only if necessary. The FTO may provide positive feedback to the new officer; however, corrective feedback is withheld unless necessary. The FTO completes a daily observation report, but it is not discussed with the new officer. The primary task of the FTO is observation. The primary task of the new officer is performance.

Third shift: The third shift is the same as the second shift. The FTO completes a daily observation report. At the end of this shift, The FTO and new officer discuss their experiences, observations, and the two completed daily observation reports. The FTO and new officer work together to better utilize the remainder of field training.

The WPOP tends to lower new officer anxiety and increase confidence. It can also be used to address cases in which new officers feel that the FTO is focusing on insignificant details. In one case where WPOP was utilized, a new officer complained that his FTO was relentlessly nit picking. The new officer, based on his years of policing experiencing, maintained that the FTO was commenting on and correcting things that were really a matter of officer discretion. Following the completion of the WPOP, the FTO reported that during the program he had seen several things that he wanted to comment on; however, he could not now remember them. Evidently, they were not serious enough to make a significant impression on the FTO. This appeared to lend credibility to the new officer's complaint.

Within Phase Emphasis Period

The WPEP is best utilized in circumstances where new officers are progressing as expected in all but an isolated area. The WPEP begins by identifying the area within which the new officer needs assistance.

1. *Issue is identified.* The new officer is not responding to more traditional interventions. The difficulty does not warrant halting the officer's field training.

2. *Design and duration of the WPEP.* This can include interventions involving specialized field assignments, classroom and scenario training, working with specialist officers, etc. Evaluation may be suspended for all, none, or for a portion of the WPEP.
3. *WPEP is implemented.*
4. *New officer's performance is evaluated as designed.* If the new officer's performance improves to an acceptable level, field training continues. The WPEP has been successful. If performance does not improve, other options must be considered. Additional options range from suspension of field training and further remedial instruction, to termination of employment.

FTO Information

Many FTOs have developed a preferred style and phase protocol for training. If the style is flexible and the protocol has been successful, all is well. If there is need for improvement, FTOs should consider these suggestions:

- In Phase I, do not move from car command too soon. Allow a reasonable period for the new officer to observe you as a model.
- In Phase II and III consider an FTO driving day for *at least* the first day of each of these phases. Traditionally, new officers have the opportunity to observe only the Phase I FTO. FTO driving days allow new officers to observe each of the FTOs as models. Also consider an FTO driving day within Phases II and III. This provides a break for new officers as well as the FTO. If you plan on doing this, arrange for it at the beginning of the phase so that the new officer does not misinterpret its meaning (like FTO dissatisfaction with new officer performance). If used, make certain that an FTO driving day fits within the department's field training philosophy.
- New officers may not respond to strategies that worked well for you when you were in field training. Also, new officers may not respond to strategies that have previously worked well for you as a trainer.
- Be creative. Individualize your field training style and strategies within the parameters of your department's FTO philosophy.
- Do not over-extend yourself in FTO or other department assignments. Engage in an occasional training hiatus to keep yourself balanced.

- Develop appropriate psychological boundaries. Think about your responsibility and limitations as an FTO. Remain mindful of the positive rewards.

Summary: Ten Considerations for Maximizing Field Trainer Effectiveness

1. Develop and implement a training program philosophy (philosophy by design). Perform consistently within your program philosophy.
2. Use appropriate verbal and nonverbal positive reinforcement. Many trainers need to increase their use of positive reinforcement. Do not over do it. Too much positive reinforcement diminishes its value. Thoughtful and balanced positive reinforcement is the most effective.
3. Remember that you are *always* a model. It is possible to unintentionally pass on good and bad behaviors. If other officers prove to be poor role models, discuss their behavior and more appropriate alternatives with the new officer.
4. Encourage encoding by periodically summarizing and reviewing new material. Assist new officer encoding by conceptualizing, categorizing, visualizing, imaging, and emotively processing new information and skills.
5. Align *content* with *message*. Remember that *delivery* can alter the *message* of any *content* (chapter 7). Avoid *content* with potential double meanings. Remain mindful of your nonverbal communication.
6. Provide deliberate and thoughtful feedback on daily observation reports *and* throughout the shift.
7. Remember the following: (1) high anxiety degrades performance and (2) reducing anxiety will allow a more accurate assessment of knowledge and skill. Use and teach relaxation breathing and other anxiety management skills.
8. Have new officers evaluate their field training experience. Use this information to improve the FTO program. New officers can evaluate their field training immediately after completion and again at some later time. The later follow-up evaluation asks new officers to reflect upon their field training experiences following some time working independently. This data can be gathered up to a year after new officers have completed their field training.

9. Be creative. You can safely exercise some discretion if you remain within the primary parameters of your training program and philosophy (WPOP, WPEP, PATROL). Share thoughts with other trainers. Meet regularly to discuss FTO consistency, FTO skill development, new officers' progress, and training program features.

10. Take care of yourself. You are a better trainer when you are motivated and feel well.

Chapter 3

Police Stress and Occupational Health

There are two primary stress intervention strategies. The first is to change your environment. The second is to change yourself. Changing yourself includes (1) learning new coping skills and (2) altering the way in which you conceptualize your environment. The first strategy acknowledges the ability to modify one's circumstances. The second strategy recognizes the transactional nature of human experience.

Stress Equals Demand

Stress equals demand—this simple equation and the confidence we can place in its accuracy comes from decades of study by many talented researchers. The implications of this equation are clear—if you wish to decrease stress, decrease demand; if you wish to increase stress, increase demand.

In terms of historical stress research, a *demand* is anything that places a need for adjustment on an organism. To illustrate this, think about what happens when you jump into a swimming pool. At first, you feel the shock of the cool water and become chilled. As you spend some time in the pool, your body adjusts to the water temperature and you feel comfortable. However, if you remain in the pool long enough, you will exhaust your body's ability to cope with the water temperature, and you will again feel chilled.

The demand in this scenario is the temperature of the water. The cool water initiates an *alarm* for adjustment (you feel chilled). The process by which your body adjusted to the water temperature is called *resistance*. When you resist the initial effects of a demand, the demand effects diminish (you feel comfortable in the water). If the demand continues, *exhaustion* occurs and the effects return (you again feel chilled). If the demand overwhelms resistance, symptoms of distress, including death, may result (if the water is cold enough and you remain in it long enough, you will die from hypothermia). The sequence of alarm, resistance, and exhaustion is called the *general adaptation syndrome* (Selye, 1974). In the general adaptation syndrome, the more intense the demand, the less we are able to resist; resulting in less time needed to produce exhaustion.

Another word for demand is *stressor*. A stressor is anything that causes a need for adjustment. The attempt of your body to adjust to a stressor is called the *stress response*. Therefore, a stressor is anything that initiates the stress response. A common way of expressing this is "a stressor is anything that causes stress." We are never without stress. Even while resting or sleeping, there are the demands for body respiration and circulation. The absence of all stress is death.

On the ends of the stress continuum lie *overload* stress and *deprivational* stress. Overload stress is characterized by too much to do, too little time, high expectations, and insufficient resources. This is how most people think about stress. It is likely that everyone has at some time experienced overload stress. The best way to manage overload stress is to decrease stressors.

On the other end of the continuum is deprivational stress. Deprivational stress occurs when there is not enough demand. Nearly every police officer has experienced deprivational stress. Most officers can easily remember slow night shifts that seemed to last forever. This circumstance is illustrated by an officer who looks at his watch and notes that it is 0300. After it feels like an hour has passed, he again checks his watch to find that it is 0310. In deprivational stress, even the perception of time is altered.

Persons who experience deprivational stress as a life pattern often report being bored and having an unexciting life. Normally, as the sense of deprivation increases, so does the level of discomfort. In extreme forms, deprivation can be punishing. This fact is well known to the captors of prisoners of war. If deprivation is extreme for an extended period of time, it is a form of torture.

If you are a parent or have otherwise used *time-out* as a child-behavior corrective strategy, you have applied the principle of deprivational stress. By having a child remain in a limited stimulus environment for a period of time following undesirable behavior, the likelihood of similar behavior in the future is reduced. In the penal system, the equivalent of time out is administrative segregation (solitary confinement).

The best way to manage deprivational stress is to increase positive stressors. Think about this for a minute...who ever thought that good stress management might mean increasing stressors?

It is possible to be in stress overload in one area of life (overworked) and in stress deprivation in another (no social life). The key to positive stressor management is finding the balance that is right for you.

The Stress Response

During the early days of stress research, the terms *stress* and *stress management* seemed like buzzwords. Back then, not much was understood about the physiological and psychological processes underlying the notion of stress. Today, you cannot read a basic psychology textbook without finding at least one chapter dedicated to the topics of stress, stress management, and the stress response.

The stress response is characterized by increases in blood pressure, increases in heart and respiration rate, increased perspiration, pupil dilation, and changes in blood flow distribution. Blood flow is altered by the constriction of blood vessels in the extremities, thereby maximizing the blood-borne delivery of oxygen and nutrients to the major organs and primary muscle groups. This is why your hands become cold and clammy when you feel under duress (blood has been constricted away from your extremities thereby lowering hand temperature, and there is an increase in perspiration). The stress response is also responsible for the popular phrase "getting cold feet" to indicate trepidation about engaging in some activity or event.

The process by which the stress response is initiated, maintained, and eventually diminished primarily involves the nervous and endocrine systems. These are the systems activated in response to stressors, and they are the systems that improve chances of survival in life threatening situations.

American physiologist Walter B. Cannon (1871-1945) termed the collection of bodily changes involved in the stress response the *fight or flight* response, in recognition of its value to the organism's survival. In survival terms, the stress or fight-or-flight response prepares the organism to flee from threatening situations or to fight off attackers (1915).

Cannon also discussed and popularized the concept of *homeostasis* (1932). Homeostasis is the process by which the body attempts to keep itself within an operational range necessary for survival. The homeostatic balance is achieved by unconscious body processes and is related to the body's ability to adapt to stressors. Homeostasis is the reason that you sweat when you are hot and shiver when you are cold. Both are attempts to keep body temperature within a functional range.

The stress response is nonspecific, meaning that it does not matter if the stressor is positive or negative. Heart rate, blood pressure, respiration, and so forth will increase whether persons have just learned of the death of a loved one or have just been informed that they have won a multimillion dollar lottery. The specific psychological/emotional response in these instances may differ (sadness in the first case and excitement in the latter), but the physiology remains mostly consistent.

In essence, the body has only one way to cope with stressors—prepare itself for action via the stress response. In earlier times, this worked well. There were many stressors that were amenable to fight or flight resolutions, such as hunting wild animals with spears, fighting off predators, running from enemies, and so on (Selye, 1974). Today, in "civilized" societies, the number of circumstances in which physical resolutions are appropriate has diminished. Persons cannot often run from or fight their problems. Therefore, the stress response has become something to manage. To manage the stress response, one needs to appropriately manage stressors.

The intensity of the stress response varies with the perceived intensity of the stressor; the perceived intensity of the stressor is influenced by one's perceived ability to cope with it. Therefore, persons can confront stressors that represent real dangers, such as a vicious dog, without any significant stress response if the dog is perceived to be friendly. Correspondingly, persons will experience a significant stress response to a dog they believe is vicious even though it is actually friendly. The intensity of the stress response in both of these "vicious dog" examples will vary with a person's perceived ability to deal with the dog. It is in this way that the stress response is said to be *transactional* (environment X person).

The fact that we respond to our interpretations of our environment (internal and external) and our assessed ability to deal with particular stressors is a fundamental element of human experience. The best we can do is to perceive, interpret, assess, respond, and reassess. It is a fundamental limitation of what we can know and how we can transact with the world.

The physiological components of the stress response are so reliable that the stress management strategy of *biofeedback* is based upon them. They also comprise the conceptual foundation of the lie detector or polygraph.

Occupational Stress

All occupations are characterized by unavoidable stressors. An unavoidable stressor is a demand which is inherent to the occupation. For example, an unavoidable stressor of school bus drivers is interacting with children, an unavoidable stressor of cashiers is handling money and credit cards, and an unavoidable stressor of trial attorneys is contending with judges and juries.

Policing has its constellation of unavoidable stressors. Some of these overlap those of other occupations, such as interacting with people, driving a car, and working in snowstorms. Others are a bit more unique, like the duty to protect others.

Some of the more commonly recognized unavoidable stressors of policing include shift work (policing is a twenty-four-hours per day, 365-days-per-year occupation), working in a paramilitary-type organization, carrying a firearm, interacting with highly emotional and violent persons, exposure to critical situations, and role over-identification.

Role over-identification of police officers is the result of a dysfunctional enmeshment of the officer with the job. The identification of some officers with the role of police officer is so complete that they say things like "Policing is not something I do. It's what I am." These officers are treading upon very thin psychological ice. This is because their sense of self is intimately tied to their job. If the job is lost, so is their sense of identity. Realistically, policing is an occupation. Like any occupation, it should be conceptualized as separate from those who engage it. For officers, there is little doubt that the job is important; however, police officers are much more than their job. They are husbands, wives, fathers, mothers, coaches, scout leaders, athletes, and so on. Police officers lose sight of this at their peril.

Police officers must also contend with the unavoidable occupational stressor of being misunderstood by the general public. Take the case of Trooper G—Trooper G was talking to Trooper L in the "opposite direction" vehicle position. This position is commonly used by police officers. It involves positioning two police vehicles in opposite directions so that the driver's door of each vehicle is facing the other. In this way, the officers remain in their vehicles, monitor radio traffic, and are able to speak to one another. Troopers G and L, parked in this position, were discussing work shift events when they received a broadcast from Dispatch: "Overturned vehicle on the interstate, unknown injuries." They engaged their vehicles' emergency warning lights and siren. They sped toward the reported accident location. Trooper G was the lead car; Trooper L was following close behind. After several miles of running code 3 (lights and siren) and passing numerous vehicles, Dispatch relayed information that the report was unfounded. Both troopers disengaged their vehicles' emergency lights and siren. They slowed to the posted speed limit. By chance, there was a highway exit close to the location where the emergency response was terminated. There was a restaurant close to the exit. The troopers decided to exit the roadway and have lunch at the restaurant.

Trooper G parked his police vehicle in front of the restaurant; Trooper L parked nearby. Trooper G exited his vehicle. He then noticed a man walking toward him. The man, who had also recently parked near the restaurant, appeared upset. When the man was within speaking distance of Trooper G, he angrily complained that it was "not right" to use emergency lights and siren to pass others on the highway just to get to a restaurant. To the man, it appeared that the troopers were abusing their authority. Trooper G explained to the man that he and the other trooper were responding to a report of an overturned vehicle farther up the interstate. He added that when it was determined the report was unfounded, the emergency response was terminated. It was just a coincidence that the troopers were at that particular exit and decided to have lunch. Trooper G offered the man the phone number of Dispatch, in the event that he wished to confirm this information. Trooper G added, "If it were you or your family members in an overturned vehicle, would you not want an emergency response from the police?" The man, taken aback by the information, replied, "I'm just sayin'," to which Trooper G responded, "Well, I'm just sayin'." The conversation ended there.

There are many circumstances in which the public has little idea of why the police do what they do. Many police actions are guided by received information, police procedure, police tactics, and officer safety concerns. Others are guided by department policy and directives. All have a rationale and a purpose. This is not to say that police officers always follow procedure or that procedures always prove adequate. Police officers can and do make mistakes. Additionally, there have been and likely will always be some police officers who betray the values of policing. These bad cops tarnish the badge and damage the reputation of all police officers. Some are unethical, some are unprofessional, and some may engage in criminal activity. The policing profession is on constant alert to indentify such officers and to remove them from the ranks of the nation's finest.

Stress Management, Life Management, Life-by-Default, and Life-by-Design

Stress management is the general term used to describe how a person controls, influences, interacts with, and confronts the stressors of life. When thinking of the stressors that comprise the totality of human experience, the term *stress management* seems inadequate. The term *stressor management* can be used to describe efforts to cope with a particular stressor, but beyond that, it also appears lacking. When thinking about the manner in which humans confront the complexities of life, the term *life management* is more satisfactory. The concept of life management is more encompassing and better captures the essence of human efforts to cope with life's complexities.

Life management can be considered from one of two primary life perspectives: *life-by-default* and *life-by-design*. These perspectives are conceptual constructs and describe a theoretical continuum along which a person can engage life. It is unlikely that anyone lives life totally by default or by design. Most people live sometimes or most times by default, and sometimes or most times by design. Life-by-default differs from life-by-design in that life-by-default is what you get if you do not practice life-by-design. Not much thought or effort goes into life-by-default. Persons who are oriented toward life-by-default often feel powerless. They subscribe to the "This is my life. What can I do about it? It is what it is. What will be, will be" life position. This is very different from the life-by-design philosophy of "taking life by the horns." Life-by-default does not mean that life experiences are or will be undesirable. Quite the contrary, life experiences can default to very desirable circumstances. It is a matter of probability. The probability that life will default to something great and wonderful is less than the probability of desirable outcomes in life-by-design.

Life-by-design is best described by a single word: *intention*. Persons oriented toward life-by-design act intentionally and accept responsibility for their decisions and behaviors. Life-by-design persons are not passive observers of life. They do not wait for life to simply unfold. They feel empowered and they act in ways to direct their lives. In life-by-design there is no illusion that all things can be directed, controlled, or even influenced. Instead, there is respect for what might be changed and what must be accepted. There is recognition of the influence of personal values, societal values, and cultural influences.

Life-by-design persons do not blindly accept the values of their childhood. They consider all values, adopt those that are appropriate for them, and live accordingly.

Life-by-design is thoughtful, mindful. To engage life-by-design, persons must accept reasonable risk, endorse the idea that they can decide many things for themselves, and use this knowledge to make a difference in their lives. Making an effort to accomplish this is the first step toward moving from a life-by-default to a life-by-design.

The Big Three—Diet, Exercise, and Self-awareness

Life-by-design means being mindful of lifestyle. The big three—diet, exercise, and self-awareness—are major components of stress management, life management, lifestyle, and life-by-design.

Diet

The word *diet* refers to what a person eats and drinks. It represents the totality of what a person consumes. *Dieting* refers to consuming less or different types of foodstuffs in an attempt to lose weight. Based on current knowledge, there are diets that facilitate health and those that are less than healthy.

The diet of most Americans is varied. Not only do Americans consume many types of solid food, they also drink many different liquids. These contribute significantly to daily caloric intake. A recent study showed that liquids comprise about 22 percent of the calories consumed by Americans (Environ International Corporation, 2002). This finding is interesting due to the fact that some Americans count only solid food calories.

All diets are primarily comprised of three elements: fats, carbohydrates, and proteins. (1) Fat is an ester of glycerol and one, two, or three fatty acids. Triglycerides are the main type of fat in food and in our bodies. (2) Carbohydrates come in simple forms such as sugars, and in complex forms such as starches and fiber. (3) Proteins are strings of amino acids, often called polypeptide chains.

Calories

A calorie is a unit of measurement. It is a measurement of energy. A food calorie (kilocalorie) is the amount of energy it takes to raise the temperature of one kilogram (about 2.2 pounds) of water one degree Celsius. Different foods contain different amounts of energy, thus different amounts of calories. A small piece of chocolate contains more energy than a similar size of lettuce; therefore, chocolate contains more calories than lettuce.

When it comes to energy, all calories are the same. A fat calorie has the same amount of energy as a carbohydrate calorie, protein calorie, or alcohol calorie. The energy produced by carbohydrates is four calories per gram. Proteins also provide four calories per gram. Fats are higher in calories.

They provide nine calories per gram. Alcohol has seven calories per gram. The amount of calories in any diet refers to the amount of energy the diet provides. If you intake more calories than are needed each day, the body stores this energy as fat ("Calories," n.d., para.1).

During sleep the human body burns about one calorie per minute. This is approximately the same as sitting on a sofa, watching television. At this level of activity, the body burns about 1440 calories daily.

It takes 3500 excess calories to gain one pound. During any period of time, if you consume 3500 calories more than you burn, you will gain one pound. To lose weight, you must burn more calories than you consume. If you produce a deficit of five hundred calories each day for a week, you will lose one pound. If you stay consistent with this deficit, you will continue to lose a pound each week. The bottom line is that if you want to lose weight, you must burn more calories than you consume (Willet and Skerrett, 2005).

When considering diet, there are three variables that can be manipulated: (1) what you consume, (2) how much you consume, and (3) how frequently you consume. By manipulating these variables, you adjust caloric intake. In conjunction with your activity level and metabolic rate, the calories you consume will determine whether you lose weight, gain weight, or remain at the same weight. Other factors can also influence weight changes. Genetic make-up, age and health status, medications and other drugs, mental illnesses, and whether you use food to respond to stress (emotional eating) seem to be involved in weight fluctuation.

Weight is different than *mass*. Weight is relative to where you are in the universe. It represents the relationship between mass and gravity. You weigh less on the moon than you do on earth. Because earth's gravity varies at different locations, you weigh less at the Equator than you do at the North Pole. Mass is invariable. Your mass remains the same regardless of where you are (Halliday et al., 2001).

Fat

Fat is stored in *adipocytes*, sometimes called *fat cells*. The average person has about 35 billion fat cells. Some people have as few as 25 billion fat cells, while others may have up to 275 billion. Fat cells accumulate differently for men and women. For men the accumulation is normally around the abdomen (the infamous spare tire), while for women, fat cells accumulate around the hips, buttocks, and thighs. Abdomen fat has a higher correlation with health risk than fat in other body locations.

Fat cells are chemically complex. They expand and contract. Much of weight loss is due to the contraction of fat cells. Cellulite is ordinary fat and is not a function of excess weight. Cellulite is caused by genetic differences in how adipose and connective tissue form. It is less likely to appear in men than women. There is no known specific health risk associated with cellulite. Unfortunately, although there are some differing opinions, physical activity seems to have little effect on reducing or altering the appearance of cellulite (Avram, 2004).

There are several types of dietary fat. Although the consumption of fat is necessary to remain healthy, eating too much can cause problems. A great deal depends on the type of fat consumed. The Harvard School of Public Health summed up the circumstances related to dietary fats: "Bad fats, meaning saturated and trans fats, increase the risk for certain diseases while good fats, meaning monounsaturated and polyunsaturated fats, lower the risk. The key is to substitute good fats for bad fats" (Griffin, 2006, 1).

Health Statistics

The U.S. National Center for Health Statistics estimates that in the United States, 49 percent of women and 59 percent of men are overweight. Nearly one-third of the U.S. population qualifies as obese. For those that were overweight and have lost weight, the statistics are grim. Within three years, about two-thirds of those who have lost weight will regain the weight they lost. Within five years, between 80 and 90 percent of those who lost weight will regain what they lost. These numbers represent those in medically supervised weight loss programs. The numbers worsen in personal programs for weight loss (cdc.gov).

Body Mass Index

Body mass index (BMI) is a way of calculating appropriate weight to height ratios. A person's BMI is weight in kilograms divided by height in meters squared (BMI=kg/m2). For example, a person 1.68 meters tall (5'6"), weighing 68 kilograms (150 pounds) would have a BMI of 24.2. A BMI below 18.5 is considered underweight. Normal weight is represented by a BMI of 18.5 to 24.9. A person is overweight if the BMI is 25 to 29.9, and obese if the BMI is over 30. If the BMI is over 40, the person is considered extremely obese. A BMI of 21 is thought to be ideal (CDC, 2009).

Cardiac Health Risk

Estimates of cardiac health risk associated with waist size and belly fat have been calculated. Research has shown that women with a waist measurement of over 35 inches measured at the belly button have a significantly higher cardiac health risk. For men, similarly measured, it is a waist size of 40 inches.

Glycemic Index and Glycemic Load

Other useful dietary information is provided by the *glycemic index*. The glycemic index is a method of ranking carbohydrate foods by their ability to raise blood sugar. The index ranges from 0 to 100. Foods below 55 are considered low glycemic foods (e.g. carrots). Foods that rank in the range of 56 to 69 are midrange (e.g. popcorn), while foods that are rated over 70 are ranked high (e.g. rice crackers).

Glycemic load is a function of carbohydrate intake and glycemic index (the amount of carbohydrates per serving). Most dieticians recommend that no more than 50-60 percent of the recommended 2000 calories consumed each day come from carbohydrates, and that no more than 30 percent of daily calories should come from fat. Many popular high-protein weight loss diets specify much lower intake levels of carbohydrates and fat.

Further dietary recommendations include the intake of less than 2300 mg of salt daily, less than 300 mg of cholesterol daily, and less than 300 mg of caffeine daily (Willet and Skerrett, 2005)

Vitamins and Minerals

Lastly, for a better understanding of diet, vitamins and minerals must be considered. Vitamins are organic compounds necessary for health. They either cannot be synthesized within the body, or cannot be synthesized in sufficient quantities within the body. Therefore, they must be taken in through diet. There are 13 vitamins for humans. Nine are water-soluble (eight B-vitamins and vitamin C) and four are fat-soluble (vitamins A, D, E, and K). Water soluble vitamins are readily eliminated in urine and need to be replenished daily. Fat soluble vitamins can be stored in the body. Similar to not consuming a sufficient quantity of vitamins, consuming too great a quantity can lead to several undesirable conditions. This is especially true of the fat-soluble vitamins.

Minerals, like vitamins, are necessary for good health. Minerals, unlike vitamins, are chemical elements and not organic compounds. Minerals and vitamins work together to perform many of the body's vital functions. Minerals in the human body are sometimes described as *macro, micro,* or *trace,* depending upon the quantity of each found in the body or required for health. Some of the body's macro minerals are calcium, iron, sodium, and potassium. Some of the body's micro minerals are copper, sulfur, and zinc. Iodine, cobalt, and silicon are among the body's trace minerals (Lieberman and Bruning, 1990).

Dietary Tips for Weight Loss

There are some tips that might help if you are trying to change eating and drinking habits for weight loss:

1. Eat smaller portions more frequently. This way you never become ravenous and overeat before your brain receives the "full" signal from your stomach.
2. Eat slowly. Research indicates that it takes about 20 minutes for your brain to get the full signal.
3. Plate your food and consume only what is on your plate, nothing more.
4. rink water. For hot drinks, try herbal teas. Stay hydrated. Thirst mimics hunger...you may feel hungry when you're actually thirsty.
5. Brush your teeth. This sends a behavioral signal to your brain that you're done eating. It is especially effective after the evening meal.
6. Do not eat from large containers or snack from big bags. Portion control becomes nearly impossible if you eat this way.
7. No eating past a certain time. Set your time, commit to it.
8. Take a temporary hiatus from certain foods and drinks. It is difficult to believe, but you can live without pork rinds, soft drinks, and the empty calories of alcoholic beverages.
9. Wait out or distract yourself from unhealthy food or drink cravings.
10. Engage an activity in the place of habitual eating (eating when not hungry), such as walking instead of eating during your work break.
11. Develop new interests or hobbies to occupy yourself so you do not eat out of boredom.
12. Make a contract with yourself or someone else which specifies the changes you are willing to make. Be reasonable. Write the contract

so that there is a high likelihood of success. Make it for a specified period of time. Renegotiate after it expires. Each renegotiation will bring you closer to achieving your overall goals. Try new things.

13. Schedule more activity. Any activity is superior to no activity.
14. Keep in mind that change takes time and effort. Do not quit. If you falter, try not to become discouraged. Do not beat yourself up. Instead, resolve to do better. Think of yourself as a work in progress.

Exercise

Metabolism is the process by which the body breaks down food for use as energy. If a person is active, metabolism increases. Conversely, if a person is inactive, metabolism decreases. Muscle is the machine that metabolizes calories and fat. Physical exercise and activity uses muscles, thereby burning calories and metabolizing fat.

There are two primary types of metabolism: aerobic, in which energy conversion takes place in the presence of oxygen, and anaerobic, where energy is supplied by processes that do not include oxygen. At rest, the body's energy is mostly supplied aerobically. As we increase activity, the demand for energy increases. If the activity is sufficiently strenuous, we soon surpass the level of energy that can be provided aerobically. This is called the *metabolic threshold*. It is the point at which energy production moves from primarily aerobic to primarily anaerobic. In anaerobic metabolism, we build up an oxygen debt. This is why following even brief periods of strenuous anaerobic activity we find ourselves breathing rapidly.

Anaerobic activity also produces by-products which contribute to muscle fatigue. Lactic acid is a well known by-product of anaerobic activity. It has long been suspected as a cause of muscle fatigue. The role of lactic acid in anaerobic activity is currently the subject of some debate, however it is often cited as one of the reasons that a person can go "all out" for only brief periods of time.

Due to the types of metabolism associated with different activities, some activities or exercises have come to be known as aerobic or anaerobic. Fast walking below the metabolic threshold is an aerobic exercise, while weight lifting is primarily anaerobic. In reference to body conditioning, each type of activity has its benefits. For cardiac conditioning, calorie burning, lessened muscle fatigue, and goals of weight loss, aerobic activity is desirable (more fat burning). For increased muscle mass and rapid performance increases, anaerobic exercises are necessary (more carbohydrate burning). The key for any exercise or activity program is *not too much too soon*. It is also recommended that you warm-up aerobically before engaging in strenuous anaerobic exercises (Maffetone, 2000).

Self-awareness: Transaction and Self-transaction

Human beings are transactional. We transact with our environment and everything within our environment. We also transact with ourselves. *Human beings are so self-transactional that we have an ongoing relationship with ourselves.* Talking and thinking to ourselves, about ourselves, is common in human experience. Self-talk can motivate, energize, and encourage. It can also demean, depress, and create anxiety. This is why self-talk is so important. It is a major factor in how we view ourselves. The human ability to maintain a relationship-with-self has much to do with the concept of self-esteem.

One of the theoretical cornerstones of the cognitive therapies is that negative thoughts drive negative emotions. In serious cases of low self-esteem, there is often self-talk of self-anger and self-hatred. The disparaging feelings that accompany negative thoughts are common in depression and other mood disorders. They often combine with thoughts of suicide and a desire to die (like the thoughts, "I'm nothing" and "I don't deserve to live"). A goal of cognitive therapy is to help persons change irrational negative thoughts to more realistic positive thoughts. Cognitive therapies have demonstrated efficacy for many years (Beck et al., 1979).

Transaction, Self-awareness, and Self-direction

To be productively self-aware, you must transact with your inner and outer worlds as an active agent. This means that you must engage life-by-design and conceptualize yourself as someone with at least some ability to directly or indirectly influence life. In the quest for increased self-awareness, questions like, "Who am I?" "What is my place in the world?" and "What do I believe, what are my values?" are common. Clarifying beliefs and endorsing particular values are necessary components of enhanced self-awareness. Living in accordance with those beliefs and values are necessary components of enhanced self-direction.

Achieving a higher level of self-awareness and thereby greater self-direction, takes thought and mindfulness. It can take some time. In the search for greater self-awareness, it would serve us well to remember the words of Chinese philosopher Lao-tzu (604 BCE - 531 BCE), "A journey of a thousand miles begins with a single step."

Self-awareness includes being "tuned in" to your body. This involves engaging in self-care. Self-care involves nurturing yourself physically, psychologically, emotionally, spiritually, and socially. Self-care is about personal and social boundaries. Boundaries are limits. When you assume responsibility for things that you cannot control, you are over your boundary. Staying within boundary is recognizing the limits of what you can do for yourself and others. If you exceed these limits for any significant amount of time, you will begin to experience the negative effects of overload stress. The more over your boundary you are, the less time it will take to notice the stressor effects. Self-care is not selfishness. Selfishness is the pursuit of desires by nearly any means, without concern for personal consequences, personal value violations, or regard for others.

In unusual or emergency situations you can exceed healthy boundaries and push yourself to extremes. However, making this a life style will significantly diminish your self-care and result in a degradation of personal well-being. Having appropriate boundaries is necessary for self-care and life-by-design. Utilizing appropriate boundaries is the opposite of "burning the candle at both ends" and being manipulated by others.

Greater self-awareness is empowering and it will increase self-direction. Together, self-awareness and self-direction is the process by which self-esteem is enhanced.

Burnout

The concept of burnout has been in existence for many years. It was first conceptualized and named by psychologist Herbert Freudenberger in 1974. *Burnout* is used to describe "someone in a state of fatigue or frustration brought about by devotion to a cause, way of life, or relationship that failed to produce the expected reward" (Freudenberger, 1980, 13). Burnout can occur in all areas of life, including work, marriage, family, sports, avocations, and hobbies.

When police officers burn out, all areas of their lives tend to suffer. This is because being burned out at work often means carrying the fatigue and frustration home. It is an unusual police officer who can feel burned out at work and remain in a positive mental state at home.

There are many indicators that an officer is burning out or is burned out. Lack of interest in work and no concern for the consequences of behavior are two of the most prominent.

As the process of burnout begins, officers work performance gradually deteriorates; they tend to answer calls or meet minimum expectations, but do little more. They slowly withdraw from the behaviors that made them successful.

For patrol officers, as burnout continues, they begin to avoid calls, "milk" calls, and become a nightmare for dispatchers trying to assign calls. This is because burned out officers feel tired and disinterested much of the time. As their performance worsens, they often draw unwanted attention from their supervisors. In some cases, supervisors will initiate performance improvement plans (PIP). Supervisory PIPs normally identify problematic areas and clarify supervisory expectations. Some officers respond well to PIPs and seem to do better. For these officers, the PIPs function as a wake-up call. Other officers, the more completely burned out officers, become more stressed and suspicious. They feel that that they are being unfairly singled out. They often say things like "my supervisor is out to get me."

Burned out officers lack insight into the causes of their problems. They do not take responsibility for their behavior and consistently blame others for their difficulties. They have a difficult time seeing things from any perspective but their own.

Eventually and inevitably, the negative behavior of burned out officers begins to affect their relationships with coworkers. This is because many officers who are not burned out frequently find it difficult to be around officers who are. If nothing is done to address this, even friends of many years will begin to distance themselves.

Burned out officers feel trapped. They feel trapped in a job that they now perceive as no longer desirable or meaningful. To them, everything seems gray, routine, and dreadful. They say things like, "If I could earn this kind of money somewhere else, I'd be outta here in a minute," "I'm sick of people," and "I'm tired of this bulls--t department."

For burned out officers, life outside of the police department is normally not much better. This is often due to the officers' lack of tolerance and ease to anger. At home, burned out officers often experience increased marital problems and family discord. They may be drinking more, smoking more, or taking more over-the-counter or prescription drugs (hopefully, not illicit drugs, but this has been known to occur). Physical symptoms increase. These range from gastro-intestinal difficulties to severe headaches. In serious cases of burnout, officers may experience eating disorders, sexual dysfunction, anxiety, low self-esteem, depression, and suicidal thoughts. Overall, due to a lack of concern for consequences, burned out officers behave uncharacteristically poor at work and at home.

Certainly, not all officers that experience burnout will follow the described sequence. Many officers struggling with burnout are able to improve their condition before the occurrence of any dire consequences.

Avoiding or Managing Burnout

To avoid or manage burnout, officers need to maintain good personal boundaries and a positive life balance. It is easy to become fatigued and frustrated with citizens, offenders, supervisors, administrative policies, failed attempts to be promoted, coworkers, departmental politics, the court system, and other work challenges. To buffer against these stressors, officers must continually remind themselves of the Occupational Imperative: *never forget why you do, what you do.*

The values of policing are noble. History is filled with accounts of police officers' bravery, commitment, and sacrifice. Anyone who has carried or carries a badge inherited this history and has contributed to it. Police officers believe in service. They believe in safety, the law, and individual freedom. They risk their lives to maintain positive social order. They do this in spite of the knowledge that there are those who would intentionally harm them. Police officers care. This is why they do what they do. When officers lose sight of the values which attracted them to policing they plunge headlong into burnout. To keep from becoming burned out, officers need to remain connected to the values that first brought them to policing.

Many burned out officers need a break. Taking a temporary respite from any stressful work environment is a welcomed relief and can be energizing. While on break, officers can reassess their careers and their desire to continue in policing. If they decide to continue in policing, even if the desire is low, they should try something different once back to work. Occupational withdrawal (trying to stay below the supervisor's radar) should be avoided. This is because continuing to withdraw from the primary elements of the job will almost certainly strengthen the symptoms of burnout. To combat burnout, what is needed is reengagement. *Burned out officers must reengage policing and reclaim their careers.* They need to rediscover their values and engage in policing behaviors which previously provided job satisfaction. They need to reassess and reinstate their personal and professional values and boundaries.

For police officers, a useful way of avoiding burnout and thinking about boundaries is circles. Officers need to recognize their *circle of control*. They must think about what can be controlled, what to accept as not controllable, and what to confront in an effort to bring about change. Just thinking in these terms will initiate the self-empowerment process. This is a counterbalance against burnout.

Outside the circle of control is the *circle of influence*. Many things that cannot be controlled can be influenced. The difference is that desired outcomes for things that can only be influenced may not be achieved. Healthy officers know this distinction and quickly recognize what can be controlled and what can be influenced. Outside the circle of influence lies everything else.

By reclaiming their careers, police officers can look forward to many more years of self-satisfaction, job satisfaction, and service to the community.

Boreout

In addition to burnout, police officers may also experience *boreout*. Boreout is a term first used by Swiss management consultants, Peter Werder and Philippe Rothlin (2007). They describe it as the opposite of burnout. Although deprivational stress is a part of boreout, being bored out encompasses more than just not having enough to do. Boreout involves being "understretched" at work. Being understretched results in feeling unchallenged. This is accompanied by listlessness and a feeling of helplessness arising out of not knowing what to do. Persons who are bored out have lost interest in what they are doing and lack any sense of identification with their job. For police officers, boreout can occur (1) after the challenge of learning how to be a police officer diminishes, (2) when officers feel underemployed or underutilized, and (3) upon being reassigned, transferred, or promoted (some officers will be overwhelmed by the demands of reassignment, etc; others will not have enough to do). To address boreout, officers need to reevaluate their position, rewrite job descriptions, initiate new programs, develop new job functions, take on rewarding challenges, contact supervisors and address assignment parameters, expand job responsibilities, and similar to burnout, *reclaim their careers*. The answer to boreout is creativity.

Life Management Skills

Developing life management skills is empowering and enhances the functionality of person-environment transactions. But what skills are needed to manage stress, cope with anxiety, and facilitate a positive life balance? To help keep yourself healthy and balanced there are some things that you can do; there are some things that may be helpful to remember.

Some Things to Remember consists of several strategies and ideas which can help you to maintain healthy lifestyle. Most are self-explanatory, some are not. This is because some are used as part of specific intervention programs and cannot be elucidated within the scope of this book. Some will be discussed in upcoming chapters.

Some Things to Remember

- Watch how you talk to yourself (relationship with self)
- Relaxation breathing-*breath through stress*-inhale nose/exhale mouth
- Maintain a high level of self-care, make time for *you*
- Keep yourself physically active, not too much too soon
- Utilize positive and appropriate coping statements
- Add survivorship: "This is difficult but I won't let it defeat me"
- Enhance your internal (self) awareness and external awareness
- Remember the limits of your personal boundary
- Practice stimulus control and response disruption
- Monitor deprivational stress and overload stress
- Use "pocket responses" when needed/consider oblique follow-up
- Apply thought stopping/blocking to negative thoughts
- Identify and confront internal and external *false messages*
- Confront negative thinking with positive counter-thoughts
- Break stressors into manageable units; deal with one at a time
- Relax, then engage in a graded confrontation of what you fear
- A managed experience will lessen the intensity of what you fear
- Only experience changes experience, look for the positive
- Reclaim your marriage; reclaim your career; *reclaim your life*
- Thinking is not doing. At some point, implement your positive plan
- Stressor strategies: confrontation, withdrawal, compromise (combination)
- Match coping strategy with stressor – strategy must address stressor

- Remember: transactions and choice points = different outcomes
- *Work*: do not forget why you do what you do (Occupational Imperative)
- Utilize your physical and psychological buffers
- Healing involves changes in intensity, frequency, and duration
- Use your shield when appropriate (psychological shield against negativity)
- Things do not have to be perfect to be ok
- Create positive micro-environments within stressful macro-environments
- Think of strong emotion as an *ocean wave*- let it in, let it fade
- Trigger anxiety— *I know what this is; I know what to do about it*
- Goal to become *stronger and smarter* (with the above = the 2 and 2)
- *Walk* off and *talk* out your anxiety, fears, and problems (walk and talk)
- Being vulnerable does not equal being helpless
- Enhance resiliency - develop and focus your innate coping abilities
- Develop and practice relapse prevention strategies
- Develop and utilize a sense of humor, learn how to smile
- Time perspective: past, present, future (positive- negative)
- Things are never so bad that they can't get worse
- Do not forget that life often involves selecting from imperfect options
- Access your power: the power of confidence, coping, and management
- Stay grounded in what you know to be true
- Keep things in perspective: keep little things little, manage the big things

Practice *Some Things to Remember* as part of life-by-design.

Stress Management and the Proactive Annual Check-in (PAC)

The Proactive Annual Check-In (PAC) is an interactive stress management program consisting of an annual meeting between police officers and the police psychologist, a member of the peer support team, or another police department support person. The PAC offers a positive exchange of thoughts and information within a confidential setting.

The Proactive Annual Check-in is comprised of six primary elements:

(1) Annual visit with the department psychologist, member of the Peer Support Team, or other police department support person
(2) Confidential meeting that does not initiate any record
(3) No evaluation - it's a check-in, not a check-up
(4) There does not need to be a problem

(5) It's a discussion of what's happening in your life

(6) Participation is voluntary and encouraged

The goal of the PAC is to provide a safe, non-threatening, proactive forum for officers to talk about their lives. It is an opportunity to exchange information with a trained support person before any significant stressor related issues arise.

Following a PAC meeting, additional meetings or the initiation of a more comprehensive support program are available if requested.

Strategy for Comprehensive Officer Wellness (COMPASS)

The Comprehensive Model for Police Advanced Strategic Support (COMPASS) is a career-long inclusive strategy for officer wellness. It begins with appropriate pre-hire psychological assessment and extends beyond retirement. The four COMPASS points are (1) officer and family, (2) health and wellness, (3) police officer career, and (4) professional and peer support.

A graphic depiction of COMPASS is included in the Police and Sheriff Peer Support Team Manual. For more information about COMPASS visit *www.jackdigliani.com*

Chapter 4

Critical Incidents

It is strange to think how to this very day I cannot sleep a night without great terrors of the fire; and this very night could not sleep to almost two in the morning through thoughts of the fire.
—Samuel Pepys, after the London fire of 1666

Critical Incidents and Trauma

Critical incidents are characteristically different from the stressors of everyday experience. While the circumstances of everyday life can be stressful, critical incidents are those that lie outside the norm of common experience. Critical incidents are often unexpected, high in intensity, and have the potential to overwhelm normal coping mechanisms. They often represent a threat to the safety and welfare of self or others. They may involve injury, death, or near death.

Involvement in a critical incident can cause varying degrees of psychological trauma. This is because the actual outcome for a person who has been involved in a critical event is determined by the complex transaction of event circumstances, personal characteristics, and the perceived elements of the incident.

Some of the variables known to influence the traumatic responses of persons exposed to critical incidents are: personality and emotional stability; personal beliefs; prior training; personal assessment of possible options; assessment of personal performance; was the action planned or unexpected; suddenness of the incident; age of others involved; degree of blood and body destruction; and specific event circumstances.

Some incidents that appear critical when viewed from the outside may cause no or little psychological trauma to those involved. Conversely, some incidents that appear non-critical to observers may cause significant psychological trauma to those involved. Another way of thinking about this is that "critical" is a feature of the incident, while "trauma" is a concept associated with human experience. This is why two officers involved in the same critical incident in similar ways can experience different degrees of traumatization. Simply stated, any incident, whether or not it appears "critical" to an outside observer, may traumatize one or all of those involved.

The degree of traumatization following a critical incident can range from no or insignificant distress to a constellation of physiological, psychological, and sociological symptoms and impairment collectively diagnosed as Posttraumatic Stress Disorder (PTSD).

History of Posttraumatic Stress Disorder

Human responses to critical incidents have been observed since ancient times. Various societies conceptualized and explained these responses in a variety of ways. Much of how they were viewed depended upon cultural beliefs and the current state of medical knowledge. Like developing medical knowledge, much of the development of traumatic exposure theory came through observations of warriors and soldiers (Cosmopoulos, 2007).

In America, as elsewhere, it was recognized that many soldiers exposed to stressful battlefield conditions complained of racing heart, sweating, chest pain, and fatigue. This syndrome came to be identified as *soldier's heart*. In 1871, this condition was described in detail by American Civil War physician and surgeon, Jacob M. DaCosta (1833-1900). DaCosta called the condition *irritable heart*. Irritable heart has also come to be known as *DaCosta syndrome*. Today, DaCosta syndrome is viewed by most psychologists as the physiological components of an anxiety disorder.

The Great War, World War I, produced the notion of *shell shock*. Shell shock was thought to be caused by neurological damage resulting from the percussion of exploding artillery. Those suffering from shell shock experienced uncontrollable tremors, developed an inability to engage their environment, and were observed to exhibit the "thousand-yard stare." Many soldiers exposed to artillery bombardment developed shell shock. The shell shocked condition of some soldiers improved once they were removed from the front. Other soldiers were not so fortunate.

It was soon noticed that soldiers who were not exposed to artillery sometimes developed symptoms similar to shell shock. Clinicians came to realize that although bombardment was implicated as a causal factor of shell shock, other circumstances could also produce the condition. However, within the science of the time, not much more could be made of this observation.

It was during World War II and under the theoretical influence of Sigmund Freud that the concept of *combat neurosis* was developed. This condition was also known by a variety of other names such as combat fatigue, battle fatigue, and war neurosis. The observation that some soldiers developed combat neurosis while others did not led to the idea that personality factors were involved. Within the conceptions of Freud's psychoanalytical child development theory, such factors were thought to have their origin in childhood. It was hypothesized that those soldiers who developed war neurosis had done so due to poorly resolved childhood conflicts.

Following the *brainwashing* and *zombie reaction* observed in captured American soldiers during the Korean War, came Vietnam. The American military in Vietnam utilized the DEROS system of deployment. DEROS was the acronym for *Date of Expected Return from Overseas*. It provided a return date for all military personnel assigned to serve in Vietnam. From the deployment date, DEROS was thirteen months for marines and one year for all other services. In the vernacular of the day, military personnel, volunteers and drafted, would arrive *in country* on one date and return to *the world* a year or so later. Thanks to DEROS, everyone who went to Vietnam (except general officers) knew before they departed, the date upon which they would return. The theoretical benefit of DEROS was that military personnel did not have to be wounded or decompensate psychologically to leave the combat environment. All that personnel had to do to leave the war behind was to make it to their DEROS date.

Initial DEROS results were promising. In Vietnam, there were far fewer evacuations for psychological symptoms than in World War II or the Korean War (Goodwin, 1987). Based on this early finding, military psychiatrists proudly announced that they had discovered the secret to avoiding combat fatigue and mental decompensation in combat. However, this optimism soon faded. Although many Vietnam veterans managed to endure their war experiences for their tour of duty, once home, they developed serious psychological problems. The psychological difficulties experienced by Vietnam veterans upon their return to the United States are now nearly legend.

In light of these observations and the growing understanding of the psychological effects of critical exposure for all persons, the American Psychiatric Association developed and approved a new stressor-related diagnosis. In 1980, the third revision of the Diagnostic and Statistical Manual of Mental Disorders (DSM-III) included for the first time ever, the diagnosis of *posttraumatic stress disorder* (APA, 1980).

The diagnostic criteria for posttraumatic stress disorder have changed several times since its inception, although *critical exposure* has remained a constant. Depending upon the number and intensity of symptoms, posttraumatic stress disorder can be thought of as ranging from mild (minimum criteria to make the diagnosis) to severe (all or nearly all of the diagnostic criteria are present in extreme form).

The critical exposure necessary for the diagnosis of posttraumatic stress disorder can include the experience of various and unusual perceptual phenomena.

Critical Events: In-progress Altered Perceptual Phenomena

Out-of-the-ordinary perceptual experiences can occur during a critical incident. One of the most common is *slow motion*. During this phenomenon, events seem to slow down and progress in slow motion, much like in some Hollywood movies. Many police officers have had slow motion experiences during critical incidents. They have reported seeing bullets fired from their guns travel slowly through the air, watching objects fall at a slow rate of speed, and seeing persons running as if they were running through water. The opposite of slow motion, faster-than-normal motion, is another perceptual distortion possible during a critical incident. The experience of faster-than-normal motion is less common than slow motion.

Other in-progress perceptual phenomena reported during critical events include time distortions, heightened visual clarity, sound distortions, automatic pilot (behavior without conscious thought), tunnel vision, and temporary paralysis (Artwohl and Christensen, 1997).

The Aftermath of Critical Incident Exposure

There are many possible responses to critical incident exposure. Some are more typical than others. A common response to critical exposure is a *heightened awareness of danger*. A heightened awareness of danger following exposure to a critical event involves the potential becoming real. To better understand this, recall the working environment of police officers. Police officers work every day with the knowledge that they could be called upon to confront dangerous persons and to respond to life threatening situations. They also realize that during their tour of duty they may be injured or killed. This knowledge is emotionally buffered by psychological defense mechanisms (chapter 7). These defense mechanisms make working in a dangerous environment easier. *Denial* (I am safe, nothing will happen to me today) and *rationalization* (I will be able to control or manage whatever comes my way) are two defense mechanisms which work to suppress the fear and anxiety associated with working in dangerous environments. When officers are involved in an incident that challenges these assumptions, these normal defenses are ripped away. Without them, the officer stands emotionally unprotected; the dangers of the work environment are no longer buffered. The *potential* danger has become *real* danger. Thoughts like "These things happen to someone else," which are common prior to a traumatic exposure, become "If this happened to me once, it can happen again." The result is a heightened awareness of danger. This occurs despite the fact that the environment was likely as dangerous the day before the incident as it was the day after the incident. The environment does not need to change. It is the *sense* of danger *in* the environment that has changed.

Anyone can experience a heightened awareness of danger following a critical incident. Victims of robbery, assault, gang violence, and so forth often talk about not feeling safe. The same is true of persons involved in serious motor vehicle accidents. Following the accident, even those who have been driving for years without fear or worry become anxious when they get behind the steering wheel, at least for a while. In these cases, the dangers represented by the road and other drivers have gone from the potential to the real.

Other after-the-fact responses to critical incidents may include anger, blaming, sleep difficulties, second guessing, emotional numbing, guilt, isolation, grief, depression, anxiety, loss of interest in sex and other activities, family difficulties, and pretty much any other experience possible for human beings.

Realtown, U.S.A.

There is no telling what might emerge as the primary issue following a critical incident. The case of Realtown, U.S.A. provides an illustration.

One of the last places a critical incident might have been expected is in the small community of Realtown (fictional name for an actual community). Realtown is comprised of less than five hundred residents. Realtown had one police officer. Several years ago, during the summer months, the police officer, who also had responsibilities to turn on the town park's irrigation system, began his work shift. As was his practice, he would leave his home, go to the park, turn on the sprinklers, and return home for a coffee break. After the coffee break, he would return to the park, turn off the watering system, and continue with his duties.

On this afternoon, he followed his normal routine. He left his home, went to the park, and turned on the irrigation. He headed home. Upon approaching his home, he heard high-pitch screaming and thought that his wife might have fallen. He entered the home from the back. He observed his wife, a woman in her 50s, face down on the floor. A man was crouched over her, straddling her. He was holding her head with his left hand. In his right hand was a knife that he had just pulled across her throat, cutting her throat as he drew the knife from left to right. She was bleeding profusely but still conscious. The officer, also in his 50s, drew his weapon and fired three times. The perpetrator was hit and fell away from the officer's wife. She managed to get up, make her way to the bathroom, and wrap a towel around her throat.

The officer called for emergency medical assistance. First responders were dispatched. First responders are persons trained to provide first aid. In small communities, where more sophisticated emergency responses may take quite some time, they are the only nearby available medical assistance. This was the case in Realtown.

As the wife held the towel around her neck, a first responder arrived. To the shock of the officer, the first responder began to treat the perpetrator. It was not until the arrival of other medical personnel that the wounds of his wife were addressed. The first arriving ambulance transported the perpetrator to the hospital. About fifteen minutes later, the victim was transported.

Upon her arrival at the hospital, she was rushed into the operating room. During a two hour surgery, she received eleven pints of blood. Her right and left carotid arteries had been injured. Fortunately, she survived her wounds and the surgery. Emergency physicians later stated that had she arrived at the hospital about three minutes later than she did, her wounds would have been fatal. She would have bled to death.

The perpetrator died. Investigation revealed that he lived in a nearby town. The officer and his wife reported that he was a total stranger to them. There was never a motive established for the assault.

A few weeks after the wife was released from the hospital, she and her husband came to my office. Although I had been advised of the incident, I was not quite certain what to expect. When they sat down, I could clearly see the results of her neck wound. By its appearance, I remember feeling surprised that she survived. As I listened to their account of the incident, I was struck by how well adjusted the couple appeared. They had come to terms with the home invasion, the seemingly random violence, the near death, the death of the perpetrator, and the defense of the wife by the husband. There was only one obstacle on the path of their continuing psychological recovery. The husband, pointing to his wife, expressed it this way, "She was dying, and the medics ignored her and were helping the bad guy!"

Shock, Impact, and Recovery

Various researchers have identified several predictable responses to critical incidents. These can be reduced to three principal phases: Shock, Impact, and Recovery. This general response pattern is frequently observed in persons exposed to critical events.

Shock—psychological shock is often the initial response to a critical incident (physiological shock may also be present). Psychological shock is comprised of a host of discernible reactions including denial, disbelief, numbness, giddiness, bravado, anger, depression, and isolation.Shock reactions, although common following trauma, are not limited to trauma. Shock can occur in response to any significant event. Football players who have just won the Super Bowl frequently respond to questions from sports interviewers by saying, "I can't believe it" (disbelief) or "It hasn't sunk in yet" (no impact).

Impact—after the passage of some time, the amount of time differs for different people, there is impact. Impact normally involves the realization that "I could have been killed" or "This was a grave tragedy." These thoughts and the feelings that accompany them can be overwhelming. Officers should never be returned to full duty while they are working through the impact of a critical incident. Police agencies should have policy directives which provide for administrative or other appropriate leave until an experienced police psychologist evaluates and clears the officer for return to duty.

Recovery—recovery does not follow impact as a discreet event. Instead, with proper support and individual processing, impact slowly diminishes. As impact diminishes, recovery begins. A person can experience any degree of recovery. No or little recovery can result in lifetime disability. Full recovery involves becoming stronger and smarter, disconnecting the memory of the incident from disabling emotional responses, and placing the incident into psychological history. Without recovery, persons remain victims of trauma. With recovery, they become survivors.

Posttraumatic Stress Disorder

The following is a summary of the contemporary diagnostic criteria for posttraumatic stress disorder (APA, 2013):

- Exposure to qualifying stressor(s)
- Intrusion
- Avoidance
- Negative alterations in cognitions and mood
- Alterations in arousal and reactivity
- Duration: symptoms for more than one month
- Distress or impairment
- Not caused by substance or medical condition

Specifiers: *with dissociative symptoms - with delayed expression*

Posttraumatic stress disorder as a diagnosis and clinical disorder is not without its detractors. Some clinicians have criticized the PTSD diagnosis on grounds that (1) it includes a clear cause (a critical event), (2) several normal reactions to less than desirable events are specified as symptoms, (3) many of the criteria of the diagnosis are seen in those who have not experienced a critical event, (4) any symptoms observed following a critical event are better accounted for by existing anxiety and depression diagnoses, and (5) because the diagnosis seems to be applicable following almost any stressful life event, it has become somewhat meaningless (Rosen et al, 2008).

Despite these issues, posttraumatic stress disorder remains an independent psychiatric diagnosis. It is likely that in light of these concerns and as it has in the past, the diagnostic criteria for posttraumatic stress disorder will continue to evolve.

Posttraumatic Stress, Posttraumatic Stress Disorder, and Acute Stress Disorder

Posttraumatic stress (PTS) is common following a critical incident. PTS is comprised of the predictable and often observed responses to a critical event. This is because by their very nature, critical incidents derail a person's normal coping mechanisms. PTS often involves some degree of intrusive thoughts, second guessing, heightened awareness of danger, appetite/sex/ sleep disturbances, and physiological arousal.

The primary difference between PTS and PTSD is that the reactions of PTS do not cause clinically significant distress or impairment. In other words, the components of PTS do not seriously disrupt the person's life as do the symptoms of PTSD. Frequently, with positive social support and the person's normal ability to process traumatic experiences, PTS will resolve within a month. This duration is another difference between PTS and PTSD; unfortunately, the symptoms of PTSD can last a lifetime.

In between PTS and PTSD is *Acute Stress Disorder* (ASD). In ASD, clinically significant distress or impairment is present, as are symptoms similar to PTSD. However, by definition, (1) ASD cannot be diagnosed until at least 3 days after the relevant incident and (2) the symptoms of ASD do not last longer than 30 days. If the symptoms of ASD are present for more than 30 days and are sufficient to meet the criteria for PTSD, the diagnosis is changed from ASD to PTSD (Appendix D).

In otherwise psychologically healthy persons, PTSD can initiate other mental disorders. The most common is depression. This is because the symptoms of PTSD are in themselves depressing. The symptoms of PTSD may also lead to high levels of suspiciousness, alcohol abuse, and marriage and family problems. Officers who suspect that they are suffering from ASD or PTSD should seek professional assistance immediately. Although treatment of PTSD may not include medication, the FDA has approved using Zoloft and Paxil to treat PTSD.

Traumatic Exposure, Vivid Images, and Visual Hallucination

Visual hallucinations in the absence of a psychotic disorder (chapter 9) can also be part of a traumatic experience. When present, the visual phenomena associated with traumatic exposure can be surprising and even frightening.

I once treated a client who was the front-seat passenger in a vehicle that had struck and killed a child the previous day. It was a tragedy. There was no driver negligence and no opportunity for the driver to avoid the child. The little girl had unexpectedly run into the street and was struck by the vehicle. When the vehicle struck the child, the force of the contact flipped the little girl onto the hood of the car and across the passenger side of the windshield. The image of the child as she rolled from the windshield to the ground was vividly impressed into the client's memory. Although shaken following the accident, the client was able to gather herself and return home following the initial police investigation.

The next morning at her home, the woman was standing at the top of the home staircase. As she moved to descend the stairs, she glanced downward. At the bottom of the stairs she saw the deceased child, standing and staring upward. She screamed and looked away. When she looked back, the child had disappeared. After dressing for work, and still a bit unnerved, she left her home and got into her car. In the rear view mirror, she could see a man sitting on the back seat of her vehicle. She screamed and instantly checked the area of the back seat. It was empty, the man had disappeared. Although she had never met the father of the deceased child, she sensed that the man she saw was the child's father. After these experiences, the hallucinations stopped.

It is also possible to experience *vivid images* during and following a traumatic event. Vivid images, while a visual perceptual phenomenon, are different from hallucinations. Unlike hallucinations, vivid images involve actual visual environmental stimuli. Consider the case of Officer M. Officer M responded to a call of a disturbance and found himself in a backyard, face to face with a seventeen year old suspect armed with a butcher knife. Officer M drew his weapon and ordered the suspect to drop the knife. The suspect did not comply and began walking toward the officer. As he was walking, the suspect began shouting "shoot me, shoot me!" Officer M, hoping to bring about a non-lethal resolution, began backing away from the suspect. By backing away, he could keep himself safe without having to shoot the young man. As the suspect continued his advance, the suspect unexpectedly drew the knife across his forehead. This caused profuse bleeding. Officer M could barely see the suspect's face.

Officer M retreated until he was backed into a corner, between a fence and a wood pile. He continued trying to reason with the young man. When he could not withdraw any further, he advised the suspect that if his advance continued, he would have to shoot him. The suspect was now approximately seven feet from the officer, still holding the knife. Officer M began to pull the trigger of his weapon. It was pointed directly at the suspect's chest. Officer M recounted, "My thoughts were at Mach I, but everything else was moving super slow." He remembered seeing the hammer of his weapon cocking back in preparation for firing. At this instant, several things happened. (1) Although the suspect was wearing a shirt, Officer M saw the suspect as bare-chested. He also observed two bullet holes in the suspect's bare chest. This was despite the fact that the suspect was still wearing a shirt and Officer M had not fired his weapon. (2) Thoughts began to run through Officer M's mind. The first thought was "Why is this weapon not firing?" (3) He thought of his children. They were close to the age of the suspect. What would they think of their father killing someone so close to their age?

About this time the suspect stopped and dropped the knife. He surrendered. To this day it remains unclear why. Maybe his anger and frustration had run its course. Maybe he realized that he did not want to die. Whatever the reason, the suspect had come very close to being killed by an officer who had literally run out of options (see *Option Funnel versus Threat Funnel,* page 85). Once the suspect surrendered, Officer M reported that everything snapped back to the present reality. His thoughts and perceptions returned to normal. The suspect was taken into custody, not shot and still wearing his shirt.

The next day, Officer M was in the shower. He was thinking about the incident and the strange experiences of the day before. Suddenly and to his surprise, he again saw the image of the bare-chested suspect. Again, there were two bullet holes in the chest. The image was so clear that it was "like a photograph." He was instantly overcome by a "deep sadness." He remembered, "Feelings flooded my body like I killed him, like I had done a horrible, horrible thing." He thought "I'm a cop. I shouldn't be feeling this way." He wondered where this image and these feelings were coming from. How were they even possible? He could not get the image out of his mind. He recalled that he thought he was going crazy. He considered quitting policing.

Visual hallucinations and vivid images are more common than believed in traumatic situations. Although the exact cause of such experiences is unknown, there is some speculation that it is related to increased levels of cortisol, a stress response hormone.

Many persons are reluctant to report hallucinations and vivid images for fear of being perceived as mentally ill or psychotic. If fact, they are neither. Visual hallucinations and vivid images are part of the brain's reaction to traumatic events. In most cases, they are short lived.

In the case of Officer M, he had experienced vivid images as the incident was unfolding, and an identical visual hallucination the following day. These images ceased, and the associated feelings disappeared soon after seeking professional treatment. Officer M returned to policing.

Psychotic and Other Stressor-related Reactions to Critical Events

True psychotic symptoms can be caused by traumatic exposure. In *brief psychotic disorder with marked stressor(s)* (previously known as *brief reactive psychosis*) several symptoms including visual and other kinds of hallucinations may be experienced. Brief Psychotic Disorder resolves within one month. If the symptoms continue for a longer period of time, the diagnosis must be changed. Other mental disorders (in addition to PTSD and ASD) that can occur as a result of traumatic exposure include adjustment disorder, conversion disorder, and a variety of mood disorders.

It was once thought that for police officers the severity of posttraumatic responses followed the *rule of thirds*. In this conceptualization, it was hypothesized that about one-third of all officers exposed to traumatic incidents would experience mild posttraumatic responses; another third would experience moderate posttraumatic responses; while the remaining third would experience significant to severe posttraumatic responses, including PTSD and other mental disorders. Although more research is needed to fully understand officer posttraumatic responses, police researchers Audrey Honig and Steve Sultan found only a 4 percent chronic PTSD rate in police officers involved in shootings. This is in contrast to 30 percent for combat veterans (2004). This suggests that the rule of thirds may be accurate for some populations and not for others. There are many variables which might account for population PTSD rate differences.

While there is little doubt that some officers experience severe reactions following critical events, others do not seem overly affected. It is not unusual following a critical event for officers to ask if it is "abnormal to feel ok." The answer is "No, it is not abnormal to feel ok." Many officers manage critical incidents quite well and suffer no long lasting ill effects.

Second-best Option

Treating the psychological aftermath of critical incidents is the second best option. The best option would be a time machine. With this, we would be able to move backward in time and change or prevent the incident. As this is not possible, the best we can do is to support those experiencing posttraumatic stress, and appropriately treat those diagnosed with posttraumatic stress disorder.

There are many considerations involved in the support and treatment of persons that have been involved in critical incidents. Several of these are discussed below, beginning with *second guessing.*

Second Guessing

Second guessing is common in human experience and it is nearly always a feature of post traumatic responses. Second guessing is the thought that your behavior might have been or should have been something other than what it was. It involves thoughts such as "Did I do the right thing?" "Why did I do that?" "I should (should not) have done X" and "Why didn't I do X."

Second guessing can be especially problematic for police officers because of the gravity of some police actions. Officers can "do everything right", act justifiably in accordance with their perceptions, training, and experience, and outcomes can still be tragic. For example, an officer who shoots a twelve-year-old child holding a toy gun, believing the child to be an armed assailant, will likely be plagued by second guessing. Second guessing in situations such as this can be psychologically punishing.

A variation of the "why" and "should" type of second guessing is the, "what if" and "if only." Officers sometimes refer to this as playing the "what if" or "if only" game. These are not intentionally played, and they are not really games. They are thought processes which seem to take on a life of their own. They replay over and over, intruding on other thoughts, disrupting activities, and disturbing sleep. The thoughts are usually something like "What if I turned right instead of left" "If only I departed a few minutes later" "What if I didn't go to the store" "If only I had stopped for coffee." This variation of second guessing is possible because of the manner in which most persons conceptualize reality - we commonly think that we could have done something other than what we actually did.

A consideration that is sometimes helpful with this type of second guessing is the understanding that in reality, even if "what if" and "if only" alternatives were possible, the outcome might not have been better. Maybe if you turned right instead of left, something even more tragic would have occurred. This is possible because we live in a world of contingency (chapter 12).

Second guessing involves evaluating a decision or action with information that was obtained after the decision had to be made or the action had to be taken. Officers can never know all of the factors involved in particular situations. This is because human behavior is ultimately unpredictable and some circumstances are so unusual, so unlikely, that officers cannot anticipate them. Persons can behave in ways which have no foundation in officer training or experience. Holding oneself accountable for failure to know, guess, predict, or otherwise anticipate the improbable behavior of others extends officers beyond the limit of human capability. The truth of the matter is that *every officer, every day*, makes decisions and takes action based on limited and sometimes flawed information. In spite of this, police officers consistently perform well. It is remarkable that in the police world of limited and often inaccurate information, officers perform as well as they do.

When confronting second guessing, officers should talk to themselves in the same manner that they would talk to another officer confronting the same circumstances. Many officers are much kinder to other officers than they are to themselves. To other officers, many officers are understanding, compassionate, and supportive. To themselves, many officers are rigidly unforgiving and overly critical. Learning to talk to yourself in the manner that you would talk to others is a functional, realistic, and productive way to address the complications of second guessing.

Single-exposure (One-shot) Learning

Single-exposure or "one-shot" learning has nothing to do with firearms or bullets. One-shot learning is a type of the classical conditioning paradigm made famous by Ivan Pavlov (1927). Simply stated, Pavlov demonstrated that an *unconditioned stimulus* could produce an *unconditioned response*. He showed this by administering meat powder to the mouth of dogs and measuring their salivation. Theoretically, the salivation upon the introduction of the meat powder did not represent learning. Salivation occurred as a natural response to the meat powder. In classical conditioning terms, the meat powder was the unconditioned stimulus, the salivation the unconditioned response. When Pavlov paired the introduction of meat powder with the sound of a metronome, the meat powder continued to produce salivation in the dogs. After a series of meat powder/metronome pairings, the sound of the metronome alone produced salivation. The sound of the metronome had become a *conditioned stimulus,* and the following salivation the *conditioned response*. The dogs had learned to salivate upon the sound of the metronome. Notice that the unconditioned response and the conditioned response are identical - salivation. The difference between the two responses is the stimulus that produced it.

One-shot learning is similar to the conditioning process observed in Pavlov's dogs with one significant difference, a series of parings is not necessary to produce learning. Instead, a single exposure to a particularly intense unconditioned stimulus can bring about a lifetime conditioned response. Often, the response is dysfunctional and unwanted. For example, consider the case of Mary G, a woman who was assaulted by a man with a beard. During the assault she experienced an overwhelming fear that she would be killed. She survived the assault and recovered from her injuries. The perpetrator was arrested, convicted, and imprisoned. However, from the night of the assault onward, Mary experienced intense fear whenever she saw a man with a beard. Mary's fear response (unconditioned at the time of the assault) had become conditioned to the previously neutral stimulus, *man-with-a-beard*. Beards had become a conditioned stimulus. Men wearing facial hair that approximated a beard produced varying intensities of fear for Mary; the actual response being dependent upon the degree of approximation. This is a process known as *generalization of conditioned stimuli.*

For police officers, one-shot learning works much the same. Following survival of a critical incident, officers can become conditioned to nearly anything, including the sight of police uniforms, police vehicles, certain odors, and the sound of police radio traffic. Conditioned fear or anxiety responses must be neutralized prior to an officer being returned to duty.

Unfortunately, historically, officers that suffered from undesirable conditioned responses managed them with alcohol, false bravado, or by simply gutting it out. Today, enlightened police agencies engage psychologists and other mental health professionals to assist officers to disconnect dysfunctional conditioned responses from the conditioned stimuli resulting from critical incidents.

Surface Lesson-Deep Lesson

Related to conditioning and one-shot learning is *surface lesson - deep lesson.* Surface lessons are comprised of specific knowledge gained from the critical incident. To illustrate a surface lesson, consider a woman who decides to walk in front of a stationary, running, unoccupied motor vehicle. She does not think twice about her crossing, as she has safely done this many times before. However, on this day, as she is walking across the front of the car, something unusual occurs and the car lurches forward. She is run over and pinned beneath the vehicle. After rescue and a hospital stay, she returns home. She suffers from a minor permanent disability, but overall is feeling well. In this case, the woman has learned that it is not always safe to walk around the front of a running automobile (the surface lesson). This is a well learned lesson and similar behavior is not likely to be repeated. After the passage of some time, her life returns to normal with one major exception. She still feels uneasy around automobiles. In fact, she feels uneasy most of the time. She is at a loss to explain it.

For the woman, the nearly constant uneasy feeling is being driven by a deep lesson. Deep lessons, like surface lessons, are learned. They may or may not be conscious. When conscious, deep lessons include an irrational cognitive component. The irrational cognitive component in the above case might be something like, "I thought that I was safe when I crossed in front of the car, I was wrong. I think I'm safe now, I could be wrong."

Deep lessons produce anxiety, involuntary heightened levels of vigilance, and the perception of unknown danger. Depending upon the intensity, frequency, and duration of the anxiety, the anxiety generated by deep lessons can prevent a person from ever feeling safe.

Surface lessons and deep lessons can arise out of any critical event. Deep lessons normally involve the sense of safety and can follow any surface lesson. Like one-shot learning, deep lessons must be disengaged from surface lessons in order to minimize their impact and influence.

The Walk and Talk

The physiology of the stress response prepares us to do something physical. Critical incidents involve stressors which initiate and maintain the stress response. This means that during a critical incident your body is in a perpetual physiological state of heightened stress arousal. The increased arousal inherent within the stress response helps us deal with the demands of the incident (fight or flight).

Once the incident is over, the need for heightened arousal ends. Your body will eventually "reset" itself to more normal levels of functioning. Until this process is complete, you will continue to experience the effects of the stress response.

You can help your body to restore system balance by engaging in the *walk and talk*. Walking and talking help to utilize the physiological arousal of the stress response for its designed purpose - action. The activity involved in walking and talking will reliably dissipate the physiological arousal associated with the stress response.

The walk and talk is an important peer support team member skill (chapter 5). Peer support team members are trained to walk and talk with officers experiencing heightened stress arousal.

Based upon what we know about the stress response, police officers should never be locked in the backseat of a patrol car or be left alone in small confined building spaces following involvement in a critical incident. Officers should be placed in a secure area, large enough to walk while they talk.

The 2 and 2 – Stronger and Smarter

Accomplishing the *2 and 2* is a primary goal for recovery following a critical incident. The first 2 is "stronger and smarter." Stronger and smarter is a guiding principle. It serves as the most, if not only, acceptable outcome following a traumatic experience. After all, following traumatic exposure, would "weaker and traumatized" suffice? Stronger and smarter endorses the idea that surviving a traumatic experience should somehow contribute to personal growth and wisdom. It is a conceptualization that helps to integrate the experience into our lives and in some way profit from it.

To avoid lifetime traumatization and to become stronger and smarter, something positive must be found in every traumatic exposure. If you are exposed to a traumatic incident and something positive is not readily apparent, you must search the experience until something positive is found. This does not mean that you ever have to view the incident as positive, but only that you must find something positive within it. To assist in your search, you must open the experience. You must look at the big picture. To focus on the worst of the experience is to provide it with power. Looking at the entire incident provides balance. It provides a more accurate and more realistic view so that positive recovery becomes possible. When searching for the positive, remember, at the very least, it is positive that you survived. But keep looking. You will find more.

The second 2 is "I know what this is. I know what to do about it." It is knowledge and skill that will help manage the nearly inevitable anxiety and strong emotion which follows most traumatic events. For anxiety, it works like this: (1) Officers are trained to identify conditioned responses and manage anxiety. (2) When anxiety is experienced in the absence of a threatening stimulus, officers are able to recognize the anxiety as triggered by a previous element of the traumatic incident (for example, feeling anxious at the sound of benign police radio traffic). (3) Once the anxiety is identified as originating from the past traumatic incident (I know what this is), officers engage anxiety reduction techniques (I know what to do about it).

Understanding the source of the anxiety and knowing how to reduce it is empowering. Officers can now interpret this anxiety as discomfort, not danger, because it is not in response to a real threat. The anxiety is little more than an unwanted reaction originating from the historical traumatic incident. This helps to remove the mystery of the anxiety. "Knowing what this is, and knowing what to do about it" involves controlling one part of the brain (emotional) with another part of the brain (cognitive). The more the officer succeeds in reducing anxiety over time, the more effective the intervention becomes. "I know what this is. I know what to do about it" is a component of "stronger and smarter." These features are the cornerstones of the 2 and 2.

Chronological History and Psychological History

Officers who have experienced critical events want to place the incident behind them and move on. The difficulty for many officers is that the incident continues to impact their lives in undesirable ways. This is because the incident, while in chronological history, is not yet in psychological history. The incident is in chronological history the instant that it is over. When thoughts and other stimuli associated with the incident evoke powerful traumatic responses after the incident, the incident is not in psychological history.

Placing the incident into psychological history involves disconnecting the memory of the incident from the undesirable and sometimes gut-wrenching emotional responses experienced during or immediately after the incident. When an incident is in psychological history, conditioned responses are minimized. Thoughts of the incident may produce emotional responses, but they will not be disabling. The officer will be able to move forward, no longer being psychologically stuck in the incident.

A major component of critical incident recovery is placing the event into psychological history.

Having the Right versus Is It Right

An issue that is especially important for police officers to consider is *having the right* versus *is it right*. Officers may need to defend themselves with lethal force. In this defense, someone may die (not all applications of lethal force result in death). Processing this thought is important for police officers. Officers know that they have the right to protect themselves and a duty to protect others. This is a legal matter and not overly difficult to sort out. But is it right to protect oneself or others if it means killing someone? This is a moral issue that should be addressed by every police officer. It is best to think and feel through this issue before it is ever confronted in reality.

Option Funnel versus Threat Funnel

The idea of *option funnel versus threat funnel* helps to place traumatic events in perspective. When there are options available, the threat to officers is usually low. As the number of options decreases, the threat to officers generally increases. Therefore, option versus threat is negatively correlated. At the bottom of the option funnel is self-defense. When this is the only option remaining for officers, the threat level increases dramatically.

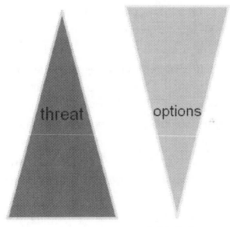

Self-defense

Police officers can be brought to the bottom of the option funnel very quickly. The case of Officer R is an example.

Officer R was one of several police units dispatched to an incident of possible domestic violence. The informant, Julia, contacted police and reported that she was concerned for the safety of her daughter, Lisa. Lisa and Lisa's husband Roy, both in their 20s, had driven to Julia's location and left their child with Julia. As this was unusual, Julia became worried about Roy's intentions. She provided police with the license plate number of Lisa's car. Officers did not have many details, only that Roy had a violent history and that he had access to firearms.

In calls like this, the goal of police officers is to contact those involved, ascertain their welfare, and make certain that there have been no criminal violations.

Officer R obtained the address associated with vehicle's license plate. He drove to the vicinity of the address in an attempt to locate the couple. After a short period of area surveillance, Officer R saw Lisa's vehicle approaching the couple's residence. He used the police radio to coordinate the response of other police units. When other units arrived, he planned to stop the vehicle and ascertain Lisa's safety.

Although Officer R did not engage his emergency lights, the vehicle stopped suddenly. Officer R maneuvered his police car behind Lisa's vehicle. The windows of Lisa's car were darkly tinted and Officer R could not see inside. He used the public address system of the police car to advise Lisa to exit the vehicle. Her exit would help ensure her safety. The passenger door of the vehicle opened and a person stepped out. It was not Lisa. It was Roy. Roy turned clockwise and began walking toward Officer R.

By this time, Officer R had positioned himself in the "V" of his police vehicle. The V is the position behind the opened driver's door, looking across the hood of the vehicle. Due to the nature of the call and standard officer safety practices, Officer R had drawn his handgun. He began to shout commands to Roy. Because of the placement of the vehicles, Officer R did not immediately see the pistol-grip shotgun that Roy was carrying. As Roy continued walking toward Officer R, he raised the shotgun, pointed it at Officer R, and fired. Officer R returned fire. The first of Roy's shots imbedded buckshot into the grill area of Officer R's police car. Roy fired a second round which missed Officer R, partially due to Officer R's evasive movements.

During the seconds-long shootout, Officer R fired seven rounds. Roy was struck by two of them. Roy was stopped only five feet in front of Officer R's position. He died of his wounds. Officer R was uninjured. Sometime after the incident, Lisa's aunt, representing the whole of the family, wrote this letter to Officer R (reproduced as written, names changed to protect identity):

Dear Officer R. First let me apologize for being so long writting this to you. I was out of town for awhile after it happened. I know you want to try to put all of this behind you & get on with your life. I am Lisa's aunt, her Mother is my Sister. Thank you for saving Lisa's life. We are sad that Roy (Rick as we knew him) had to die at such an early age & in this manner. But I am glad he is out of our lifes. We tried to help him by accepting him into the family. He really made Julia & her families life pretty much "hell" in the 2 years he & Lisa were married. He was a time bomb waiting to explode & He did. Justice was served & I praise & thank God that no one else was hurt or killed. I pray you can put all of this behind you. Please don't feel guilty in any way. You did what you had to do. Thank you. God bless you in your job & in your life as you serve your community in this way. Sincerely, Catherine Parker (reprinted with permission)

Note: Persons who are unfamiliar with police tactical defense might ask, "How is it that Officer R fired seven rounds and only two struck the suspect?" In this case, Officer R is point shooting. He is attempting to stop an advancing, moving threat by pointing and firing his weapon. This is different than sight shooting, where an officer has time to acquire a sight picture over the target sights of a weapon. Point shooting is often the only option available to police officers. It tends to become more accurate as a moving target advances and the distance between the shooter and the target is reduced. The suspect was also point shooting.

Lisa as well wrote to Officer R. She wrote three pages of hand written text. Below are some excerpts. It began:

Dear Officer R, sorry its taken me so long to get this to you but I haven't had much spare time . . . I really wanted you to know how sorry I am for everything you have been through . . . I have absolutely no hard feelings towards you . . . I'm so relieved you were not hurt or killed . . . I hope you will continue to be a police officer . . . The force needs all the good men & women it can get . . . Finally, I would like to thank you for saving my life & the life of the baby inside me. If Roy would have taken you out, he would have probably taken me next. Because of you I'm alive & the baby's holding on . . . There's no way I could ever really thank you enough. I guess this sums up what I needed you to know ... You ... will be in my thoughts & prayers for a long time to come. Sincerely, Lisa

Second Injury and Secondary (Vicarious) Trauma

The concept of second injury acknowledges the fact that persons can be traumatized or further traumatized by the way in which they are treated following a critical incident. In policing, treating an officer like a suspect following involvement in a critical incident, especially an officer-involved shooting, will almost certainly create a second injury. Unless there are specific reasons to interact with an officer in this way, the last thing officers need following a fight for their lives is to be treated like a criminal. Police officer second injury can also be caused by insensitive press stories, undeserved criticism from city leaders and activists, comments by spouses and family, statements of relatives of the suspect, and many other sources.

For police agencies, buffering their officers against second injury should start long before officers "hit the streets." It should start with orientation training in the police department pre-service skills academy. It should continue through the careful design of protocols and policies which guide the actions of department members following critical events.

Second injury is different from secondary trauma. Secondary or *vicarious* trauma is the term used to describe the traumatization of those who are exposed to persons who have been traumatized. This includes those attempting to help traumatized persons by listening to their account of their experiences. Mental health professionals, peer support team members, police officers, and police family members are at risk for secondary trauma. The concept of secondary trauma recognizes the fact that interacting with traumatized persons can itself be traumatizing. Those exposed to traumatized persons must seek support and assistance for themselves in order to avoid or manage secondary trauma.

Pocket Responses

Many times following a critical incident, involved officers will be approached by others who wish to know details about the event. Providing an account of the incident over and over to curious acquaintances can in itself retraumatize. To avoid being retraumatized and appearing discourteous, officers should consider using pocket responses. A pocket response is a previously thought out (kept in your psychological pocket) reply to undesired inquiries. For instance, the response, "I'm ok. Thank you for asking. Good to see you" is a pocket response to a question about your welfare. A pocket response to the question, "What happened?" is "It was something. I'm fine. Thanks for asking." With pocket responses, officers do not have to think about what to say. The pocket response is used; stress and retraumatization (or simply annoyance) is avoided.

Officers can add an *oblique follow-up* to the pocket response. A useful oblique follow-up is saying something like "Got to go, take care" and walking away. By using the oblique follow-up, officers remove themselves from a situation wherein they can be asked further questions.

Any reply can be used as a pocket response. Officers should construct pocket responses that best fit their personalities and best meet their needs in various anticipated circumstances.

Administrative and Criminal Investigations

There are many circumstances that can cause a police agency to initiate an investigation of its police officers. Some have to do with suspected wrongdoing; some are a matter of protocol. In officer-involved shootings and some other critical incidents, two investigations will be conducted: administrative and criminal.

The administrative investigation is conducted to determine if there has been a violation of agency policy. The criminal investigation is completed to determine if there has been a violation of law. Police officers know about these investigations. They know that if they are involved in a shooting, the circumstances and their actions will be investigated. This is a fact of police life. However, knowing this does not make such investigations stress free. It is always stressful to be the subject of investigation, even if the officer knows that there was no violation of either policy or law.

There are particular civil rights that accompany criminal investigations. Hollywood has made famous the U.S. Supreme Court ruling in *Miranda v. Arizona* (1966), which mandates that police read suspects their constitutional rights prior to a custodial interview: "You have the right to remain silent. Anything you say can and will be used against you in a court of law. You have the right to talk to an attorney and have an attorney present with you while you are being questioned. If you cannot afford to hire an attorney, one will be appointed to represent you before any questioning if you wish. You can decide at any time to exercise these rights and not answer any questions or make any statements." Police officers, like others, have the full protection of the Constitution in criminal investigations. They have the right to remain silent, and so forth.

Administrative investigations are somewhat different. Under the U.S. Supreme Court ruling which arose out of *Garrity v. New Jersey* (1967), police employees do not have the right to remain silent. In fact, they must cooperate with an administrative investigation or have their employment terminated. The following paragraph is part of an actual employee advisement (sometimes called a Garrity Advisement) of a police agency. The advisement is read and communicated in writing prior to an employee interview during an administrative investigation:

> You must cooperate with this investigation. Failure to cooperate will result in termination. Anything you say in this investigation cannot be used in any subsequent criminal investigation.

This paragraph highlights the relationship that exists between the two types of investigations. Information from a criminal investigation may be utilized in an administrative investigation, but information developed in an administrative investigation cannot be used in a criminal investigation. This is because in the administrative investigation, cooperation is mandatory (at risk of employment termination), while in a criminal investigation, police employees have the constitutional protections set out in the Miranda advisement.

Trauma Intervention Program

The Trauma Intervention Program (TIP) is a critical incident protocol guide for police agencies. It consists of several recommended components and strategies designed to assist officers and their families with the physical, emotional, and psychological aftermath of a critical incident.

The Trauma Intervention Program works best for officers when certain precursors have been completed. These are: (1) comprehensive pre-hire psychological assessment, (2) stress inoculation and trauma management training in the pre-service skills academy, (3) participation in the PATROL program during field training, and (4) involvement of spouse/family in agency familiarization and specialized education.

The Trauma Intervention Program: (1) has some elements that are implemented simultaneously and some elements that are implemented sequentially, (2) is flexible and may be modified to meet the needs of any agency, (3) may be modified to fit within available resources, (4) incorporates a police psychologist and a properly supervised peer support team, and (5) may be adjusted to accommodate circumstances wherein the involved officer was injured.

The Trauma Intervention Program is presented in outline form with elaborative information in italics.

Trauma Intervention Program

Precursor Programs—Pre-hire psychological assessment, pre-service skills academy training, PATROL, and spouse/family education.

1. *On-scene support*—provided by the police psychologist and the peer support team. *On-scene support begins with the police psychologist and/ or selected members of the peer support team. The officer becomes the client of the police psychologist so that confidentiality privileges are established.*
2. *Critical incident debriefing or small group/individual intervention*—as needed, provided by the police psychologist and peer support team. *Debriefings are best utilized for critical incidents where a need for debriefing has been identified. Often, individual interactions or small group interventions are adequate. The appropriate interventions are decided upon by the police psychologist with input from the peer support team. Members of the peer support team play a significant role in this part of the TIP. Officer participation in any group intervention is voluntary.*
3. *Considerations for intervention*—police psychologist. *The police psychologist initiates a counseling support program and continues to work with the officer and family. The following represent some of the issues which are considered. (Adjusted if the officer has been injured or is hospitalized):*

   - obtain contact numbers
   - criminal and administrative investigation issues
   - officer and officer's family security
   - spouse/children/family considerations
   - history—background and current status (bio-psycho-social)
   - medical, medications, psychological, social-support
   - support interventions: assessment and implementation
   - supportive therapy (cognitive/emotional/EMDR)
   - memory—stress response and frequent outcome

- photographs and recordings—as appropriate
- reports—review as needed
- educational and informative material—as appropriate

4. *Current work status: administrative leave or other*—modified work status in accordance with policy. *The police psychologist works with agency administrators to ensure that an agency contact person is appointed, that agency support continues, that any obligations that existed prior to the incident are managed in a satisfactory manner, and that the officer is not further traumatized.*

- department contact person
- *ongoing* department support
- administrators, supervisors, and peers
- officer and family security
- court, training, meetings, and so on
- police vehicle and equipment
- modified-duty considerations

5. *Equipment and other stimulus reintroduction if necessary*—anxiety triggers (uniform, patrol vehicle, radio traffic, etc). *This component of the TIP is unnecessary in some cases and absolutely necessary in others. Much depends upon whether there has been an acquired undesirable conditioned response to a previously neutral stimulus.*

6. *Incident site visit*—visit to location of incident from a psychological perspective. *Although the officer may have returned to the location of the incident for investigative purposes, this is insufficient to accomplish what is intended in the TIP site visit. TIP site visits are informative, experiential, sometimes emotional, and are used to help the officer further process the incident. They are also used to rule out the presence of anxiety triggers and other conditioned responses.*

7. *Firing range*—shooting exposure for shooting incidents (non-qualification, qualification). *If the critical incident involved the use of an officer's firearm, prior to returning to work, the officer shoots a non-qualifying course of fire for exposure (can be a loaner weapon). This is to ascertain whether the officer has any difficulties handling a firearm post-incident. The timing of this exposure is critical to the officer's recovery and is to be determined by the police psychologist. Later, prior to returning*

to duty, the officer shoots a qualifying course of fire. If the actual firearm used in the incident was taken for evidence, the officer shoots a qualifying course with the weapon once it is returned. The psychologist or a peer support team member may accompany the officer if requested or otherwise assessed appropriate.

8. *Officer Wellness Assessment*—as a component of the psychologist's support intervention (clinical interview, mental status examination, symptom assessment, rule out clinically significant incident-related distress or impairment). *The OWA is utilized to: (1) determine if the incident generated a stress disorder that would prevent the officer from safely returning to duty, (2) determine if the incident exacerbated a pre-existing condition that would prevent the officer from safely returning to duty, and (3) help determine optimal timing for the initiation of graded reentry.*

9. *Graded reentry*—return-to-duty protocol (RTD). *Graded reentry allows the involved officer to work with a partner and gradually resume the responsibilities of solo duty. An actual RTD is presented below.*

10. *Additional involvement of peer support team*—as needed. *The need for continued support from the peer support team is assessed and provided as requested or deemed appropriate.*

11. *Other considerations*—specific to the officer and incident. *This component of the TIP assesses, acknowledges, and addresses issues specific to the officer. Other persons or agencies may become involved if needed to address specific issues.*

12. *Follow through for the year of firsts*—first birthday, Christmas, and other meaningful dates, since the incident. *A member of the peer support team is chosen by the officer to provide support throughout the first year. This PST member helps the officer process any issues that might arise on holidays, the anniversary date of the incident, or any other date significant to the officer.*

Return-to-duty Protocol

Return-to-duty protocols specify the graded reentry for police officers. They have varying lengths and components, depending upon the assessed circumstances. RTD protocols that consist of less than thirty-five hours are not recommended. In most cases, a thirty-five-hour RTD will accomplish the goals of the protocol. The goals of the protocol include allowing a supported return to duty, re-exposure to the environment within which the incident occurred, anxiety management skills application, and checking for the presence of conditioned anxiety stimuli.

The following is an actual thirty-five-hour RTD utilized for a deputy sheriff following a robbery and shooting incident wherein the suspect was killed by deputies. The names have been changed to protect the identity of the deputies. Each shift is comprised of ten hours.

Recommended Return-to-duty Protocol for Deputy Bart Collins

Deputy Collins and I have visited on several occasions since the incident of (date). I am pleased to report that Deputy Collins has completed all phases of his Trauma Intervention Program. Deputy Collins is cleared for return to full duty effective (date). There are no patrol duty restrictions. Deputy Collins should not resume his duties as firearms instructor or function in any other special assignment until his Return-to-duty Protocol (RTD) is completed.

The following return-to-duty protocol is recommended. Any deviation from the protocol may prove detrimental to Deputy Collins and undermine the return-to-duty preparation work previously accomplished.

1. (*date*). Deputy Collins should work the entire shift as a partner to Deputy Land. Deputy Collins should function as a car partner/back-up officer and should not assume primary call handling or reporting duties. Deputy Land should drive his (Land's) assigned patrol vehicle with Deputy Collins accompanying.
2. (*date*). For the first half of this shift, Deputy Collins should accompany Deputy Land as specified in #1. For the second half of this shift, Deputy Collins should drive his (Collins's) patrol vehicle and assume primary call handling responsibilities with Deputy Land functioning as a car partner/back-up officer. *An actual change of vehicle from that assigned to Deputy Land to the vehicle assigned to Deputy Collins should take place mid-shift.*
3. (*date*). Deputy Collins and Deputy Land should work as specified for the last half of #2.
4. (*date*). For the first half of shift, Deputy Collins should work with Deputy Land and function as they did in #3. At the halfway point of this shift, Deputy Land should depart Deputy Collins's patrol vehicle and conclude the remainder of the shift independently. Deputy Collins works the rest of this shift solo. The RTD protocol has been completed.

Reflections of a Police Psychologist

5. (*date*). Deputy Collins works as normally assigned and assumes all normal departmental responsibilities.

Deputies Collins and Land have been briefed on the RTD. Additionally, a *safety net* comprised of several telephone communications between Deputy Collins and myself has been set in place. These communications are strategically placed within the RTD. In this way, the return process can be monitored, assessed, and adjusted if needed.

A follow-up meeting for Deputy Collins has been scheduled for (*date*). This is several weeks after the completion of the RTD protocol. The follow-up meeting allows for a brief assessment after Deputy Collins has worked solo for a period of time. Meetings beyond (*date*) will be scheduled only if deemed necessary.

Thank you and the Sheriff's Office for your support of my efforts to assist Deputy Collins. Your care and concern for the welfare of Deputy Collins is admirable and appreciated. Please do not hesitate to contact me if you have any questions or if clarification is needed.

Critical Incident Information: Officers and Spouses

Many officers have asked about how much incident information should be provided to their spouses. There are several factors that should be considered. Two of the most important are (1) is the officer retraumatized by recounting the information and (2) how much information is desired by the spouse.

For some officers, talking about their critical incident is not problematic. They can recount the event and their experiences without difficulty. For others, this is not possible. For them, each recounting of the incident is retraumatizing. In the latter cases, responding to a spouse's repeated request for more information may be detrimental to the officer.

Following a critical incident, some spouses want to know every detail. They want to see photographs, read case reports, listen to dispatch tapes, and so on. Other spouses desire or can tolerate only a broad description of the incident. For these spouses, providing more than general information may result in vicarious traumatization. This is especially true if the incident details involve blood, body damage, and gore.

To keep officers from being retraumatized and spouses from being vicariously traumatized, a healthy balance must be struck between how much information officers can provide without detriment to themselves, and how much information is desired by spouses.

A particularly difficult circumstance arises when the officer's need to talk about the incident exceeds the capacity of the spouse to listen. Capacity may be overwhelmed by the nature of the incident or the sheer number of times that the spouse has heard the story. Even if the officer is still struggling with the incident and feels better after talking about it, at some point most spouses will become *incident-info saturated*. They want to move past the event and get back to normal. For these spouses, like the spouses that cannot tolerate much incident detail, further exposure may result in vicarious traumatization.

Although things generally improve with time, there may be no getting back to what was previously normal. Some traumatic events will change persons and relationships forever. The officer and spouse (the entire family) must find a new normal and live on from there. The new normal may be better than the old, but the opposite is also possible. Some police officer relationships do not survive critical incidents. The incident either creates new and unbearable difficulties or intensifies previously existing problems. Some relationships collapse under the strain, and the couple separates. Other relationships appear to be strengthened by the pulling together of couples following traumatic exposure.

Suggestions for Supporting Officers Involved in Shootings and Other Trauma – Colorado Statutes and Other Jurisdictions

The following "Suggestions for Supporting Officers Involved in Shootings and Other Trauma" were written by Alexis Artwohl and published in her book, *DEADLY FORCE ENCOUNTERS*, co-authored by Loren Christensen (1997). My comments are represented in italics (added with permission). This information can be easily adapted to all jurisdictions.

1. Do initiate contact in the form of a phone call or note to let a traumatized officer know you are concerned and available for support or help (don't forget to acknowledge their significant others). In the case of a shooting, remember that the non-shooters who were at the scene are just as likely to be affected by the incident as the shooters. Remember that there are many other events besides shootings that traumatize cops. When in doubt, call. *Do not fall into the trap that*

"others will do it, so I don't have to." Your expression of support will be appreciated.

2. Offer to stay with a traumatized officer/friend for the first day or two after the event if you know they live alone (or help find a mutual friend who can). Alternatively, you could offer for the officer to stay with you and your family. *This type of support for an officer living alone can be quite beneficial for the first few days following a critical incident.*

3. Let the traumatized officer decide how much contact he/she wants to have with you. They may be overwhelmed with phone calls and it may take a while for them to return your call. Also, they and their family may want some "down time" with minimal interruptions. *As in the past, the Peer Support Team (PST) will continue its efforts to advise through email or other appropriate means when involved officers need a communication hiatus.*

4. Don't ask for an account of the shooting, but let the traumatized officer know you are willing to listen to whatever they want to talk about. Officers may get tired of repeating the story and find "curiosity seekers" distasteful. Be mindful that there is usually no legally privileged confidentiality for peer discussions. *Legal confidentiality privileges exist for particular relationships. These include licensed mental health professionals, attorneys, licensed or ordained clergy members, spouses, physicians, and some others. In Colorado, members of law enforcement, firefighter, and emergency medical service peer support teams are protected from testifying without consent in state courts under C.R.S. 13-90-107(m). However, this protection is limited and does not apply to federal courts. Because of these limitations, peer support team members should not talk about the incident with involved officers. Peer support team members are ethically responsible to specify the limits of their confidentiality protections prior to engaging in any peer support interaction.*

5. Ask questions that show support and acceptance such as, "Is there anything I can do to help you or your family?" *In some cases where the pre-existing relationship will support it, just doing instead of asking is appropriate.*

6. Accept their reaction as normal for them and avoid suggesting how they "should" be feeling. Officers have a wide range of reactions to traumatic events. *If part of their reaction is thoughts or feelings of*

homicide or suicide, or should you observe behaviors consistent with the "gravely disabled" mental illness criteria of C.R.S. 27-65-102, you should contact the police psychologist or a member of the PST immediately. Do not leave the officer alone.

7. Remember that the key to helping a traumatized officer is nonjudgmental listening. *Just listening without trying to solve a problem or imposing your views can go a long way to support traumatized officers.*

8. Don't say, "I understand how you feel" unless you have been through the same experience. Do feel free to offer a BRIEF sharing of a similar experience you might have had to help them know they are not alone in how they feel. However, this is not the time to work on your own trauma issues with this person. If your friend's event triggers some of your own emotions, find someone else to talk to who can offer support to you. *It's worthwhile to keep in mind that individual officers will frequently perceive a traumatic incident in a somewhat unique way. However, there is enough overlap in our experiences to allow us to relate to the experience of involved officers. A good rule to follow: If the involved officer asks you a question about your experience or how you handled a past incident, respond fully to the question, then re-focus on the officer. If additional questions are asked, respond in a similar fashion . . . the officer is requesting more information from you. Your responses are likely to normalize the feelings, thoughts, and behaviors which may be new or strange to the officer. Keep your responses concise and talk in plain language. Do not get stuck in your own unresolved issues. The last thing an officer who has experienced a critical incident needs from you is to become your therapist.*

9. Don't encourage the use of alcohol. It is best for officers to avoid all use of alcohol for a few weeks so they can process what has happened to them with a clear head and true feelings uncontaminated by drug use. *Remember, alcohol is a behavioral disinhibitor in small dosages and a central nervous system depressant in larger quantities. It is best not to be affected in either of these ways when attempting to process a traumatic event. Additionally, in order to avoid over stimulation and symptoms of withdrawal, caffeine intake should remain close to normal. Caffeine is a diuretic and vasoconstrictor. Its stimulant properties increase autonomic arousal and can cause a jittery feeling. Even small amounts of caffeine can interfere with*

sleep onset and maintenance in those not accustomed to it. Officers should stay within their normal limits of caffeine consumption.

10. Don't "congratulate" officers after shootings or call them names like "terminator" or otherwise joke around about the incident. Officers often have mixed feelings about deadly force encounters and find such comments offensive. *Mixed emotional responses can include feelings of elation that the officer survived the incident and performed well, while at the same time realizing that he or she had to injure or kill another person in order to survive. Mixed feelings, along with a heightened sense of danger, are two of the most common after-effects of shooting incidents.*

11. Offer positive statements about the officers themselves, such as, "I'm glad you're O.K." *Critical incidents frequently bring forward emotions and thoughts not present in everyday living. Making positive statements demonstrates support and caring. This frequently helps officers deal with the issues inherent in traumatic experiences.*

12. You are likely to find yourself second-guessing the shooting, but keep your comments to yourself. Critical comments have a way of coming back to the involved officer and it only does harm to the officer who is probably second-guessing him/herself and struggling to recover. Besides, most of the second-guessing is wrong anyway. *Keep in mind that the best anyone can do is to make reasonable decisions based upon perceptions and the information available at the time. No one really knows what it was like for a particular officer to be involved in a particular incident. Saying things such as "I would have done . . ." or "He (or she) should have . . ." is almost always damaging.*

13. Encourage the officers to take care of themselves. Show support for such things as taking as much time off as they need to recover. Also encourage the officer to participate in debriefings and counseling. *Officers involved in shootings and other serious traumatic incidents are engaged in peer support, debriefings, and counseling as appropriate. Remember, employees may, at any time, seek confidential assistance from the staff psychologist, the PST, or the Employee Assistance Program for any event or ongoing stressor. To access the names of PST members, contact Dispatch.*

14. Gently confront them about negative behavioral and emotional changes you notice that persist for longer than one month. Encourage them to seek professional help. *A general rule of confrontation:*

confront to the degree that the underlying relationship will support. In other words, if done in a caring way, the closer you feel to a person, the more you can confront without jeopardizing the relationship or creating harm. If this rule is followed, the likelihood of the officer responding positively to the confrontation is maximized.

15. Don't refer to officers who are having emotional problems as "mentals" or other derogatory terms. Stigmatizing each other encourages officers to deny their psychological injuries and not to get the help they need. *Getting through critical incidents is difficult enough. We do not need to make it more difficult by derogatory labeling. This includes general attitudes communicated in everyday speech as well as specific comments following a particular event.*

16. Educate yourself about trauma reactions by reviewing written materials or consulting with someone who has familiarity with this topic. *The police psychologist and PST have informational materials that can assist you in learning more about trauma and traumatic responses. Contact any member of the PST to obtain this information.*

17. Officers want to return to normality as soon as possible. Don't pretend like the event didn't happen but do treat the traumatized officers like you always have. Don't avoid them, treat them as fragile, or otherwise drastically change your behavior with them. *It is normal for officers who have been through a traumatic experience to become a bit more sensitive to how others act toward them. This increased sensitivity is usually temporary. You can help the involved officer work through this sensitivity as well as larger aspects of the incident aftermath by just being yourself.*

18. Remember that in this case, your mother was right: If you don't have anything nice to say, don't say anything at all. *In the final analysis, we cannot know which side of a critical incident we will find ourselves: an officer looking to others for support or an officer attempting to provide support. Our strength and defense lies in how we treat each other.*

Police Shootings and Officer Safety

Many officers respond to the news of an officer-involved shooting by better applying officer safety strategies. This is true even for officers who have become somewhat complacent. Unfortunately, this renewed effort for officer safety does not seem to last long. After some time without additional similar incidents, some officers again fall into unsafe "routine" police practices. These can be seen in the manner in which they conduct vehicle stops, deal with juveniles, respond to business alarms, position themselves when talking to suspects, and so on. Like many things in policing, officers become complacent at their own risk.

Recovering from Traumatic Stress

Recovering from traumatic exposure takes time. Trauma causes a "mental injury" which requires time and support to sufficiently heal. Conceptualizing traumatization as a mental injury instead of a mental disorder or mental illness is a positive way to support healing. This is especially true for persons diagnosed with PTSD..."Living with a mental illness can feel oppressive, incomprehensible, and hopeless. Living with a mental injury offers hope of healing" (Zimbardo, et al, 2012, xxi). This is because most persons expect to heal from an injury. This is not always the expectation when persons are told that they have a mental disorder or are suffering from a mental illness.

The most difficult challenge for action-oriented officers is to be patient in recovery. If you are traumatized during a critical incident, accept your feelings even if they surprise you. Many "tough" cops have reported crying like a baby following shootings and other critical incidents. They describe this experience of strong emotion as *having lost it*. They are talking about feeling as if they lost control—control of their emotions. In fact, they have not lost anything. Instead, they have found something. They have found the emotion that underlies their traumatic experience. When strong feelings surface, let them in, let them fade. Experience and explore the emotion. It is a natural part of being human and a natural part of emotional recovery. Imagine intense emotion as an ocean wave. It will come and it will go. Although it may feel overwhelming, you can manage it. You know what it is: it is the healthy expression of strong emotion. You know what to do about it: you breathe through it.

Keep in mind that physical symptoms sometime accompany strong emotion. These will normally subside as recovery continues. Additionally, remember that family members may not fully understand your experiences. Try not to become angry. They cannot know what it is like for you. Be kind to yourself. Be kind to those you care about. Assume an active role in your recovery. Seek assistance if you feel stuck. You do not have to go it alone.

Posttraumatic Stress Disorder and Disability

The nature of policing places officers at greater risk for exposure to work-related critical incidents. If an officer develops PTSD following a critical incident, and the symptoms are severe and enduring, the officer may become *totally* or *occupationally* disabled. Total disability occurs when the severity of the symptoms renders an officer incapable of engaging in any employment. Occupational disability occurs when an officer experiences disabling symptoms in the policing environment, but remains relatively symptom free in other work environments. This renders the officer incapable of returning to policing, but able to perform other work. This sometimes happens because traumatic experiences have the power to "split" environments. That is, whereas officers are normally PTSD-symptom free in their work environment prior to the critical incident, following the incident their work environment transacts to produce posttraumatic symptoms. In such cases, the officer cannot be returned to the type of environment that produced the traumatic event. In essence, work environments have been split into symptom and non-symptom producing environments.

Law Enforcement Critical Incident Handbook

The Law Enforcement Critical Incident Handbook provides practical information for officers involved in critical incidents. To download a copy of the Law Enforcement Critical Incident Handbook at no cost visit *www. jackdigliani.com*

Chapter 5

Police Peer Support Teams

A police officer should never not have a place to go.

- peer support team motto

Police peer support teams may be single or multi jurisdictional. Team members are specially trained in the principles of peer support, and may be trained to facilitate critical incident debriefing.

History of the FCPD/FCPS Peer Support Team

In 1986, the Fort Collins Police Department (FCPD), renamed *Fort Collins Police Services* (FCPS) later that same year, created its first ever peer support team. This small group was comprised of four police officers and was called the Traumatic Incident Debriefing Team (TIDT). As one of the four police officers that comprised the team and author of much of the policy that created it, I was selected to serve as the TIDT coordinator. At that time no one could anticipate how the Traumatic Incident Debriefing Team would develop or how integral a part of FCPS it would become.

Work to develop a peer support team within the FCPS had started several years prior to 1986. FCPS staff was generally supportive of the idea of a peer support team; however, they remained concerned about several issues. One of the concerns was summarized by an FCPS division director who stated, "If we have a team like this, officers won't take their problems to their supervisors." I remember my response: "They don't take their problems to their supervisors now. We can give them someplace to go." Thoughts about this response later evolved into a peer support team motto. I still use it today. Although it is bad grammar, it captures the essence of those committed to the concept of peer support, "*A police officer should never not have a place to go.*"

Another staff concern involved team member confidentiality. In 1986, the state of Colorado did not include peer support team members in the law that prohibits testifying without consent. This meant that there were no legal protections for the information obtained in peer support interactions.

In an effort to provide some protection for peer support team interactions, the proposed FCPS policy included this statement, "Issues discussed during any peer support interaction involving a member of the Traumatic Incident Debriefing Team shall be considered confidential and not subject to questioning during an administrative/criminal investigation." If approved, this statement would provide some protection for TIDT members from internal investigators, but would it protect team members from investigators who were not subject to FCPS policy? No one knew for certain. Despite this question, and with a willingness to explore new territory, then chief of police Bruce Glasscock on June 1, 1986, approved and signed into effect FCPS directive No. 58, *Traumatic Incident Policy*. This policy not only created the Traumatic Incident Debriefing Team, but also provided for team member confidentiality.

In 1986 the idea of peer support was relatively new to the field of policing. The FCPS endorsement of such a sweeping peer support team confidentiality standard was generally unheard of. Directive No. 58 demonstrated the significant commitment of FCPS staff to the principles of peer support.

Incidentally, the division director which I spoke of earlier, after observing the actions and results of the TIDT for a period of time, became one of its most ardent supporters. (Note: in 1986, an officer at the rank above lieutenant and just below that of chief of police was designated *division director*. This FCPS rank level has undergone several nomenclature changes since then, including, *deputy chief, commander,* and *captain.* Today (2015) at FCPS, an officer of this rank is once again designated *deputy chief.*)

In 1989, the Traumatic Incident Debriefing Team was renamed the *Critical Incident Team* (CIT). This name change was implemented because it seemed to be more descriptive of the team's mission and activities.

As CIT coordinator, I remained concerned about the provisions for peer support team confidentiality and relied primarily upon directive No. 58; however, several years had passed and there were no difficulties involving confidentiality. The CIT had doubled in size. Through its work, it had established credibility and had demonstrated its value. Personally, I was doing more individual counseling through CIT than ever before. The demand on my time for counseling became so great that late in 1989, I was granted one day out of each four-day work cycle for peer support counseling with other police employees.

In mid-1989, with my graduate studies nearly complete, I intended to separate from FCPS. I was planning to depart at the end of the year. My plan was to establish a private practice specializing in police psychology. Although I had not submitted any formal communication to FCPS staff, my plans became known. I am not certain how this occurred, most likely via the grapevine. I was approached by staff with a proposal. They proposed that I continue my career with FCPS. If I agreed, I would remain a police officer and be assigned to a full-time counseling position. I would also be permitted to design and develop the position within appropriate legal, ethical, and departmental parameters. To this day, I remain flattered and humbled by this proposal. I accepted. On January 1, 1990, I was honored to become the first ever FCPS Director of Human Services (DHS).

During this period, I was also developing professionally. Soon after being appointed the DHS, I was licensed as a professional counselor. Shortly thereafter, I was licensed as a psychologist. I was the only fully commissioned police officer/licensed psychologist in the state of Colorado.

As part of my duties as the Director of Human Services, I remained the coordinator of the CIT. I also became the CIT clinical supervisor.

Over the years, FCPS directive No. 58 evolved into General Directive 30, which later became FCPS Directive A-5. Directive A-5 continued to protect the confidentiality of CIT member communications. Directive A-5 has since become FCPS Policy 817.

Peer Support Team Confidentiality

As a licensed mental health clinician, my counseling communications were well protected by statute. But what of the peer support interactions involving CIT members? We had Directive A-5, which had served us well for many years. Was there more? There were two Colorado statutes that I considered relevant. It was with these two statutes that I would defend the confidentiality of peer support team interactions in the event of a challenge. Colorado Revised Statutes (C.R.S.) 13-90-107, *Who may not testify without consent*, paragraph (g) and 12-43-218, *Disclosure of confidential communications*, specify the confidentiality protections of licensed mental health professionals (among others). They also provide similar protection for those who are supervised by licensed mental health professionals. It was under the umbrella of clinical supervision that I conceptualized the confidentiality privilege for CIT members. Had Colorado not passed legislation which now includes peer support team members in C.R.S. 13-90-107, I would yet be prepared to present the "umbrella of supervision" argument. Whether this argument would have withstood a courtroom challenge remains unknown. A legal challenge to the peer support team privilege of confidentiality never materialized.

Critical Incident Team to Peer Support Team

In 2001, upon my departure from FCPS, the FCPS Critical Incident Team was renamed the Peer Support Team (PST). I endorsed this change because it reflected the growing standardization of nomenclature of peer support teams throughout the country.

Legislative Action

In 2005, the Colorado legislature considered a bill to add a paragraph (m) to C.R.S. 13-90-107, *Who may not testify without consent*. This bill proposed the inclusion of "law enforcement or firefighter" peer support team members to those protected under the statute. The bill became law the same year (2005) and established Colorado as the fourth state to provide some confidentiality protection for peer support team members. In 2013, C.R.S. 13-90-107(m) was amended to include "emergency medical service provider or rescue unit peer support team" members.

Specified peer support teams must meet several criteria to be afforded the privileges of C.R.S. 13-90-107(m) (Appendix C).

Confidentiality Complexities

The protection against testifying without consent afforded to those specified in C.R.S. 13-90-107 applies to courtroom testimony within the state of Colorado court system. For peer support team members, this protection is specifically limited. One significant peer support team member limitation is that the protections of C.R.S. 13-90-107(m) do not apply in cases where "there is information indicative of any criminal conduct."

Peer support communications are protected from disclosure during internal or administrative investigations by applicable department policy and adopted peer support team operational guidelines. If these protections are not written into department policy and/or guidelines, there is no PST protection in internal or administrative investigations.

The prohibition against testifying without consent for peer support team members specified in C.R.S. 13-90-107(m) does not apply to the federal court system. In a federal court proceeding, the information exchanged in peer support interactions becomes subject to disclosure. This is important to remember because incidents involving municipal, county, or state officers move to the federal court system when there is an allegation of civil rights violations. These claims are normally pursued in federal court under Section 1983, Title 42, The Public Health and Welfare, United States Code. In such actions, peer support team members can be compelled to testify. This is the reason that peer support team members should support officers involved in critical incidents *without discussing the incident*. While it is often helpful for involved officers to discuss their actions and experiences during and following a critical incident, such discussion is best left to state and federally protected confidential resources such as spouses, attorneys, psychologists, and clergy. Peer support team members must not be lulled into a false sense of security or confidentiality by the provisions of C.R.S. 13-90-107(m).

The Riverhouse Incident—Loveland Police Department

The Riverhouse incident occurred in Loveland, Colorado, on January 3, 1989. This incident, so called because it ended at the Riverhouse Restaurant, involved Larimer County sheriff's deputies as well as Loveland police officers.

Briefly, it began when officers responded to a reported domestic disturbance. As a deputy sheriff and a police officer met alongside the roadway leading to the residence to discuss their approach, the suspect drove up to them and shot the deputy. The suspect, still armed, fled the scene and drove to the Riverhouse Restaurant. There he took many customers hostage. As police and sheriff's deputies surrounded the restaurant, the suspect fired from his location within the restaurant, wounding a police officer. After some time, a police sniper observed the suspect holding one of the restaurant waitresses in front of him, pointing a gun to her head. The sniper fired, hitting the suspect. The suspect was not killed. The wounded suspect then fired a bullet into the head of the waitress, killing her. Immediately after that, he fired a bullet into his head, killing himself.

During the confusion that followed these gunshots, a hostage within the restaurant attempted an escape by diving through a restaurant window. The window was dressed with a curtain similar in color to the suspect's jacket. A police officer, seeing a flash of the curtain color and believing the escaping man to be the suspect, shouted commands for him to stop. When the commands were not followed, in a split-second decision, the officer fired. The man was killed. It was later determined that man attempting escape was hearing impaired.

The police officer and deputy sheriff that were shot during this incident survived their wounds. When it was over, three persons including the suspect, were dead. The Loveland Police Department requested assistance from the FCPS Critical Incident Team. I and other members of the CIT responded. It was not long after this incident that the Loveland Police Department established a peer support team.

The Riverhouse incident was my introduction to the Loveland Police Department. In 1990, through a contract arrangement, I became the Director of Human Services and peer support team clinical supervisor for the Loveland Police Department.

Brief History of Peer Support

In a sense, peer support has always existed. Eons before the arrival of the modern day conception of peer support, members of various groups relied on one another for support and solace. One can imagine ancient peoples sharing their thoughts and comforting one another when confronted with various challenges. Ancient writings and more recent historical documents are filled with such accounts.

In modern times, the power of peer support and mutual aid became especially evident in cases of alcohol addiction and attempts for sobriety. In America, in the 1870s the Drunkards Club was formed to assist those who wished to stop drinking. This was followed in 1914 by the creation of the United Order of Ex-Boozers, an organization with similar goals. Other sobriety support groups were created during this period. Most, like the Drunkards Club and the United Order of Ex-Boozers, eventually failed. Alcoholics Anonymous (AA), which was established in Boston in 1935, outlasted all of its predecessors and remains a force in the treatment of alcoholism and addiction. Whether successful or failed, all of these groups recognized the supportive power of the peer group and peer interactions.

Peer support groups are known for their endorsement of the *helper principle*, the idea that one is helped by helping others. This principle has long been a part of the foundation of AA and similar groups. The benefits of peer support to those who provide it are now universally recognized. This is not to say that providing peer support cannot in itself be stressful. Those persons providing peer support must practice self-care and must also be supported.

The principles and practice of peer support has been extended to include various populations, ranging from students to persons with mental disorders to emergency service workers and military personnel.

Peer Support Interactions – Level I and Level II

Peer support differs from counseling and psychotherapy. Peer support is a non-professional interaction wherein a one person attempts to support another person with whom they have something in common. Counseling involves a professional relationship in which a clinician attempts to help clients achieve specified goals. Psychotherapy is a form of counseling that is used to treat mental, emotional, or behavioral disorders through the application of psychological theory and intervention, with the goal being relief of symptoms, personality alteration, or increased functionality.

Peer support is based upon similar experiences, backgrounds, or history. These and other commonalities provide the "power of the peer" in peer interactions.

When thinking about peer support, it is useful to differentiate two levels. Level I peer support can be thought of as "traditional" peer support. This level of peer support is found in the everyday interactions of friends, co-workers, and others providing support to one another. Level I peer support is characterized by "friends talking" and "giving advice." It can consist of a one-time contact or ongoing interactions. For police officers, this level of peer support includes the *B and B* (booze and buddies) strategy for stress management. The B and B strategy of peer support has been around for awhile and is known to produce variable results. The outcomes of the B and B, like any Level I peer support, can range from very effective to quite dysfunctional.

Level II peer support has much in common with Level I, but there are some important differences: (1) Level II peer support is provided by members of an agency-recognized peer support team functioning within C.R.S. 13-90-107(m) and/or department policy, (2) Level II peer support is provided by persons trained in peer support, (3) Level II peer support interactions are characterized by elements of functional relationships which encourage exploration, empowerment, and positive change, (4) Advice giving is avoided in Level II peer support - independent decision making is encouraged, (5) Level II peer support is guided by ethical and conceptual parameters – this makes it different than just "friends talking," (6) Level II peer support has positive outcomes as its goal – this is not always true in Level I peer support interactions, (7) Peer support team members are clinically supervised by a licensed mental health professional - this provides a "ladder of escalation" if consultation or referral is needed. A structured ladder of escalation is not available in Level I interactions, and (8) Level II peer support, while non-judgmental, includes a safety assessment – it has an evaluative component. If a peer support team member assesses that the recipient of peer support is dealing with an issue that exceeds the parameters of peer support or if it is assessed that the recipient is or may be overly stressed, depressed, or suicidal, the peer support team member is trained to act upon the assessment. This is accomplished by providing information about available resources, making appropriate referrals, moving up the ladder of escalation, or emergency intervention.

Peer support team members capable of providing Level II peer support may continue to provide Level I peer support. Level I peer support occurs when peer support team members are not acting in their peer support team member role. However, when peer support team members are not acting in their peer support team member role, the confidentiality privileges afforded to peer support team members during peer support interactions do not apply.

Level II Peer Support

Level II peer support is not simply agreeing with whatever a person says while thinking that such agreement is "supportive." It makes no sense to agree with persons who are making decisions or behaving in ways that are degrading their lives. Instead, Level II peer support encourages the development of interpersonal rapport so that appropriate confrontation and positive change becomes possible.

Like Level I peer support, Level II interactions can consist of a one-time contact or an ongoing supportive relationship. Many times a person will initiate contact with a peer support team member only to ask a question or to obtain some information. Other times, peer support is utilized regularly or intermittently over a period of time.

Level II peer support can exist independently or function as a part of a comprehensive professional counseling program. Such professional programs can involve the police psychologist, the agency Employee Assistance Program, or a community psychotherapist. In many cases, peer support is sufficient and no other intervention is warranted. In some circumstances it can be more effective than professional counseling.

High-functioning peer support teams do not rely solely upon the initiative of others to engage members of the peer support team. History has demonstrated that many employees who are open to and would benefit from peer support do not initiate peer support contacts. There are several reasons for this, ranging from lack of knowledge about the peer support team to an exaggerated sense of self-reliance ("I don't ask for help from anybody"). Recognizing this, peer support teams should include in their operational guidelines a *reach-out* provision. This feature permits peer support team members to take the initiative in cases where it is suspected that proactive peer support would be beneficial. Reach-outs must not be intrusive, embarrassing, or be conducted in such a manner that they create or exacerbate a problem.

The Early Days of Police Peer Support

In the early days of police peer support, support groups (not trained peer support teams) were the order of the day. Police support groups were comprised largely of officers who had been involved in shootings or other critical events. These officers and the Level I peer support they provided, more often than not, were not officially sanctioned by the department. The groups that formed were more representative of officers reaching out to each other, sometimes to the dismay of department administrators. It was group support in its most rudimentary form. Officers became involved in these early peer support groups or interactions by default. That is, in order to provide or receive peer support, an officer had to have been involved in a shooting or other critical incident. During this period of police peer support development, it did not seem to matter whether the officers offering support had successfully processed their critical and often traumatic experiences.

As time passed, and more became known about what was then called *trauma syndrome, post-shooting syndrome,* and *post-killing syndrome,* some police agencies came to rely upon officers who had survived armed confrontations to help other officers involved in similar incidents. These officers answered the call and did everything possible to support other traumatized officers. The difficulty was that there were no formal departmental structures to support the officers that were trying to support other officers. The officers that were giving all they had to support other officers were at times providing this assistance at the expense of *their* psychological health. In fact, left to themselves, many officers were negatively impacted or retraumatized by their efforts to help other officers. This created the unfortunate situation wherein both officers, the supporter and the supported, were or became susceptible to psychological and emotional decompensation. It was not long after this realization that enlightened police agencies began to develop programs to prevent or manage the possible negative psychological outcomes associated with police shootings and other critical incidents. These programs included the availability of professional psychological services and trained peer support teams.

Peer Support Team Members

Police peer support team members may be sworn or civilian, employees or volunteers. Regardless of their status, peer support team members, like FTOs, (see chapter 2, p. 35) should possess an aptitude for helping and three primary characteristics: interest, commitment, and credibility (ICC):

(1) A peer support team member must have an interest in helping others and in the fundamental principles of peer support. Without interest, even the most skilled peer support team members eventually fail. Team members lacking interest are perceived by peer support recipients as distant, inattentive, and uninvolved in the peer support process. Interest is a vital component of functional peer support.

(2) With interest, a peer support team member must have commitment; commitment to the ideals of peer support, commitment to the peer support team, and commitment to the recipients of peer support. This is expressed in their willingness to respond to requests for assistance at all hours of the day, and to function in compliance with peer support team policies and guidelines.

(3) Peer support team members must be credible. Credibility is established by ethical personal and professional behavior over time. The perception of credibility has a great deal to do with reputation. For example, it is not likely that an officer with a reputation for gossiping would also be seen as a person who can keep confidences. Therefore, officers with such a reputation lack the credibility necessary to become members of a peer support team. New employees should have at least two years of service before being considered for a peer support team. They will need at least this amount of time to become known in the department and to establish credibility.

Reflections of a Police Psychologist

Peer Support Team Structure

Police (and other) peer support teams can be organized in several ways and remain in compliance with C.R.S. 13-90-107(m).

The *Team Coordinator* (TC) model utilizes an appointed peer support team coordinator. The team coordinator can assume any of the responsibilities specified within agency policy and the team's operational guidelines. The TC model is best applied in agencies where there is no or little funding. While not recommended, the team coordinator model is preferable to not having a peer support team. The most significant shortcoming of the TC model is that there is no program-endorsed licensed mental health professional providing clinical support for the members of the peer support team. Without such support, peer support team members are left to make decisions best made with professional consultation.

The *Clinical Advisor* (CA) peer support team model utilizes a licensed mental health professional to advise peer support team members. The clinical advisor contracts with the agency not only to provide consultation for peer support team members, but also to meet monthly with the team to enhance team cohesion and provide ongoing training. The CA model includes the appointment of a team coordinator and can be established with modest agency funding.

The preferred, albeit the most expensive peer support team model is the *Clinical Supervisor* (CS) model. The clinical supervisor of the agency's peer support team is a licensed mental health professional who is either an employee of the agency or a contracted professional. The clinical supervisor assumes all of the responsibilities of a clinical advisor and additionally provides direct counseling services to agency employees and their families. The actual services provided by the clinical supervisor are determined by either a job description or elements of a contract. In fully developed CS models, the clinical supervisor assumes the departmental position of staff or police psychologist (if licensed as a psychologist). (Note: In Colorado, there are four mental health licenses - psychologist, social worker, professional counselor, and marriage and family therapist. All are title protected. A doctorate is required to be licensed as a psychologist. The other licenses require a master's degree.) As with the CA model, the CS model utilizes a team coordinator. All models may include peer support team assistant coordinators.

Peer Support Team Policy and Confidentiality

Regardless of the peer support team model, all police peer support teams looking to establish the privilege granted in C.R.S. 13-90-107(m) must be formally founded. The best method of doing this is to create a peer support team policy. The policy should establish the team and specify its parameters. It should also adopt the team's operational guidelines. Rather than engaging in a lengthy discussion about what should be included in a peer support team policy, it would better serve to provide an example. A draft policy is presented below. The draft is written for the clinical supervisor model but it can be readily adapted to accommodate the clinical advisor or team coordinator models.

The core of information included in the draft has served several police agencies very well for many years. Any police (or other) agency within or outside Colorado wishing to establish a peer support team should edit the draft to meet its particular needs.

Draft Colorado Police Peer Support Team Policy

Policy Directive XXX-XX

The Peer Support Team (PST) is established to provide peer support and debriefing services to department personnel experiencing personal or work related stress. The PST also provides support services for family members of department personnel.

PROCEDURES

1. *Organization and administration*: The PST is comprised of department employees and volunteers. It operates under the clinical supervision of the PST clinical supervisor and the administration of the PST coordinator.
2. *Selection of team*: *Coordinators*: The PST coordinator is designated by the chief of police. The assistant coordinators are selected by the team coordinator and the clinical supervisor. Applicants for the assistant coordinator positions must submit a letter to the team coordinator outlining their interest and qualifications for the position. *Team members*: PST applicants submit a letter stating their interest and qualifications to the PST team coordinator. Applicants are interviewed by the PST coordinator and selected members of the PST.

Any PST member may provide input before an applicant is considered for appointment. The team coordinator submits a list of qualified applicants to the chief of police for final approval and appointment. All members of the PST serve at the discretion of the chief of police.

3. *Confidentiality*: PST member confidentiality is specified under C.R.S. 13-90-107(m), *Who may not testify without consent*. PST members are subject to all disclosures mandated by law. PST members functioning in their PST role shall not be interviewed or examined as part of an administrative investigation without the consent of the recipient of peer support. (*Note: Agency administrators should not be overly concerned with the preceding statement. In the many years that I have practiced as a police psychologist, a negative issue has never arisen in reference to peer support team members being protected from inquiry by internal investigators. This protection is necessary to make the peer support team functional. After all, what officer or employee would seek peer support if the information discussed could be obtained by internal investigators without consent? Without this protection, the potential benefit that a peer support team can provide to an agency is significantly limited.*)

4. *Clinical supervisor*: The chief of police shall appoint a licensed mental health professional as the clinical supervisor of the PST. The PST clinical supervisor must be kept informed of all PST interactions.

5. *Availability of team*: The PST is available on a twenty-four hour call-out basis. PST members may be contacted directly or through dispatch.

6. *Team response*: PST team members functioning in their peer support role may respond (1) to the scene of any incident serious enough to warrant a clear need for PST support, (2) to any other location to meet with incident-involved personnel, (3) to any location at the request of an employee or a supervisor, and (4) to any location at the request of the PST team coordinator or clinical supervisor. PST members should make every effort to contact the team coordinator prior to responding to a critical incident. If this is not possible, PST members must notify the team coordinator as soon as practical.

7. *Use of team*: Peer support team members acting in their peer support role shall not be utilized for incident investigation or other assignments except under emergency circumstances.

8. *Critical incident debriefing*: Debriefings and other group interactions conducted by the PST clinical supervisor are confidential within

the limits prescribed by law. Debriefings are conducted in those circumstances where it is assessed by the PST clinical supervisor to be the most appropriate group support intervention. Debriefing attendance is voluntary.

9. *Request for PST member*: If an employee involved in a critical incident requests a particular on-duty PST member, supervisors shall make reasonable effort to release the requested PST member from any previous assignment so that the requested PST member may respond.

10. *The team provides personal contact as follows*:

   o Self referral—Any employee may engage PST assistance for any reason.
   o Supervisor request—Supervisors may request or recommend that personnel under their direct supervision contact the PST for assistance with a perceived difficulty or stressful circumstance. Supervisory requests or recommendations do not constitute a supervisory order. Supervisors shall not order a subordinate to contact a member of the peer support team for the purposes of peer support.
   o Reach-out program—PST members may engage in proactive contact in an effort to assist a person with a perceived difficulty or stressful circumstance.

11. *Administrative investigations*: Employees involved in any type of administrative investigation, including internal investigations and supervisory inquiries, who wish assistance in dealing with the stress inherent in such investigations, may contact the PST clinical supervisor or uninvolved members of the PST for support and assistance.

12. *Operational guidelines*: The peer support team operates within the parameters set forth in the department approved Peer Support Team Operational Guidelines.

Peer Support Team Operational Guidelines

The peer support team's operational guidelines play an essential role in the appropriate functioning of the team. Each agency should develop operational guidelines that meet their needs. For instance, if the agency is utilizing the clinical advisor peer support team model, the role of the clinical advisor should be specified. This will be different than the role of a peer support team clinical supervisor.

Peer support teams must operate within written guidelines to meet the criteria set forth in C.R.S. 13-90-107(m). Some information included in the draft peer support team policy is repeated in the draft peer support team operational guidelines. This is by design. It is necessary because the peer support team policy and the peer support team operational guidelines must address several critical areas independently. The PST policy provides for the structure of the PST, establishes PST parameters, and is readily available to all employees. In contrast, the PST operational guidelines represent the working document of the PST. They can be easily amended to address new or unanticipated issues. Additionally, while the PST guidelines are not confidential, they are not included in the department's policy directives. Therefore, they may not be as readily available to department employees. For these reasons, PST policy and operational guidelines must be able stand independently of one another. It is possible to combine the PST policy and operational guidelines into a single document; however, this would create a document with much information not normally found in policy directives.

A draft *peer support team operational guidelines* is presented. The draft is written for police agencies within the state of Colorado using the clinical supervisor model, opting for PST debriefing facilitation. The draft operational guidelines can be modified to meet the particular needs of any agency.

Draft Colorado Peer Support Team Operational Guidelines

The Peer Support Team functions as a peer support and debriefing resource for personnel of the police department and their families. In order to effectively meet this responsibility, the Peer Support Team (PST) adopts the following operational guidelines.

I.   Peer Support

Members of the Peer Support Team are committed to functioning within the limits of their peer support training. Peer support interactions may continue as an adjunct to comprehensive professional counseling or any other ongoing professional or self-help program.

II. Clinical Supervision

The Peer Support Team is clinically supervised by the department-appointed licensed mental health professional. This person is designated the PST *Clinical Supervisor*. The clinical supervisor is responsible for the clinical supervision and the ongoing in-service training of the Peer Support Team.

III. Team Coordinator

The PST team coordinator is appointed by the chief of police. The team coordinator is the primary spokesperson for the PST and represents the team in matters involving department staff, agency, and interagency issues. The PST team coordinator is administratively responsible for the PST's operational status. The team coordinator and the clinical supervisor function as co-chairpersons during PST team meetings.

Assistant team coordinators will be selected in compliance with department policy. Assistant team coordinators assist the team coordinator and clinical supervisor in the performance of their duties. They function as the PST coordinator in the absence of the team coordinator. An acting team coordinator will be appointed by the team coordinator during periods of absence of the team coordinator and assistant team coordinators.

IV. Primary Obligations of Peer Support Team Members

Professional Supervision

Peer Support Team members have a primary obligation to communicate their peer support activities to the PST clinical supervisor. Due to the varying nature of the issues involved in peer support, some peer support team member activity may be communicated at regularly scheduled PST meetings. In circumstances where more timely supervision or consultation is needed, team member activity should be communicated to the clinical supervisor as soon as practical. In emergencies or circumstances involving critical intervention, PST members should contact the clinical supervisor immediately.

If the information pertaining to a member's peer support activity is assessed by the team member as inappropriate for discussion in a regularly scheduled group PST meeting, the PST member should arrange to discuss the interaction(s) with the clinical supervisor privately.

Confidentiality

Issues discussed during peer support are confidential within the parameters specified by law, department policy, and clinical supervision. Safeguarding acquired information is a primary obligation of team members. Subject to the limitations of law, information received in confidence shall not be revealed without the express consent of the person involved. Express consent to reveal information constitutes a waiver of confidentiality. In cases where express consent is granted, information will be provided only to those specifically designated to receive the information.

The statutory privilege for peer support team member confidentiality is specified in C.R.S. 13-90-107(m), *Who may not testify without consent.*

Team members must advise all persons with whom they interact in a peer support role of the limitations of peer support team member confidentiality. This includes that the information discussed will be communicated to the clinical supervisor.

In the event that information received in a peer support interaction must be revealed by mandate of law, PST members shall reveal such information only after an effort to elicit the person's voluntary disclosure has failed. In cases where it is appropriate, the peer support team member should inform the person of the obligatory actions necessary. Information revealed under such circumstances shall be provided only to the appropriate persons and public authorities.

In the unlikely event that a PST member receives information during a peer support interaction that there is a viable threat of harm or violence toward another person or persons, a *duty to warn* exists. This information is not confidential. The PST member must warn the threatened person(s), contact the team coordinator or clinical supervisor immediately, and take any other actions deemed appropriate for the circumstances.

PST Scheduled Meetings

Attending scheduled PST meetings for the purpose of group clinical supervision and PST cohesiveness is a primary obligation of all PST members. The Peer Support Team meets monthly to allow for clinical supervision, on-going training, and team cohesion. Peer Support Team members endeavor to attend monthly meetings. If a team member is unable to attend a meeting, he or she should:

1. notify the team coordinator or an assistant team coordinator in advance of the meeting when possible or contact the team coordinator or an assistant team coordinator as soon as practical after the scheduled meeting,
2. obtain a copy of any training materials presented at the meeting, and
3. schedule an individual supervision meeting or otherwise contact the clinical supervisor if he or she has engaged in any PST interactions since the previous supervisory contact.

Excessive absences from the PST monthly meetings and training will be addressed by the team coordinator, assistant coordinators, and the clinical supervisor on an individual basis. Continued excessive absences may result in the team member's removal from the PST.

V.   Duty to Take Action

Peace officer members of the PST are required to make an arrest in cases where there is probable cause that a crime has been committed within a domestic relationship. Peace officer members and other PST members who are mandatory reporters must also take action in cases of actual or suspected child abuse or neglect, and in cases of at-risk adults and elders.

VI. Clarification of Peer Support Interactions

Peer Support Team members are responsible for clarifying the role in which they are functioning when interacting with others. Peer Support Team members must remain aware of potential conflicts of interest when providing peer support to individuals with whom they work or who they may directly or indirectly supervise.

VII. Availability for Call-out

The Peer Support Team will provide Dispatch with a list of team members. In the event that PST support is requested through Dispatch, Dispatch will contact the team coordinator. If the team coordinator is unavailable or unresponsive, an assistant coordinator will be contacted. The coordinator or assistant coordinator contacted will assess the circumstances and arrange for appropriate PST intervention.

In the event that the PST coordinator and assistant coordinators cannot be contacted, Dispatch will continue to call team members in the order listed in Dispatch until a team member is contacted. The team member contacted will then act as coordinator. This team member will assess the circumstances and arrange for appropriate PST intervention.

VIII. Compensation

Peer Support Team members do not maintain a paid on-call status. Therefore, PST members are not eligible for on-call compensation. Peer Support Team members who are called out or otherwise function in their PST capacity during off-duty hours will be compensated as specified by department policy.

IX. Debriefing and Debriefing Process

PST members may facilitate debriefings when appropriate. All PST debriefings must be approved by the clinical supervisor. Approval is required because of research which suggests that debriefing participants may be retraumatized or vicariously traumatized during the process. Prior to the start of PST debriefings the "Limits of Confidentiality: Debriefing Statement for Peer Support Team Members" must be read. Debriefing attendance is voluntary.

Various debriefing protocols may be utilized depending upon the actual circumstances. Team members recognize that the debriefing process is dynamic. Peer Support Team members remain flexible and facilitate debriefings in a manner that best meets the perceived needs of participants.

Peer Support Team members may invite persons not directly involved in the incident to attend a debriefing if it is thought that they can positively contribute to or benefit from the debriefing process. All such invitations must be approved by the clinical supervisor, team coordinator, or an assistant coordinator.

Debriefing participants may be accompanied by personal support persons. Personal support persons may attend debriefings if their participation is not prohibited by other sections of these operational guidelines.

X. Media

Media representatives are prohibited from attending debriefings. Any PST information released to the media will be accomplished as specified in department policy.

XI. Attorneys

Personal attorneys are prohibited from attending debriefings. This restriction is not intended to deprive any participant of legal representation. However, it is thought that the presence of a personal attorney inhibits the group process. Debriefing participants are encouraged to communicate to their attorneys that debriefings facilitated by licensed mental health professionals are confidential within the limits prescribed by law.

XII. Other Agencies

The PST may be utilized to assist other agencies. The PST provides such assistance as specified by mutual aid policies or at the direction of the chief of police or designee.

XIII. Team Actions

Peer Support Team administrative concerns shall be discussed and decided at scheduled monthly meetings. Decisions or actions required by exigent circumstances may be made, implemented, or otherwise carried out by the clinical supervisor, team coordinator, an assistant coordinator, or acting coordinator.

XIV. Referral to Professional Counseling Services

Peer Support Team members may find it appropriate to inform those involved in peer support of available options for additional counseling. Available options include the clinical supervisor, the Employee Assistance Program, community private practitioners, self-help groups, and the various helping agencies within the community. It may also be appropriate to refer a person to specialized resources including but not limited to attorneys and financial advisors.

XV. Reach Out

Peer Support Team members may initiate a reach out. In a reach out, a PST member initiates supportive contact with a person who has been exposed to a critical incident, a life-circumstance change, cumulative stressors, or other known or suspected stressor.

XVI. Leave of Absence

Peer Support Team members may request a leave of absence from the PST for up to one year. A request for a leave of absence must be submitted in writing to the team coordinator. If the team coordinator wishes to request a leave of absence, the request must be submitted to the clinical supervisor. Any request for a leave of absence must specify the length of absence requested and the date of anticipated return to active status. During a leave of absence the PST member may attend monthly or otherwise scheduled PST training.

XVII. Resignation from the Team

Peer Support Team members may resign from the team at any time by submitting a written resignation to the team coordinator. Any team member considering resignation must be certain that all ongoing peer support interactions are appropriately terminated, referred to other team members or the clinical supervisor, or referred to professional counseling resources.

XVIII. Removal from the Team

> "All members of the PST serve at the discretion of the chief of police" (Policy Directive XXX-XX).

The chief of police may remove any team member from the Peer Support Team. The team coordinator in consultation with the clinical supervisor may request that the chief of police remove from the Peer Support Team any member who has been determined to have acted in violation of law, departmental policy, or the PST operational guidelines. Such a request may also be presented when a team member has been determined to have acted in a manner that undermines the credibility or fundamental ethical principles of the Peer Support Team.

XIX. Compliance with the Peer Support Team Operational Guidelines

Peer Support Team members are required by policy to function in compliance with the Peer Support Team Operational Guidelines:

> The peer support team operates within the parameters set forth in the department approved Peer Support Team Operational Guidelines. (Policy XXX-XX, paragraph XX).

Remaining in compliance with the peer support team's policy and operational guidelines is imperative for the proper functioning of the peer support team. Once established, any changes in the PST operational guidelines must be approved by the chief of police.

Peer Support Team Considerations

It is important to remember that peer support teams do not work in opposition with administrative staff. There is no "us versus them" mentality in agencies with high-functioning peer support teams. When initiated and properly maintained, peer support teams soon become an integral part of the department. In many ways, once established peer support teams become nearly indispensible.

Many police administrators do not recognize the need for peer support teams. This is because most agency employees have access to a jurisdiction-wide employee assistance program (EAP). Most EAPs are comprised of a number of mental health professionals who contract with the jurisdiction to provide counseling services. Usually, the number of employee visits to the EAP is limited, anywhere from six to twelve visits per year or issue. There are many excellent EAPs.

The availability of EAP counseling for police officers represents a significant advancement in the delivery of counseling services. However, for officers, EAPs, although helpful, appear insufficient. They are helpful in that they are utilized by some officers who might not otherwise seek assistance. They are insufficient in that despite their availability, they do not and cannot meet the needs of many police officers. This is also true of a police psychologist. Peer support teams occupy a niche that cannot be readily filled by either an EAP or a police psychologist. If the agency wants to do the best it can to support its officers, a peer support team is necessary. Incidentally, a peer support team is one of the most valued resources for a police psychologist. Many police psychologist counseling programs are designed to incorporate the efficacy of peer support.

Frequently Asked Questions

Being a member of a peer support team can be challenging. There are many questions that arise for peer support team members. Some of the more frequently asked are:

As a peer support team member . . .

Do I need to check with my clinical supervisor or team coordinator before I engage in a peer support interaction? No. As a trained peer support team member, you may initiate or respond to a request for peer support. Independent peer support team member interactions, which are in compliance with law, the peer support team policy, and operational guidelines are appropriate and encouraged.

How do I respond to a person who asks if peer support interactions are confidential? When asked if peer support interactions are confidential, you should fully explain the limits of peer support team member confidentiality. Remember to include that PST information must be provided to your clinical supervisor. An unacceptable reply to this question would be some cursory remark such as "Yeah, they're confidential. There's a law . . ."

What happens when the person I have been providing peer support waives the privilege of confidentiality? When a person to whom you have been providing peer support waives confidentiality, the content of your communications become available to those identified in the waiver. A person waives confidentiality for some reason, usually so that you can communicate with family members, supervisors, lawyers, and so forth. Regardless of the reason, under the waiver, information relating to the recipient as well as the peer support team member becomes available. A peer support team member should always remain aware that the information discussed and the actions taken within peer support interactions, including what the PST member said and did, may at some point become available to others. Additionally, keep in mind that the prohibition against revealing peer support information without consent (within confidentiality limits) restricts only the peer support team member. The person with whom you are involved in a peer support interaction is free to discuss any or all of the peer support interaction. In other words, the recipient of peer support does not need your permission to reveal any information you provided. This includes anything that you said and anything that you did, and this information can go *anywhere*. Bottom line, remain professional.

Do confidentiality waivers have to be in writing? Although there is a common practice that allows verbal confidentiality waivers in certain circumstances, it is best to have a written waiver before disclosing any protected information.

What do I do if a person confesses to a crime or talks about criminal behavior during a peer support interaction? To answer this question fully would involve addressing all possible combinations of several variables. For our purposes, suffice it to say that in this situation, peer support team members should contact their clinical supervisor immediately. The appropriate action will be decided upon and implemented.

Some of the variables that must be considered are (1) whether you advised the person of the limits of peer support team member confidentiality (if yes, this likely means that the information was communicated because the person wants to confront the consequences of behavior with your support), (2) you failed to advise the person of the confidentiality limitations (it may be that the person communicated this information with an expectation of confidentiality, which does not make it confidential), (3) the type of information presented, (4) whether you are a mandatory reporter of actual or suspected child abuse or neglect, (5) whether you are a police officer, and (6) whether the information involves a crime within a domestic relationship.

Regardless of the circumstances, you should (1) stop the conversation in this area immediately, (2) continue peer support, (3) advise the person that information indicative of criminal conduct is not protected, (4) tell the person that it would be better if a confidential resource was contacted to discuss this information, (5) inform the person that you must contact your clinical supervisor, (6) contact your clinical supervisor, and (7) assist the person to contact a confidential resource (all referral resources have the responsibility to advise the person of any limitations of their confidentiality).

Discussion: Stopping the conversation when a person begins to discuss information indicative of any criminal conduct is not a peer support effort to assist the person to conceal or cover-up a crime. Quite the contrary, peer support interactions encourage honesty and the assumption of personal responsibility. Instead, stopping the conversation and following up as indicated recognizes the fact that you can better assist the person if you are not placed in a position where you might become a witness in a possible prosecution. As it is, you may be required to take action and/or testify based upon the information already presented. No matter what the specifics are in any case, if persons present information indicative of any criminal conduct, *do not leave them alone*, especially if the person is a police officer. Stay with the person until otherwise directed by your clinical supervisor. Peer support team members are committed to helping others; however, *peer support team members are not required to and do not jeopardize themselves professionally or ethically by concealing ongoing or past criminal activity.*

What do I say to an internal affairs investigator who asks me about my peer support conversations with an employee being investigated? The draft policy prohibits a peer support team member from disclosing information in an administrative investigation without consent. This is necessary for the proper functioning of the peer support team. If you are contacted by an administrative investigator and asked about your peer support interactions with an employee, you should politely remind the investigator that to respond to the inquiry would amount to a violation of the department's peer support team policy. If the recipient of peer support wishes to waive confidentiality for the investigator, you may communicate freely.

Administrative, and for that matter, criminal investigators should not be permitted to "fish" the peer support team in an effort to determine whether an employee has sought peer support assistance.

What do I say to a criminal investigator who asks me about my peer support conversations with an employee being investigated? Information indicative of any criminal conduct in peer support interactions is not protected by law or department policy. The first thing you should do is contact your clinical supervisor. Together, you will determine whether there is information that is indicative of any criminal conduct. If it is determined that the recipient of peer support provided you with information indicative of criminal conduct, you must respond as you would if you received this information in a non-peer support interaction.

To avoid complications and undermining the credibility of the peer support team, you must remember to specify the confidentiality limits of peer support team members *before* beginning your peer support interactions.

Am I covered by my agency's policy and operational guidelines if I am providing peer support to personnel from other agencies? Yes, within the parameters of your agency policy. Under mutual aid policies and the draft operational guidelines, there are provisions for assisting other agencies. Your coverage is dependent upon meeting and remaining within the criteria specified in your policy and operational guidelines.

Should I keep records or notes in reference to my peer support interactions? No. As long as you remember to bring your PST interactions under supervision, there is no requirement or need to keep a record. Many persons would be reluctant to utilize peer support if they thought that peer support team members were maintaining a record of their interactions. It is acceptable to record the number of your peer support contacts and the amount of time that you spend in your peer support role. This is for statistical purposes only and it can be used to determine the activity and utilization of the peer support team. Some agencies require that this information be recorded, and you can do so without concern.

Why is clinical supervision necessary? It is not required by C.R.S.13-90-107(m). Of the three discussed options for peer support team structure, the most professionally developed is the clinical supervisor. Clinical supervision is intended to enhance the delivery of peer support services. It provides for PST clinical oversight, support for PST members, and is a resource for PST referral. In itself, C.R.S. 13-90-107(m) does not require any type of peer support team structure. It requires only that written guidelines be developed and that PST members function within them. However, if a PST was not concerned about the protection specified in this statute, it would not need written guidelines. *The statute does not require that peer support teams meet its standards.* The statute was intentionally written so that each PST interested in having the protection could develop a PST that best served their needs and funding capabilities. This is accomplished through the PST written guidelines. In this way, the statute serves the guidelines, not vice versa. When clinical supervision is required by the PST guidelines, it is because the agency has endorsed the values inherent in PST clinical supervision.

What if I fail to bring a peer support interaction under supervision? This question pertains to peer support team members structured under a clinical supervisor, but it may also apply to peer support teams organized with a clinical advisor. An intentional violation of any of the primary obligations of team members as specified in the operational guidelines is a serious matter. It is not difficult to keep your PST interactions under supervision. Failing to bring your peer support interaction under supervision represents a serious breach of PST member ethical standards of conduct. In the event that such behavior is discovered, peer support team administrative censure, up to and including removal from the peer support team, is likely.

What happens if I fail to act in compliance with the peer support team policy or operational guidelines? An intentional act of non-compliance with the peer support team policy or operational guidelines is a serious breach of trust and commitment. It is justification for removal from the peer support team. Unintentional non-compliance or well-intentioned errors can be evaluated on an individual basis, but may also result in removal from the peer support team.

It is not difficult to remain within the boundaries of the team policy and operational guidelines. To stay within the boundaries of these documents requires periodic review. You cannot act within the behavioral standards of the peer support team if you do not remember what they are. The policy and guidelines exist to protect the peer support team member, the recipient of peer support services, and to provide for the highest possible quality of peer support.

The draft policy and guidelines establish peer support clinical supervision so that there is a ladder of escalation. This means that the peer support team member has a specified course of action in cases that exceed the limits of peer support. The team's monthly meetings and in-service training encourage the enhancement of fundamental peer support skills. Peer support team members endorse these values. A peer support team member that has lost connection with these values cannot continue with the peer support team. To do so would damage the peer support team and worse, may damage those that the team is committed to supporting. There is no faster way to undermine the efficacy of the peer support team than by having one of its members operating outside its policy or guidelines. One peer support team member has the ability to defeat years of successful peer support team performance. *The reputation of a peer support team and the willingness of employees to engage in peer support are truly this fragile.*

Police and Sheriff Peer Support Team Manual

The Police and Sheriff Peer Support Team Manual is a reference and resource manual for law enforcement peer support team members. To download a copy of the Police and Sheriff Peer Support Team Manual at no cost visit *www.jackdigliani.com*

Chapter 6

Critical Incident Debriefings

The efficacy of critical incident debriefings has been the topic of recent debate. For several years, conducting debriefings after a critical incident has been the standard of intervention for emergency service personnel. However, recent research has provided some evidence that formal debriefing may not always be helpful, and in some cases may be harmful.

The National Center for Posttraumatic Stress (NCPTSD) identified several types of incident debriefings. It further described the possible negative outcomes of formal critical incident stress debriefing (CISD). The NCPTSD makes the following distinctions:

- *"Operational debriefing* is a routine and formal part of an organizational response to a disaster. Mental-health workers acknowledge it as an appropriate practice that may help survivors acquire an overall sense of meaning and a degree of closure.
- *Psychological or stress debriefing* refers to a variety of practices for which there is little supportive empirical evidence. It is strongly suggested that psychological debriefing is not an appropriate mental-health intervention.
- *Critical Incident Stress Debriefing* (CISD) is a formalized, structured method whereby a group of rescue and response workers reviews the stressful experience of a disaster. CISD was developed to assist first responders such as fire and police personnel; it was not meant for the survivors of a disaster or their relatives. CISD was never intended as a substitute for therapy. It was designed to be delivered in a group format and meant to be incorporated into a larger, multi-component crisis intervention system labeled Critical Incident Stress Management (CISM). CISM includes the following components: pre-crisis intervention; disaster or large-scale demobilization and informational briefings (town meetings); staff advisement; defusing; CISD; one-on-one crisis counseling or support; family crisis intervention

and organizational consultation; follow-up and referral mechanisms for assessment and treatment, if necessary.

Currently, many mental-health workers consider some form of stress debriefing the standard of care following both natural (earthquakes) and human-caused (workplace shootings, bombings) stressful events. Indeed, the National Center for PTSD's Disaster Mental Health Guidebook (which is currently being revised) contains information on how to conduct debriefings. However, recent research indicates that psychological debriefing is not always an appropriate mental-health intervention. Available evidence shows that, in some instances, it may increase traumatic stress or complicate recovery. Psychological debriefing is also inappropriate for acutely bereaved individuals. While operational debriefing is nearly always helpful (it involves clarifying events and providing education about normal responses and coping mechanisms), care must be taken before delivering more emotionally focused interventions.

A recent review of eight debriefing studies, all of which met rigorous criteria for being well-controlled, revealed no evidence that debriefing reduces the risk of PTSD, depression, or anxiety; nor were there any reductions in psychiatric symptoms across studies. Additionally, in two studies, one of which included long-term follow-up, some negative effects of CISD-type debriefings were reported relating to PTSD and other trauma-related symptoms. Therefore, debriefings as currently employed may be useful for low magnitude stress exposure and symptoms or for emergency care providers. However, the best studies suggest that for individuals with more severe exposure to trauma, and for those who are experiencing more severe reactions such as PTSD, debriefing is ineffective and possibly harmful" (2003).

Concerns with Critical Incident Stress Debriefing

The formal CISD process is comprised of several phases: introductory phase, fact phase, feeling phase, information phase, and reorganization phase (Mitchell, 1983). Some of the concerns that have evolved from outcome research of the CISD process as it currently employed include:

1. Lack of choice—Many agencies mandate participation in debriefings.
2. Poor timing—CISD recommends the debriefing take place between forty-eight and seventy-two hours of the incident. This may be too soon for some persons.

3. Retraumatization—Persons may be retraumatized by the intensity of particular CISD phases, especially the fact and feeling phases.
4. Vicarious traumatization—Others in the debriefing that are not significantly traumatized may become traumatized by listening to the account of the incident.
5. Interference – CISD debriefing may interfere with the normal processing of a traumatic event.
6. Superficiality—CISD may not adequately address the more serious issues of those participating in the debriefing (Carr, 2003).

The Case for Critical Incident Stress Debriefing

Jeffrey Mitchell, president emeritus of the International Critical Incident Stress Foundation Inc., responded to reports that CISD may be ineffective or even harmful in an article entitled "Crisis Intervention and Critical Incident Stress Management: A defense of the field." Mitchell reported that thousands of clinicians have chosen to ignore the negative outcome research on CISD and continue to conduct debriefings. He identified numerous research studies that support the efficacy of CISD. In part IV of the article, he criticized the negative outcome research, indicating that: "A) No evidence has been found that any of the *negative outcome* researchers have been trained in the field of CISM or the CISD small group crisis intervention tool, B) Inappropriate target populations have been chosen by the researchers, C) Inappropriate interventions were provided under circumstances for which the CISD group process was never intended, D) The negative outcome researchers have engaged in a mixing and blending of terms to a point that it is difficult to tell what was done to who and by whom, E) Major flaws exist in all of the negative outcome studies, F) Randomized controlled trials are *not* the only way to measure outcomes, G) Inappropriate outcome measures were often applied, H) The "Type III" error was present in every case." (Type III error involves faulty model implementation). Mitchell summarized, "More research is clearly needed. But instead of trying to prove that something does or does not work, efforts should be made to more clearly understand what interventions should be implemented for which populations and at what times and by whom" (2004, 52).

There are efforts underway to determine just this. In the meantime, there has been a move toward a resiliency-based group intervention following critical events. One such approach has been described by Slawinski and Blythe (2004).

It involves a service offering meeting, group resiliency briefing, individual resiliency briefing, follow up, and additional resources information. The service offering meeting (SOM) takes place within twenty-four to seventy-two hours after the incident. During the SOM, involved personnel are provided information and options for support. Although done in a group setting, the SOM is not a psychological debriefing. Following the SOM, for those that are interested, there is a *group resiliency briefing* (GRB). The GRB allows for group discussion of the incident, but the focus is on support and health. Graphic reenactments of the incident are avoided. People may share their reactions, but without reprocessing distressing facts. Crisis professionals facilitate the GRB and offer individual assistance to those wishing more support. *Individual resiliency briefings* (IRB) are provided as needed. The IRB is a personal meeting that takes place in a therapeutic setting. This allows for individual treatment without concerns of traumatizing others. *Follow up* is conducted at various intervals for up to one year, and information about *additional resources* are provided to assist involved persons to use and develop resiliency techniques.

Freezeframe Model for Group Support

The freezeframe facilitation model for group support (Digliani, 1992) was originally developed to provide an alternative to the prescribed phases of CISD. It was developed out of necessity. Its conception originated from a debriefing situation wherein the phases of CISD appeared difficult to utilize. Although freezeframe can be used to process facts and feelings, it is easily adaptable to a resiliency or strength-oriented group process. The freezeframe model for operational debriefing has proven its value on many occasions.

The freezeframe model utilizes an exploration within various "frames" of an incident. To use the freezeframe method, the primary facilitator requests information from the group. When the information indicates a point of significance, the facilitator freezes that frame and initiates processing. This sequence continues until all pertinent elements are processed. Freezeframe facilitation is especially useful when processing large groups, complex events, and incidents where several persons were involved.

Actual freezeframe processing: Freezeframe processing can be easily started by asking a question similar to "How did this call come in?" If through dispatch, the events in the dispatch center become the first frame to process. Once this frame is frozen, group information can be processed. The facilitator continues until all issues within the frame are processed. If discussion begins to drift out of the current frame, the facilitator refocuses the group on the frame being processed. Frames range from "narrow" to "wide" and will vary during the processing. When processing within a frame is completed, the facilitator offers a *brief* summary. The frame is now cleared, and the facilitator can engage the group to discover the next frame. The facilitator can make mental or discreetly written notes about significant issues that have surfaced. These are addressed when appropriate. This might be within a frame, between frames, or following the processing of all frames.

Timing is important when using the freezeframe. If the facilitator moves too fast through the frame, or from one frame to another, some group members may not have the opportunity to process appropriately. If the facilitator moves unnecessarily slow, the group will feel that the process is heavy and cumbersome.

Following a critical incident, if a group intervention is deemed appropriate, a skilled group facilitator can utilize freezeframe to disseminate information, normalize responses, and strengthen resiliency.

Debriefings and Police Agencies

Should police agencies continue to debrief following a critical incident? A good working hypothesis is *yes, with consideration*. Based on current research, police agencies should continue to engage in operational debriefings. These debriefings have anecdotal efficacy and lack any clear research-established negative outcomes. More formal psychological debriefings, such as CISD, in the manner traditionally practiced, should at least for now be used only with great caution. It is irresponsible to ignore the research indicating that CISD may cause harm to some people. Resiliency and strength-based group interventions following a traumatic event represent a viable alternative to the criticisms and possible negative outcomes of traditional CISD. Until additional research helps to clarify the conflicting and confusing current state of affairs, police agencies should err on the side of safety.

Mandated or Voluntary Participation for Debriefings

In the early days of police psychology, mandating officers to attend a debriefing was thought to remove any stigma associated with voluntary participation. In those days, there was much concern over the issue that officers would not be able to overcome their desire to appear tough, and thereby would not attend debriefings. This concern is not near as great as it once was. Most police officers and other emergency services workers now see debriefing as part of a positive supportive process. Many officers look forward to operational debriefings. They have heard or know from experience that such debriefings can be helpful. With this perceptual change and the fact that several other types of support interventions are available for officers who might opt out of debriefings, the mandatory provision for debriefing attendance has outlived its usefulness. In the final analysis, there is little to recommend mandated debriefing attendance. Unless and until some notable efficacy is demonstrated, debriefing attendance should be voluntary.

Debriefing Confidentiality—Licensed Clinicians

Prior to the beginning of a debriefing, clinicians should specify the confidentiality limitations of group discussion and clarify the responsibilities of group members. In Colorado, this can be easily accomplished by reading the "Limits of Confidentiality—Operational Debriefing Statement for Licensed Clinicians." This statement endorses debriefings as a group therapy process, contrary to the position of Mitchell and Everly (1995). However, without this, debriefings would not be protected under Colorado confidentiality statutes.

The argument that critical incident debriefings are therapy and thereby protected by state confidentiality laws is supported in developing case law. Although to date there has not been a debriefing confidentiality challenge in the Colorado courts, the Iowa Supreme Court, in *City of Cedar Falls v. Cedar Falls Community School District* considered a motion for discovery filed by the school district. In its opinion the court stated, "The City resisted discovery and the (police) officers refused to answer questions concerning the sessions on grounds the information discussed at these 'critical incident stress debriefings' was protected by the mental health professional/patient privilege." The court held that "We agree with the City that the matters discussed at the debriefing sessions are privileged. The record indicates the sessions were conducted by a licensed mental health professional for purposes of assisting the officers to deal with the stress of the traumatic incident they had just experienced" (2000).

Limits of Confidentiality—Operational Debriefing Statement for Licensed Clinicians

Clinicians should read the following paragraphs aloud to the group prior to the start of the debriefing. Written copies may be provided to each participant.

1. Debriefing conducted by a (psychologist, etc) is a group therapy process. Participants in a debriefing have a legal obligation to respect the confidentiality of information disclosed by others during the course of the debriefing.

2. Colorado Revised Statute 12-43-218, *Disclosure of confidential communications,* states in part, "A (psychologist, etc) . . . shall not disclose . . . nor shall any person who has participated in any therapy conducted under supervision of a (psychologist, etc) . . . including, but not limited to . . . group therapy . . . disclose any knowledge gained during the course of such therapy without the consent of the person to whom the knowledge relates." Further, C.R.S. 13-90-107(g), *Who may not testify without consent,* provides that, "...a licensed psychologist, etc . . . shall not be examined. . . nor shall any person who has participated in any psychotherapy, conducted under the supervision of a psychologist, etc . . . including but not limited to group therapy . . . be examined . . . without the consent of the person to whom the testimony sought relates."

3. There are some legal limitations pertaining to debriefing confidentiality. Psychologists, police officers, firefighters, as well as several other professionals are required to report: (1) actual or suspected child abuse or neglect, and (2) actual or suspected abuse or exploitation of at-risk elders. Therefore, any information indicative of such abuse, neglect, or exploitation is not confidential. Additionally, information or observations indicating that a person is mentally ill and due to such mental illness is a danger to self or others, or gravely disabled (as defined by C.R.S. 27-65-102) may be disclosed in an effort to ensure that the person receives appropriate treatment.

4. (Read the following if there are peace [police] officers in the group.) Lastly, in accordance with C.R.S. 18-6-803.6, *Duties of peace officers*

and prosecuting agencies—preservation of evidence, peace officers who determine that there is probable cause to believe that a crime or offense involving domestic violence has been committed are required to make an arrest without undue delay. Therefore, such information is not confidential in this debriefing.

5. Is there anyone who does not understand the confidentiality limitations or obligations under Colorado law?
6. Now that our confidentiality limitations and obligations are clear, we are bound by the provisions of these statutes.
7. You control the information that you present. However, if you have any legal questions or concerns, it is recommended that you not discuss it here. Instead, you should consult with an attorney or another legal professional.

Colorado Limits of Confidentiality—Peer Support Team Members

Under the current version of C.R.S. 13-90-107(m) there is no confidentiality privilege afforded to peer support team members functioning in a group setting. Unless and until this changes, debriefings facilitated by peer support team members are not confidential.

Appropriately trained peer support team members can facilitate debriefings (chapter 5). Many emergency services personnel have been helped in operational debriefings facilitated by qualified members of a peer support team. The situations in which peer support team members can safely conduct debriefings are those in which a critical incident does not generate a concern for the appropriateness of the actions of emergency services responders; for example, a traffic accident where a child was killed or injured. Investigating such a tragic event may traumatize investigating officers and others, but there is little question as to the officers' behavior relative to the accident itself. This is very different from a police involved shooting, where the issue of appropriate officer behavior might arise. In the latter category of cases, debriefings, if appropriate, should never be facilitated by anyone lacking group statutory confidentiality protections.

In cases deemed appropriate for debriefing by Colorado peer support team members, the following advisement is recommended (*required* if the draft operational guidelines are adopted).

Limits of Confidentiality—Operational Debriefing Statement for Police Peer Support Team Members

Peer support team facilitators should read the following paragraphs aloud to the group prior to the start of the debriefing. Written copies may be provided to each participant.

1. In a group setting such as a debriefing, peer support team members do not have a statutory privilege of confidentiality. *Therefore, information discussed during the debriefing is not confidential.*
2. Participants in a debriefing have a primary ethical obligation to respect the information disclosed by others during the course of the debriefing. It is ethically inappropriate to discuss or gossip about the information presented by others during the debriefing.
3. Police officers, firefighters, psychologists, physicians and certain additional medical workers, clergy, as well as many other professionals are required to report: (1) actual or suspected child abuse or neglect, and (2) actual or suspected abuse or exploitation of at-risk elders.
4. Peer Support Team members of the police department have an obligation to discuss debriefing information with our clinical supervisor and staff psychologist, Dr. X.
5. (Read if you are not a mandatory reporter.) Dr. X is a mandatory reporter. *Therefore, any information relating to actual or suspected child abuse or neglect, or elder abuse will be reported.*
6. (Read the following if you are a peace officer or if there are peace officers in the group.) In accordance with C.R.S. 18-6-803.6, *Duties of peace officers and prosecuting agencies—preservation of evidence,* peace officers who determine that there is probable cause to believe that a crime or offense involving domestic violence has been committed are required to make an arrest without undue delay. Therefore, be advised that peace officers must take action under such circumstances if they are disclosed in the debriefing.
7. You control the information that you present. However, if you have any legal questions or concerns, the Peer Support Team recommends that you not discuss it here. Instead, you should consult with an attorney or another legal professional.

Chapter 7

Police Marriage and Family

The secret of a happy marriage remains a secret

- Henny Youngman

Whether or not you are inclined to agree with comedy legend Henny Youngman (1906-1998), most married people would agree that marriage is work. Marriage is work in the sense that when people choose to marry (or otherwise live together) they have to make accommodations and compromises for one another. However, good marriages are not *hard* work. They are not hard work because they are founded upon solid principles of positive interpersonal transaction. Good marriages are loving, functional, supportive, and rewarding.

Marriage

There are many types of marriage. Social anthropologists have identified various marriage arrangements in various cultures throughout the world. These include polygamy-polygyny (one husband-more than one wife), polygamy-polyandry (one wife-more than one husband), group marriage (more than one husband-more than one wife), and monogamy (one husband-one wife). In America, monogamy is the civil and legal standard for marriage (Schultz and Lavenda, 2006). However, as in other parts of the world, alternative forms of marriage are known to exist within the United States. Polygamy-polygyny appears to be the most common.

Although many aspects of the following discussion apply to all relationships, it is presented in terms of the monogamous marriage.

Marriage Roman Style

In the Julian marriage laws of 18 BCE, No.120, *Men Must Marry*, roman emperor Augustus Caesar (63 BCE-14 AD) declared, "If we could survive without a wife, citizens of Rome, all of us would do without that nuisance; but since nature has so decreed that we cannot manage comfortably with them, nor live in any way without them, we must plan for our lasting preservation rather than for our temporary pleasure" (Lefkowitz and Fant, n.d., para.,1). The first part of this sounds a bit like the modern expression "can't live with them, can't live without them" used by some men when discussing women. Can it be that not much has changed in over two thousand years? The second part was an attempt on the part of Augustus Caesar to increase the number of children born to citizens of Rome.

Hopefully, in the twenty-first century, men do not continue to think of marriage and having a wife in the same manner as the emperor!

Families

Married couples have at least three families: the *immediate family*, the *family of origin*, and the *extended family*. The immediate family is comprised of the husband, wife, and any children. The family of origin is the family from which one came, for example, a person's mother, father, and siblings. The extended family is comprised of all other relatives such as aunts, uncles, cousins, in-laws, and so forth.

Reconciling family of origin values and practices with that of a new spouse, who is also bringing family of origin values and practices to the marriage, is a primary task of married couples. Without some degree of reconciliation, differences in family of origin values and practices can negatively impact or destroy the immediate family relationship. Problems can arise when one person's family of origin values or loyalties conflict with those of the spouse. These conflicts often surface in marriage therapy. In the defense of their respective positions, spouses say things like, "I can't help it. It's how I was raised" or "I can't disappoint my mother." Much of the work of marriage counseling in these instances involves helping the couple to see that they can now decide for themselves how they will transact with one another. This may also mean learning new ways to transact with their family of origin - quite the challenge. But, it is self-defeating to have negative or dysfunctional values and behaviors of childhood express themselves in adult marriages.

In today's world of divorce and remarriage, blended families, half brothers and sisters, and step-relatives, it is easy to see how complex families can become. There is no doubt that managing various family demands can be difficult. Finding a balance and remaining sensitive to those you care about can be a challenge. When thinking about the difficulties inherent in family demands, and observing the struggles of persons involved in complex family systems, I have often been struck by a single thought: *family issues are tough*!

Family Culture

Families are culturally diverse. They are multi-generational, evolve a system homeostasis, and have various structures, combinations, alliances, coalitions, rules, and myths. The homeostasis of a family system is reflected in how the family functions (the "steady-state" of the family system). It relates to the behavior of family members, their interactions, family values, and so forth. Some families have a high-functioning homeostasis; others are quite dysfunctional. All families default to a homeostasis, regardless of the level of family functionality. The homeostatic level of functionality can be altered by inputting energy into the family system. Such energy is represented by efforts to change unwanted or dysfunctional interactional patterns. If successful, family systems move from a default homeostatic position to a homeostatic system by design - but altering a family system is not easy. Theoretically, there are system forces that operate to maintain the family homeostasis, regardless of whether it is functional or dysfunctional (Lebow, 2005).

Family Rules, Myths, Alliances, Rituals, and Relationships

Rules are common in families. One of the most important rules is, "Who makes the rules?" The answer to this question defines the power broker(s) in families. Rules can be explicit (you must be home before midnight) or implicit (do not discuss sex). Myths too are common. They are comprised of family beliefs that are exaggerated or mostly false. They get passed from one generation to another. Some of the more common family myths have to do with how the family conceptualizes itself, such as "We are special and better than others" and "We don't have problems." Rules and myths function to define and govern a family unit.

Alliances and coalitions describe the relationships of some family members. For instance, a father and daughter might be allied together against the wife-mother. Such an alliance would "triangulate" the family, where the father and daughter represent a coalition. This would permit joint action against the wife-mother. In this dysfunctional scenario, the daughter has been elevated to the level of a spouse, and the wife has been relegated to the position of a child. The position of the daughter is empowered by the father.

Reflections of a Police Psychologist

This would make even appropriate mother-to-daughter guidance, influence, and discipline nearly impossible. In such cases, the parent-child structure of the family has been damaged.

Rituals are family events that serve to communicate or reinforce family ties. Having a family dinner every evening serves as a bonding ritual for most families. Rituals can look a lot like rules, depending on how non-participation in the ritual is managed by the family. Rules, myths, alliances, and rituals are observed in all family systems. They may be functional or dysfunctional.

An interesting perspective on family rules, the parent-child relationship, and the structure of family was provided by actor Ricardo Montalban (1920-2009). In a column of syndicated writer Ann Landers circa 1975, he penned this letter to his son:

> Dear Son: As long as you live in this house you will follow the rules. When you have your own house, you can make your own rules. In this house we do not have a democracy. I did not campaign to be your father. You did not vote for me. We are father and son by the grace of God, and I accept that privilege and awesome responsibility. In accepting it, I have an obligation to perform the role of a father. I am not your pal. Our ages are too different. We can be many things, but we are not pals. I am your father. This is 100 times more than what a pal is. I am also your friend, but we are on entirely different levels. You will do, in this house, as I say, and you cannot question me because whatever I ask you to do is motivated by love. This will be hard for you to understand until you have a son of your own. Until then, trust me. Your father.

Pre-marital Mentality

Ever wonder why things seem to go so well at the beginning of a relationship? This period can last from months to years. It is sometimes called the honeymoon period, and it seems to be characterized by the best behavior of each person in the couple. Then, as time passes, something seems to change. There are greater demands for perfection, less flexibility, and less tolerance for differences. This results in more disagreement and discord. The couple slowly drifts emotionally from one another. They do not seem to have fun anymore. In some cases, they begin to live as roommates, or describe their marriage as emotionally flat. In more serious cases, the couple becomes *emotionally divorced*, a condition wherein there is little or no emotional connection. Sometimes such couples will stay together to co-parent, or because of finances or religious beliefs. Some emotionally divorced couples have set a date for actual divorce. It usually coincides with their youngest child's eighteenth birthday.

Being emotionally divorced is a difficult way to spend years of your life. These couples may live fairly separate lives, may be constantly at odds with one another, or experience some variation of both. If none of this describes your relationship, congratulations. You are doing well. If it is descriptive of your relationship, and your marriage is not beyond saving, it is time to do something about it. It is time to reinvest in your relationship and rekindle your emotional connection. If you had a good marriage and somehow lost it, you should work together to recover it. Do this by looking back to the time when the relationship was good. How is the marriage different now? How is your behavior different now? This historical survey is the first step toward relationship enrichment.

What can you do to reestablish the positive? Try opening up dormant lines of communication, schedule a date night, show an interest in your spouse's activities, and do more things together. Seek professional help if necessary. Most importantly, as in all life-by-design strategies, *reclaim your marriage*.

Some persons approach marriage with the *safety valve* mentality. The safety valve mentality is "If I don't like marriage or if it doesn't work out, I can always get divorced." Is this a good thought for married couples or for those considering marriage? It implies a degree of uncertainty and a lack of commitment. It is very different from the *marriage commitment* mentality "There is no issue that we cannot resolve." If a couple has this thought prior to marriage, and maintains the thought throughout their relationship, the probability of staying happily married is greatly enhanced.

Three Relationship Counseling Positions

When a couple initiates counseling, they usually start in one of three positions: (1) we are committed to staying together, help us to make our relationship better, (2) we have decided to separate, help us to separate in the best way possible, or (3) we are unsure if we want to stay together, help us figure this out. The position of the couple often determines the course of therapy.

It is possible for a couple to be in a mixed position. The most likely mixed position is a combination of position one and three. One person reports being committed to the relationship, while the other is unsure about continuing. In this mixed position, it is usually the emotional connection which has eroded for the person who is unsure. They say things such as, "I love him, but I'm not in love with him," "I haven't felt anything in this relationship for a long time. What's the point of staying," and "I'm just here to give it one more chance."

In counseling, some couples are able to find what they once had; a loving, functional relationship. This is because everything necessary to improve the marriage still resides within the couple. Other marriages have moved too far down the dysfunctional marriage track. Their marriage is a train wreck waiting to happen. Dysfunction has gained too much momentum and cannot be stopped. In such cases, at least one of the couple will conclude that there is no option but to separate.

Functional Relationships

Functional relationships are characterized by a balance between relationship rights and relationship responsibilities. The importance of this balance cannot be overstated. It can best be achieved by maintaining a solid relationship foundation. The stronger the foundation, the more balanced and functional the relationship. This is true not only of marriages but of all relationships. The Foundation Building Blocks of Functional Relationships describes the primary components of functional relationships.

Foundation Building Blocks of Functional Relationships

1. *Emotional connection.* All relationships are characterized by feelings or the emotional connections that exist between or among relationship members. Feelings frequently alter or influence perceptions and behaviors. Love is a common emotional connection. The emotional connection established between persons can alter, or be altered by, any or all of the other blocks.
2. *Trust.* Trust is a fundamental building block of all functional relationships. Trust is related to many other components of functional relationships including fidelity, dependability, and honesty.
3. *Honesty.* Functional relationships are characterized by a high degree of caring honesty. There is a place for not hurting others feelings and not addressing every issue. However, consistent misrepresentation or avoidance to avoid short-term conflict often results in the

establishment of negative outcomes such as long-term resentment and invalidation.

4. *Assumption of honesty.* With trust, we can assume honesty in others. A relationship in which honesty cannot be assumed is plagued with suspicion. Such relationships are characterized by trying to mind-read the "real" meaning of various interactions.

5. *Respect.* Respect is demonstrated in all areas of functional relationships—verbal communication, nonverbal behaviors, openness for discussion, conflict resolution, and so on. Without respect, relationships cannot remain functional and problem resolution communication is not possible.

6. *Tolerance.* The acceptance of personal differences and individual preferences are vital to keeping relationships working well. A degree of mutual tolerance makes forgiveness possible and relationships more pleasant. It also reduces points of conflict.

7. *Responsiveness.* Your responsiveness to others helps to validate their importance to you. It reflects your commitment and demonstrates relationship meaningfulness. Responsiveness is especially important in families and in hierarchical work relationships.

8. *Flexibility.* Personal rigidity frequently strains relationships and limits potential functional boundaries. Highly functional relationships are characterized by reasonable flexibility so that when stressed, they bend without breaking. Many things are not as serious as they first seem. Develop and maintain a sense of humor as part of flexibility.

9. *Communication.* Make it safe for communication. Speak and listen in a calm manner. Allow others to express thoughts and feelings without interruption. Stay mindful of the difference between *hearing* and *listening*. Safe and functional communication is characterized by listening.

10. *Commitment.* Long term functional relationships are characterized by commitment and a willingness to work on problems. This is accomplished by acceptance of personal responsibility, attempts to see things from other perspectives, conflict resolution, and the ability to move beyond perceived transgressions.

In troubled marriages the fundamental blocks of the relationship foundation have been damaged. Because the blocks are the foundation upon which the marriage is built, the damage in the foundation is reflected in the relationship. The couple will experience a degree of marital discord commensurate to the foundation damage. Most persons in troubled marriages do not seek help until marital dysfunction reaches some crisis. By this time, the foundation may have sustained too much damage for the relationship to be successfully repaired.

Special Status

All of us have *special status* people. Spouses, significant others, partners, and so on are special status people. They are the only persons in the entire universe that hold this unique status in our lives. It is ok to do some things differently for those with special status...for instance, yielding in an argument. Doing this for special status persons increases the likelihood that they will return the favor. For special status persons and others, model the behavior that you wish in return. A useful way to remember this is, *you often get what you give.*

Intimacy Enhancing—Intimacy Distancing

Intimacy is not sex. Sex is not intimacy. Intimacy is an emotion. Sex is a behavior. People can be intimate without sex. People can have sex without intimacy. Intimacy involves a feeling of closeness and connection. The closer a person feels to another person, the more intimate the relationship. High functioning relationships are characterized by a high degree of intimacy. In high functioning marriages, this makes sex with intimacy possible—a very good situation indeed.

Many behaviors are intimacy enhancing. Intimacy enhancing behaviors are those that encourage feelings of interpersonal connectedness. Intimacy enhancing behaviors are limited only by the imagination. A kiss on the cheek, a thoughtful gift, a well-timed wink, and establishing a date night are all examples of intimacy enhancing behaviors.

Special occasions such as birthdays, anniversaries, Valentine's Day, and so on are ideal times for enhancing intimacy. Thoughtful gifts, activities, and cards on special occasions are often much appreciated and work to enhance intimacy. Forgetting or minimizing special occasions will often distance intimacy (in spite of your spouse's statements to the contrary). So remain mindful of special dates. Also, do not underestimate the intimacy enhancing power of the occasional card or gift for no reason other than spousal appreciation. These seemingly simple things keep relationships fresh, interesting, and rewarding.

Many behaviors are intimacy distancing. These behaviors are emotional wedges which force people apart. Yelling, consistently criticizing, inconsideration, invalidation, threats, minimizing, and physical violence are examples of intimacy distancing behaviors. Intimacy distancing behaviors are common in dysfunctional relationships. Relationships can be improved by avoiding intimacy distancing behaviors and increasing the frequency of intimacy enhancing behaviors.

More on Communication

Communication is vital to functional relationships. There are many thoughts about human communication. There are theories about verbal communication, nonverbal communication, mass communication, persuasion, the list goes on and on. Some theories are simple, others quite complex. A simple, easy to remember, and useful way to think about verbal communication is the triad *content-message-delivery*. Within the triad, *content* refers to the actual words chosen to send a message. The *message* is the meaning of what is communicated. The *delivery* refers to how the content is spoken. Delivery includes nonverbal behavior when the verbal communication is in-person. Nonverbal behavior in these circumstances helps to define the message of the content. For example, pointing a finger at someone while saying, "I'm talking to you" can intensify the message.

The content of verbal communication can impart various messages. This is because words, phrases, and sentences have inherently differential meanings.

A person can use the same content to send different messages. This is accomplished by altering the delivery. For instance, "You're bad!" said in a serious and stern voice would indicate disapproval. However, in the present day, if said in an animated, enthusiastic tone, the same sentence might mean "You're great!"

A person can also use different content to send the same message. For example, when speaking to someone who has recently completed a difficult task, "I think you've done a great job" sends a similar message (approval) as "I'm impressed with your work and how well this turned out."

It is clear that delivery can alter the message of content. Most police officers are well familiar with this feature of communication. Many citizen complaints are founded in the grievance, "It's not what he said (content), it's how he said it" (delivery).

A fundamental component of delivery is *intensity*. Intensity can be thought of as ranging from a low of 1 to a high of 10. For most couples, verbal communication in excess of intensity level 5 brings the conversation out of "problem solving territory." In conversations with an intensity higher than 5, the focus usually changes from the issue being discussed to the issue of power. Once people start yelling at one another, the core of the exchange becomes an argument over who is dominant. When the argument changes to a fight for dominance, spouses are arguing for their place in the relationship. So, a complaint about not replacing the toothpaste cap after brushing becomes, "Who are you to tell me what to do!" The ironic thing is that once a conversation evolves into a power fight, the issue that initiated the discussion seldom gets addressed. It becomes lost in the greater argument.

To keep discussions in problem solving territory, couples must monitor their verbal intensity. This involves remaining mindful of one's emotional state, vocal emphasis, and vocal volume. It is not possible to demonstrate verbal intensity on the pages of a book, but varying communication intensities can also be expressed in writing. Written intensity involves text selection (content), semantics (meaning and message), letter case, fonts, underlining, and punctuation (delivery). For example, which sentence reads with greater intensity? "Leave me alone" or "LEAVE ME ALONE!" What about "Leave *me* alone" and "Leave me alone?" Most of us can literally "hear" the differences in these sentences. It is the same for verbal communication. Volume and emphasis can determine the message of identical content. Combine this with nonverbal behaviors and environmental context, and the framework for communication is complete.

Overall, communication improves when content aligns with the intended message and the intensity of the delivery is respectful and appropriate.

Message-to-Content

A dysfunctional content-message-delivery communication pattern which can cause considerable distress for couples is the "message-to-content" transaction. This negative behavioral pattern involves using benign or even complimentary content, but delivering it in a way that sends an insulting or attacking message. Then, if the sender is confronted on the attacking nature of the message, the sender defends it by referring to the content. An example will help to illustrate this pattern: A husband walks into the couple's messy kitchen, looks around, and sarcastically says to his wife, "I see that you've been working on keeping the house clean." The wife, responding to the criticizing message, responds, "Stop picking on me! I'm doing the best I can. It wouldn't hurt you to help out more!" The husband, now reacting to his wife's challenge, takes on the innocent, good guy role. He responds, "What's wrong with you? All I said was that I saw that you've been working on the house. I was giving you a compliment! You must be crazy!" The message-to-content pattern of communication, when used habitually, is very destructive. It is an intimacy-distancing behavior which damages several blocks of the couple's relationship foundation.

What if in the example above, the husband was actually trying to give his wife a compliment? After all, isn't it possible that his good intention might have been misinterpreted? Of course this is possible. However, if it were true in this case, the husband would not have been sarcastic in his delivery. The delivery of the content would have been different.

In communication, the possibility of being misunderstood is ever present. This is because communication is transactional. The message you receive will influence your response. It may not be the message intended by the sender. This is why feedback is so important. Communication is imperfect. Feedback is sometimes necessary to improve communication accuracy. To avoid miscommunication you should remember the communication imperative: *a person will respond to the message received and not necessarily the message you intended to send*. This is also true for you. You will respond to the message you receive and not necessarily the message intended by the sender. If you are unclear about the message you received or it is upsetting or seemingly unjustified, you can ask the sender to clarify the meaning.

To improve communication, think about speaking in suggestions, proposals, and preferences. For instance, which would you rather hear; "We're staying in tonight because I'm tired." or "I'm a bit tired tonight. What do you think about staying in?" The first sentence uses content that can be perceived as domineering and controlling. If the listener is sensitive to these issues, this sentence will trigger an argument or result in quiet resentment. The latter sentence is more likely to be received non-defensively. Its content validates the listener as a factor in decision making. From this point the couple can negotiate the evening's activities.

A word about negotiation. If during negotiation you agree to something, you forfeit your right to complain about it later. The time to argue and complain is during the negotiation, not afterward. Once you agree to something, stand by your agreement. Do not punish others by agreeing to do something, such as going out for dinner when you wanted to stay home, and during dinner do little more than act badly. This is not good faith negotiation. It is part of a dysfunctional behavior pattern and should be avoided. Good-faith negotiation improves poor relationships and helps to sustain good ones.

If all this seems too complicated remember that good communication requires more energy than poor communication, at least at first. Once functional communication patterns are established it takes little energy to maintain them.

The *Northeast* Communication Style

Remain aware of the Northeast communication style (named by my wife due to my previous communication propensities). The Northeast communication style is characteristic of dysfunctional verbal communication and should be avoided. It is comprised of five communication style components which are best described as dominating the conversation, simultaneous talking, talking over, formulating the response, and the pause jump.

Dominating the conversation is nearly continuous talking without regard for others. Although the speaker achieves personal expression, no one else is provided this opportunity. Dominating the conversation monopolizes the transaction and normally fatigues listeners. In *simultaneous talking*, if everyone is talking simultaneously, who is listening? Everyone is so concerned about making their point that there is no consideration for the views of others. Is this communication? Not really. It is more like a struggle to establish interaction dominance. *Talking over* is a milder form of simultaneous talking. It is the occasional cutting off the communication of another by simply interjecting your response over their communication. It does not matter if they are mid-sentence, just making a point, and so on. Talking over can be a feature of superior rank or dominance in a relationship. It invalidates the speaker and shuts down a mutual exchange. *Formulating the response* is a communication pitfall. It is characterized by not listening. In the place of listening, the person is formulating how to respond to make a point, regardless of the speaker's information. While formulating the response, vital pieces of the speaker's communication may be missed. This is because most of us cannot fully attend to another's communication while actively thinking about making our point. The internal process of formulating the response is often reflected in nonverbal facial expressions. Observation of these expressions sometimes prompts the speaker to ask, "Are you listening to me?" The last of the NE communication style components is the *pause jump*. The pause jump occurs when a NE communicator perceives even the slightest pause in the communication of others as an opportunity to jump in. This often provokes the response, "I wasn't finished!" or worse, "You never let me finish talking." To avoid the pause jump, NE communicators must realize that different communication styles are composed of different length pauses within communication transactions. The NE style maintains very brief pauses. When all parties are NE communicators, this is not much of a concern. It can be annoying, but at least everyone is on the same hectic page. When NE communicators are speaking with non-NE communicators, it can become a problem. The problems are often similar to those seen in talking over. For NE communicators, moderating the elements of the NE communication style will likely improve the functionality of existing communication transactions.

Police Marriages and Relationship Counseling

Many police marriages are highly functional. In these relationships, the couple works together in ways that enhance one another. Regardless of whether the officer is the husband, wife, or both are officers, straight or gay, married or living together, many officers report a high degree of satisfaction in their relationships. This is reflected in police officer divorce rates. The U.S. Department of Health and Human Services reports that on average, from 40 to 50 percent of first marriages end in divorce. Although some police marriages end in divorce, there is growing evidence that the divorce rate for police officers is similar to or maybe *less* than that for the general population. This is counter to the long held belief that police officers experience a higher than average divorce rate. In one study which compared the divorce rates of those in various occupations, several occupations had divorce rates higher than police officers. These included dancers, bartenders, massage workers, and telemarketers. Police officers, optometrists, clergy, and podiatrists, were characterized by lower than average divorce rates. The factor that emerged as the most significant influence on the probability of divorce was the state of residence (McCoy and Aamodt, 2009). Audrey Honig, chief psychologist for the Los Angeles Sheriff's Department, reported that the higher than average divorce rates historically reported for police officers is a modern myth that has its roots in the research and tales of the 1980s (2007).

Police marriages have much in common with other marriages. When police marriages become troubled, they are troubled by the same issues present in many marriages. The usual suspects in troubled marriages are the lack of emotional connection, money, spending of money, child discipline, sex, anger, use of alcohol, perceptions of mistreatment, life philosophy differences, and family issues. Occasionally, occupational stressors will surface as the primary problem area in police marriages. These stressors might involve spousal frustration with the officer's work schedule, frustration with the police agency, the officer's behavior at home (acting like a cop with family members—most family members do not like being treated as suspects), a perception that the officer is prioritizing the job before the family, and having firearms in the house. Rarely, the spouse of the officer is upset by the risks inherent in policing. This is because most police spouses manage this fear by trusting in police training, tactics, and technology. However, for some spouses the fear that the officer will be injured or killed on the job becomes unbearable. Several former police officers have ended their careers due to such fears of their spouses.

Work Stress and the Police Family

Work can be stressful. Police officers (and others) should avoid returning home from work without any fuel in their *stressor management gas tank* (SMGT). The idea of SMGT helps us gauge the amount of coping energy available for continued stressor confrontation. With some practice, anyone can become adept at SMGT level awareness. The hypothetical example of Officer D will help clarify SMGT.

Officer D has had a difficult workday. During his shift, he made three arrests, investigated six crime reports, investigated a vehicle accident, and wrote four traffic tickets. During one of the arrests, he was slightly injured. During another, the suspect spewed out insult after insult. Two of the recipients of traffic tickets told him he should be out catching real criminals. One questioned why he was picking on the honest citizens who pay his salary. To top things off, his sergeant mentioned that a citizen had filed a complaint in reference to one of his traffic stops the week before. As the day wore on, Officer D was becoming more frustrated and angry. He needed greater amounts of self-restraint to remain professional. By the end of his shift, Officer D had pretty much reached his limit with people. His coping energy, the energy needed to deal with others, was nearly depleted. This meant that his SMGT was precariously low. Officer D was hanging on by a thread. We will return to Officer D shortly.

The desire for, or tolerance of, external stimulation is relative. Some persons enjoy a great deal of environmental stimulation. Others find minimal outside stimulation desirable (a factor to be reckoned with in marriages where individual stimulation preferences are widely different). For most persons, there is an optimal range of stimulation. If they fall much below the optimum, they become bored and restless. If they are much above the optimum, they become overstimulated, irritable, and overstressed. In the latter circumstances, their limits for coping with stimulation (demands) have been exceeded.

Now back to Officer D. Officer D has been overstimulated. He has experienced too many demands during his workday. In his effort to manage the excess stimulation, he has depleted his coping resources. There is little fuel remaining in his SMGT. He is a raw nerve, a powder keg ready to explode at the least of provocations. And now he is going home.

For Officer D, once home, it would not take much to ignite family conflict. In fact, something as simple as his child asking him to play catch might do it. Imagine this. Officer D's child, happy to see her dad, asks him to play catch. Normally, this would not be a problem for Officer D. However, in his current, SMGT depleted condition, where his toleration for additional demands is nearly zero, he yells at her, "I don't have time for you right now!" The child walks away disappointed and confused. At eight years old she cannot understand what she did to make daddy angry. Officer D's wife, having watched the exchange, yells at him, "What's wrong with you! Why are you treating her that way?" Officer D responds, "You don't know anything! Get off my back!" He stomps to the refrigerator, grabs a beer, and walks outside. This is not good, and worse, the evening has just begun.

Fortunately for Officer D, future similar scenarios are avoidable. In order to prevent another similar occurrence, Officer D needs to renegotiate his *internal* and *external* interface.

Internal and External Interface

The internal interface represents the relationship that persons have with themselves. It is related to the notions of self-concept, self-esteem, personal values, and self-control. The internal interface is made possible by the complexities of human consciousness. By renegotiating his internal interface, Officer D can learn to practice techniques and use strategies that help to prevent or manage stimulus overload. This will help maintain SMGT levels. In the event that these internal interface strategies occasionally prove insufficient, he can renegotiate his external interface. The external interface is best described by how a person relates to everything outside of self, including other people. By renegotiating his external interface, he would have replenished his SMGT prior to arriving home.

As a police officer, if you have had a stressful workday, your SMGT may be depleted. You can learn to recognize low levels of coping energy by increasing your self-awareness. If you feel that you cannot handle much more without blowing up, you have little left in your SMGT. What should you do? You should engage internal and external interface management strategies. You should do this to keep from arriving home in a stressed out frame of mind.

Internal and External Interface Management

When you feel stressed out after a workday, with little fuel in your SMGT, do not go home. (1) Stop. Hang around the station for a few minutes. Practice relaxation breathing and other stress management strategies. Talk to friends. Talk about something other than police work. Calm yourself. (2) Think about your family. Think about the fact that you will need to continue to cope with stressors when you get home. If you have children, keep in mind that they may be waiting for you. Consider that when you get home, your spouse may need a break from the kids. This means that you may need to go from police officer to parent as soon as you arrive. (3) Think about all that is good in your life. By accessing these thoughts, you add some fuel to your SMGT. (4) On your way home, listen to some favorite music. Continue your relaxation breathing. Think about a recent pleasant family outing. (5) Stay out of the bars. Coming home stressed and intoxicated is never a good way to improve family transactions. (6) Upon arrival home, *check yourself*. Checking yourself involves calming yourself and preparing for family transactions. Tap into your replenished SMGT. (7) Refuse to allow the stressors of your workday to follow you home. Really, would you want the suspect that you arrested today to affect you in ways that cause you marital or family problems? You might as well bring the suspect home! We do not bring suspects home physically, and we cannot afford to bring them home psychologically. Keep the bad guys out of your head, out of your home, and out of your family. The same holds true for all work stressors. (8) At home, if needed, ask your family for a few minutes alone. Always follow up this request with something like, "I'll be back shortly. Then we can catch up on things." During your down time, recharge, then reengage. (9) Try to think outside yourself. You are an important figure in your family's life. It is important for your family to have you available. It is not a bad thing to have your family excited to see you. (10) If you are a parent, *remember that your family behavior today is creating your children's future childhood memories*. What kind of memories would you like your children to have? Certainly, coming home from work and terrorizing the family is not one of them. The worst of who we are should never be acted out against those whom we care for most.

Engagement—Disengagement

Related to *optimal levels of environmental stimulation* are the concepts of *engagement* and *disengagement*. These are useful ideas when trying to understand stimulation-based difficulties. Simply stated, when persons are overstimulated, they seek disengagement from others. When understimulated, they seek to engage others. On any given day, officers that have been overstimulated at work may return home to a spouse that has been understimulated (or vice versa). This creates a substrate for conflict. For example, after a stressful day, an officer might seek solitude at home. Meanwhile the spouse, being bored most of the day, might seek social contact and interaction once the officer arrives home. The worst cases of such a circumstance might end in heated exchanges such as "Talk to me!" (an attempt to engage) and "Get out of my face!" (an attempt to disengage). Of course, most engagement/disengagement conflicts are not this severe; however, couples should be on guard for the difficulties that can arise out of engagement/disengagement conflicts. Because anyone can become over or understimulated, these situations can arise even in cases where the spouses are nearly identical in their preference for environmental stimulation.

Love Is Not Enough

One of the myths of marriage is that love will keep the couple together. Love can keep a marriage together, but there are no guarantees.

Love can keep a marriage together even when the marriage becomes dangerous. Every officer is familiar with the response of some battered wives when asked, "Why do you stay with this guy?" She often replies, "Because I love him." This is usually followed up with something like "He's not always bad. He just loses his temper." In seriously dysfunctional relationships, officers sometimes hear "It's my fault that he hits me."

In cases like this, there is always the question of whether the woman is truly speaking of love. It could be that she is unknowingly describing suppressed fear or emotional dependency. Regardless, couples like this are in need of immediate intervention. Left untreated, this kind of marriage represents a significant threat to the wife. Too many times such relationships end in serious injury or death.

Some couples split despite confessing their love for one another. When "loving" couples divorce, it is usually because of a violation of the marriage agreement. For many couples, infidelity is one such violation; bad behavior associated with alcoholism is another. Some couples separate due to the sheer exhaustion of trying to live together when significant personality or preference differences exist.

Another myth of marriage is that love will keep the couple happy. Although necessary, love is not sufficient to create a happy marriage. To have a happy marriage, the remainder of the relationship foundation blocks must also be present. In happy marriages, each of the foundation blocks is strong and sturdy.

A third myth of marriage is that the other person will never leave. The fact is that anyone can treat another so badly for so long, that the person will consider terminating the relationship. This marriage myth is founded in denial and narcissism. The person with this belief is convinced that the spouse is so in love, that the thought of leaving is not possible (denial). And even if the spouse thought about leaving, it would not be possible because of the specialness (narcissism) of the believer. Case in point—a police officer in a metro police department had engaged in numerous affairs during the past several years of his marriage. One of his affairs produced a child with a local prostitute for which he and his wife were paying child support. His wife begged him to stop the extramarital relationships. She had begged him for years. During this period, they entered marriage counseling at least three times. On each occasion, the wife would tell him that she loved him and wanted the marriage to work. He would promise to be faithful. On each occasion, the officer terminated counseling after a few sessions, dismissing it as "not helpful."

Several months after the officer terminated the most recent marriage counseling, his wife discovered that he had begun a new affair. This time she had reached her limit. She contacted an attorney and filed for divorce.

Upon learning this, the officer went into a psychological tailspin. His friends arranged for him to see the police department psychologist. In counseling, he said that he could not believe that she would actually leave. He asked, "What's going on? Why did she spring this on me? I had no warning!"

The serving of the divorce papers functioned as the critical stimulus. This act punctured his wall of denial. It became clear to him that he could not fix things this time. He had lost her. The divorce papers also stripped away his narcissistic defenses. He became very depressed and suicidal. He had to be relieved of duty. His firearms were collected and placed into lockdown due to concerns for his safety. Because of the severity of his depression, he entered a residential treatment facility. He did not reengage the department's psychological services.

Couples Counseling

In counseling, police wives often discuss their husband's in-home behavior in less than flattering terms. In these troubled marriages, officers are often described as angry much of the time, over-controlling, suspicious, demanding, verbally abusive, impatient, and intimidating. Such descriptions frequently conflict with the work reputation of these officers. At work, they are known to be professional, competent, compassionate, caring, and kind. They exercise good judgment and authoritative discretion. They are respected and well liked by their peers. They seldom receive citizen complaints. So how is it that very little of this behavior is seen at home? When asked this question, officers respond nearly universally, "There are consequences at work. I don't want to lose my job or get in trouble. I want to get promoted. If I feel angry or frustrated at work, I handle it. I want to look good. Work is work. When I get home, I want to be myself. I don't want to have to watch how I act."

These officers are describing *role driven* behavior. The role is *police officer*, and the behavior is that which they see as appropriate for the role. This way of thinking is not in itself dysfunctional. All of us alter our behavior to some degree when acting in particular roles. However, within the officers' responses, there are three interesting and clinically significant underlying implications:

- The first implication is that the officer believes there are no consequences for bad behavior at home ("There are consequences at work..."). *No consequences? The officer is sitting in the office of the police psychologist due to relationship problems. He may be close to losing his family. This is an extreme consequence.*

- The second implication is that the "real" person, when not being driven by the role of police officer, is not a very nice person ("When I get home, I want to be myself..."). *Is this true? Can it be that the compassionate, understanding, coping professional person seen at work is nothing more than a sham, a facade? No. If the officer is a kind and compassionate person at work, he can be a kind and compassionate person at home. Period.*

- The third implication is that stress coping strategies can stop at home ("If I feel angry or frustrated at work, I handle it...") *Where did police officers ever get the idea that stress coping strategies can stop at home? This idea has no merit whatsoever. Officers must continue to utilize stress coping strategies at home. They must present their best thoughts, feelings, and behaviors to those they care about most.*

For happier marriages, officers must avoid getting caught in the police role driven behavior trap. It is unfortunate that some officers will treat peers, citizens, and even suspects kinder than they treat their spouses and other family members.

The Popeye Philosophy and PYLM

There is another trap lying in wait for police (and other) couples. This is the *Popeye philosophy*. The Popeye philosophy is represented within the cartoon character's often said statement, "I yam what I yam." Well, everyone is what they are, and there is something to be said for simply accepting oneself. This is normal and can be healthy. However, if this gets carried to an extreme, it becomes a rationalization for bad behavior. This philosophy can destroy efforts to improve behavior, and it can destroy relationships. In essence, the extreme of the Popeye philosophy is another way of saying, "I'll behave as I want, and you'll just have to deal with it." This is seldom a good way to maintain a happy marriage.

Just how far should persons go in self-acceptance? It seems to depend upon values and goals. Sorting out what is appropriate for self-acceptance and what should be targeted for improvement is a major challenge to everyone living a life-by-design. When confronting this challenge, it is important to keep in mind that self-acceptance and self-improvement are not mutually exclusive.

It is possible to accept yourself for who you are *and* target behaviors or traits for improvement. This helps to maintain self-esteem while continuing efforts for desired change.

Frequently observed within the Popeye philosophy is the *prove you love me* (PYLM) transaction. PYLM transactions are characterized by behavior in which one member of the couple seems to consistently test the loyalty and love of the other. This is done by behaving badly (being overly rigid in disagreements, pouting, and outright challenges "If I'm so bad, why don't you leave!?"). Following PYLM behavior, the perpetrator waits and observes the reaction of the other. If the other's response is satisfactory (sufficiently consoling, contrite, apologetic, etc) the goal has been accomplished. The person has "proved" their love. If the response is not satisfactory, the intensity of the PYLM transaction is increased until the desired "proof" is presented. PYLM transactions are often motivated by an internal and sometimes repressed sense of relationship or personal insecurity. They also involve dominance, manipulation and control.

PYLM transactions undermine relationship authenticity and are therefore undesirable. The issues that underlie PYLM transactions can be serious and are best confronted directly, with professional assistance if necessary.

My Job—Your Job

In addition to the Popeye philosophy and PYLM, there is the *my job-your job* (MJYJ) transactional pattern. Officers must be aware of MJYJ because it can cause significant marital problems. The MJYJ pattern is being played out when the officer diminishes or disregards the job stress of the spouse, based on the intensity of the stressors inherent in policing. It goes something like this: The spouse expresses a work frustration. The officer responds "Do you realize what *I* deal with everyday? It's danger. It's life and death. I can't get excited because some janitor didn't clean your office. That's nothing compared to the stress of my job." The MJYJ minimizes the importance of the issues identified by the spouse. It frequently leads to the spouse feeling invalidated and unimportant in the relationship. This is intimacy distancing and thereby dysfunctional.

Although policing includes unavoidable stressors and personal risk, listening to and supporting spouses when they are upset or overwhelmed by their job stressors (including the stressors of being a stay-at-home spouse or parent) is a fundamental feature of functional police marriages.

Psychological Defense Mechanisms and Police Marriages

There are many theorized psychological defense mechanisms. Some of them have been previously introduced. Psychological defense mechanisms were first discussed by Sigmund Freud as part of his approach to the treatment of anxiety (1920). Freud hypothesized that psychological defense mechanisms operate unconsciously. This means that they exist outside of conscious awareness.

Defense mechanisms are thought to protect us from undue psychological harm. They allow us to cope with stressful circumstances without actually changing them. *Denial* is a defense mechanism. So are *rationalization, intellectualization, suppression,* and *projection,* to name a few. In denial, we fail to recognize personal difficulties that may be obvious to others. Rationalization allows us to create false but credible explanations for our thoughts and behaviors, as well as the actions of others. Intellectualization is the process by which we use theoretical thinking to justify our thoughts and behavior. Suppression involves pushing stressful thoughts out of our consciousness. Projection is the process by which we attribute to others our own unacceptable thoughts and feelings.

In themselves, there is nothing pathological about psychological defense mechanisms. In fact, they can be thought of as adaptive in many circumstances. It is only in their overdevelopment that problems can result. Because defense mechanisms operate unconsciously, persons struggling with difficulties caused by defense mechanism overdevelopment have no insight into the cause of their problems. One particularly interesting psychological defense mechanism is *emotional insulation.* Emotional insulation is the process whereby feelings and emotional reactions are dampened. It is especially useful for police officers because they are required to remain calm in emotionally charged and stressful situations. Remaining calm in these situations permits police officers to better process information and achieve resolutions based on fact, not emotion. Emotional insulation helps to make this possible.

There are several factors that encourage the development of emotional insulation in police officers. The first is the work itself. In policing, unavoidable stressors include the exposure to domestic violence, traffic accidents, child abuse, natural death and homicide, violence, and personal danger. Without some sort of psychological protection against the negative effects of such exposure, officers would soon overload their coping capacity.

The second is police officers themselves. There exists a social value among police officers for calmness in situations which normally evoke strong emotion in others. It is not that officers never express emotion in the presence of one another, but only that there is a value placed on remaining calm. Case in point—an officer contacted two suspects for a minor violation. The suspects became uncooperative and attacked the police officer. During the altercation, the officer was able to radio for assistance. As other police units arrived and the suspects were taken into custody, the first thing the slightly injured and roughed up officer said was "How did I sound on the radio?" Many officers have suffered the taunts of other officers for "freaking out" or "screaming like a little girl" on the radio. One of the last things officers want is to be seen by their peers as fearful, excitable, or overly emotional.

The third is the court system. The court system encourages police officer emotional insulation by placing a premium on objective, uninvolved, and unemotional testimony. In fact, if an opposing attorney can demonstrate officer emotion in reference to a case, the officer's testimony is discredited. Such attorney arguments usually center on "Officer, isn't it true that you were upset and angry? And isn't it true that your actions were based more on your anger than on appropriate police behavior?" and so forth. Another way that an officer's testimony can be impeached is if the opposing attorney can show some emotional connection of the officer to anyone involved in the case. This last circumstance is not quite the same as emotional insulation, but it is another example of the testimonial standard of objectivity expected of police officers.

Emotional insulation helps officers to function professionally in stressful situations. Its development is encouraged by repeated exposures to stressful events. What then is the problem? Problems, especially relationship problems, arise when officers' insulation becomes too "thick", too rigid, and impermeable. In clinical cases of emotional insulation, the officer appears emotionally numb. For the officer, the experience of emotion, on and off the job, becomes almost painful. Hence emotion is repressed. If emotional connections remain, they are often only with peers—not citizens, not family. The payoff for the officer is that no uncomfortable feelings are experienced. However, the down side is that the insulation works in both directions. Although there is protection from external stressors, the *expression* of emotion is also muted. Soon, the emotional shut-down becomes a factor in the officer's marriage. In response to lack of feelings expressed by the officer and the perceived withdrawal from the relationship, spouses often find themselves withdrawing, thereby widening the emotional gap between the couple.

Living with an overly insulated officer is difficult. This is because the officer acts more robot-like than a caring person. Wives of these officers describe the marriage relationship as cold and unfeeling. Sex, if it is occurring at all, is unemotional. One wife described it as "Wham bam, thank you, ma'am." Other family activities are also affected. Family transactions become brief and seem mechanical. If there is any emotion expressed by the officer, it is usually anger. Not much of any other emotion can penetrate the insulation.

On the other side, emotionally insulated officers complain that their spouses do not understand them. They say that their wives have become intolerant and "bitchy." Officer and wife appear to be at an impasse. Neither knows how their marriage got to this place. Wives of emotionally insulated police officers, when looking at their husbands in the psychologist's office, say "This is not the man I married. I don't know who this is." The officers say little until some comment provokes an angry response.

The course of therapy for such couples depends upon the actual situation. Mostly it involves finding a way to reduce emotional insulation so that the couple can emotionally reconnect.

Police officers must remain on guard to avoid the overdevelopment of emotional insulation. Good communication helps. Talking to spouses, staying involved in family life, and not living police work every day are buffers against emotional insulation. Taking time for one another and sharing couples activities (without the kids) are also important. Good boundaries are imperative. Happily married police officers strive to have a life outside of the police department. This helps the officer and the relationship to stay fun, interesting, balanced, and functional.

Dysfunctional Relationship Patterns

Dysfunctional relationship patterns are predictable sequences of behavior which result in undesirable or otherwise negative outcomes. For instance, have you ever wondered why you *always* end up leaving the house in a rage when you and your spouse try to discuss how family income should be spent? If this describes your relationship, you are experiencing a dysfunctional relationship pattern. As you might expect, dysfunctional patterns can involve any topic and vary in degree of dysfunction.

When couples are locked into dysfunctional patterns, they often see each other as adversaries. It feels as if it is husband against wife, wife against husband, partner against partner. This feeling energizes the dysfunction and contributes to its maintenance. Couples can better alter undesirable patterns if they think about teaming up against them. This approach allies the couple in an effort to disrupt the pattern. It works like this: whenever either perceives the startup or presence of the dysfunctional pattern, it is identified and the couple's coping responses are engaged. The coping responses include a myriad of interventions such as taking a short break and reengaging, calming down and reengaging, lowering the intensity of the communication, and so on. In this way, the old pattern is disrupted and the probability for a better outcome is increased. When a couple thinks about attacking a dysfunctional pattern instead of each other, it changes the focus from *prevailing over each other* to *prevailing over the pattern*. As they succeed in their efforts, the new, more functional pattern is reinforced. With continued success, the previously dysfunctional pattern is eventually replaced.

To increase the probability of dysfunctional pattern replacement, both persons must agree beforehand to engage coping responses upon the request of the other. Such agreement is necessary because as the dysfunctional pattern unfolds, its habit-strength will naturally carry the couple to its undesirable outcome. Without a previous agreement, and following a call for pattern disruption (sometimes initiated by the use of a prearranged codeword), the other person may well want to continue fighting. The couple must trust one another to use dysfunctional pattern disruption coping strategies only when appropriate and not as a means to exert control over or otherwise manipulate the other. The coping strategy for dysfunctional pattern disruption must not be transformed into another element of relationship dysfunction.

At first, the person who identifies the dysfunctional pattern and calls for coping responses may feel weak, as if it is tantamount to backing down. That is, by refusing to participate in acting out the old pattern, it may feel that the other person has somehow won. While the feeling of backing down is common, it is not truly reflective of the circumstances. When dysfunctional patterns are interrupted and improved outcomes achieved, both persons win. The reward is an improved relationship. In fact, it is usually the stronger person in the couple that first breaks the habit-strength of the dysfunctional pattern.

Reflections of a Police Psychologist

Protect Less—Communicate More

In highly functional relationships, there is less protecting and more communicating. So *protect less-communicate more*. This is accomplished by a reduced effort to protect the relationship from disagreement and a greater effort on initiating discussion when appropriate. This does not mean that you should become hypersensitive to everything. There is a place for just letting things go and moving on. Do not get caught up in the minor and unimportant aspects of everyday living. It is not necessary to confront every issue. However, if it is important to you, you should open a discussion. If your partner approaches you with something important, remain open minded. It may be difficult to listen to an account of how your actions hurt or otherwise affected your spouse, but try to understand without judging. "That would not have bothered me" or "You're too sensitive" is never a good response. Focus on the pattern. Work together to resolve problems and to prevent similar future occurrences. Apologize—this should not be difficult with your special status person. Make an effort to alter your behavior based on the discussion. This is a wonderful courtesy that can be extended to your spouse. Remember, a courtesy rendered frequently results in a courtesy returned.

Keep the communication functional. Good relationships are characterized by good communication. Do not forget the relationship imperative: *Make it safe!* Making it safe involves remaining calm and attentive. A single conversation wherein you "blew your top" or appeared disinterested can discourage communication for years. Spouses should be able to come to one another with *any* issue and expect respectful discussion. In the end, discussing and successfully resolving a perceived difference, no matter how minor, is intimacy enhancing.

Complaint versus Criticism

Every person has a right to complain. If your husband says he will do something, and he fails to do it, you should register a complaint. "You said that you were going to get the car washed, and you didn't. I'm disappointed that the car is not clean." Complaints are valid and are factually based. They differ from criticism. Criticism attacks the person, "You said that you were going to get the car washed, and you didn't. You always let me down. You can't be trusted to do anything!"

Notice that in complaint, the wife (as complainant) is talking about herself, "*I'm* disappointed that the car is not clean." In criticism, the wife (as criticizer) is talking about her husband, "*You* always let me down. *You* can't be trusted to do anything." Complaints encourage continued communication and improve the prospects for problem resolution. Similar to *protecting less and communicating more*, resolving a complaint is intimacy enhancing and strengthens the relationship. Criticism damages the relationship and should be avoided. Criticism is intimacy distancing and weakens the couple's bond (Gottman and Silver, 1999). Of course, the best way to avoid a complaint and enhance intimacy is to follow through on what you say.

Extramarital Affairs

There is a true test of marital fidelity. The test has three components: (1) you are attracted to a person not your spouse, who is also attracted to you, (*yes, it is possible to be attracted to a person who is not your spouse*), (2) the person makes it known to you that he or she is available and willing to engage in romantic or sexual activities, and (3) you believe that you can engage in such activities and not be discovered. You pass the test if you walk away and redirect your emotional energies to your spouse and into your marriage.

Some marriages are troubled most of the time. Some marriages are troubled some of the time. Many marriages are not troubled at all. Having an extramarital affair will normally cause trouble for most of the time in a marriage. Although affairs are frequently the result of an unhappy marriage, they can also destroy "good" marriages. Persons who have had an affair sometimes say "I don't know what I was thinking. I have a good marriage."

Marriages can survive affairs. However, even if the marriage survives, it is changed forever. The emotional wounds caused by affairs seldom completely heal. These emotional injuries, often deeply repressed, will remain with the offended party for life. These feelings are so much a part of the offended person that they will continue to exert their influence after the death of the unfaithful spouse.

Some couples say things like, "The affair was a good thing. It helped us seek counseling and focused our problems." Although an affair may be responsible for the initiation of counseling and the focusing of problems, I have never known an affair to be good for a marriage. For most, statements like this help to rationalize the affair and distribute responsibility ("It's part your fault that I had an affair because you . . ." or "It's part my fault that you had an affair because I . . ."). Rationalization serves the purpose of allowing the couple to move forward, and in this sense is useful. As demonstrated, it is seen in the offended as well as the offending party. Unfortunately, in some cases, once this initial purpose is served, regardless of the rationalization, at least one of the couple will decide that the marriage is over.

There are at least three general categories of extramarital affairs: (1) the emotional affair, which may involve little or no physical contact, (2) the infamous one night stand, and (3) the ongoing affair, which can last from days to years. Some marriages do not survive emotional affairs, in spite of claims from the offending spouse that "I didn't do anything wrong" (did not have sex). In such instances it is normally the sense of emotional betrayal that causes the breakup. Other marriages seem to endure after years of known sexual infidelity. The reasons for these differences? Too numerous to specify. As you might expect, the actual effect and outcome that an affair has on any marriage is dependent upon complex interactions among various psychological, emotional, economic, and social factors.

In some cases, both spouses have had affairs. These can occur concurrently or years apart for various reasons. Sometimes they occur as a component of revenge or "getting even." No matter, it normally spells trouble for the relationship.

There are various rationales for having an affair. One of the most common is "I had an affair to save my marriage." The rationale is "I am unhappy in my marriage. If I act on this, I'll have to divorce. I don't want to divorce (for the kids, religious reasons, money, ongoing emotional attachment to spouse, etc). So I had an affair to compensate for what is lacking. This way, I meet my needs and my marriage is saved."

Another affair rationale is "If I can get it, why not take it. You only live once." This rationale is readily understood and has to do with self-centeredness and the pursuit of personal pleasure. It disregards any sense of marital commitment and the emotional well-being of the spouse.

A third rationale is "It just happened." It is difficult to make headway in counseling with this rationale. This is because the person is not accepting responsibility for personal behavior. Such an explanation for an affair normally leaves the spouse plagued with thoughts that similar behavior could easily be repeated. Affairs do not "just happen" . . . intentional behaviors must be engaged.

There are other rationales for affairs. Sometimes the rationale includes a myriad of factors. No matter, extramarital affairs are difficult to overcome.

This is true regardless of whether the couple remains married or chooses to divorce. Affairs can be so emotionally difficult to manage that some persons resort to violence, including homicide, suicide, or both after learning of an affair.

Affairs and Sex Addiction

Are some affairs related to an addiction to sex? Can a person be addicted to sex? This is a current controversy in psychology. There are many clinicians that advocate for the authenticity of sex addiction. They specialize in treating persons considered to be addicted to sex. Supporters of this position not only maintain the belief that sex addiction is real but also feel that it is acted out in various ways, including affairs.

The current Diagnostic and Statistical Manual of Mental Disorders (fifth edition) (DSM-5) (APA, 2013), does not recognize sex as an addiction. The DSM-5: "...groups of repetitive behaviors, which some term *behavioral* (or *process) addictions*, with such subcategories as "sex addiction," "exercise addiction,", or "shopping addiction," are not included (in this manual) because at this time there is insufficient peer-reviewed evidence to establish the diagnostic criteria and course descriptions needed to identify these behaviors as mental disorders" (481).

For those clinicians that support the idea of behavioral or process addictions, sex could be considered an addiction even though there is no such designation within the DSM-5. There is a clinical conception of "excessive sexual drive," which includes *nymphomania* (uncontrollable sexual desire in a woman) and *satyriasis* (uncontrollable sexual desire in a man), but this is not intended to describe sex as an addiction per se.

Incidentally, in contrast to an excessive sexual drive, it is also possible to experience a less than normal sex drive. While it is normal for a person's sex drive to wax and wane, if low sex drive is persistent and certain other conditions are present, *female sexual interest/arousal disorder* (302.72) or *male hypoactive sexual desire disorder* may be diagnosed (302.71)(DSM-5).

When considering sex drive, you may have heard that "sex is ninety-five percent psychological and five percent physical." While this statement captures the importance of being "turned on" when it comes to sex, low sex drive and sexual performance difficulties can have their origin in physiology (this is also true for excessive sexual drive). One of the most common physical causes for low sex drive and an inability to perform sexually is the inadequate production of sex-related hormones. This condition can be readily diagnosed and treated by qualified physicians.

The treatment of low sex drive often includes the administration of supplemental sex hormones, a treatment not without risk. Persons experiencing low sex drive or other sexual difficulties should discuss the possible benefits and risks of available treatments with their physician.

Housekeeping and Sloppy Factor

A major complaint in some officers' marriages is housekeeping. This may sound like a minor problem, but it can have serious consequences. This problem often gets expressed in statements like "I work all day, and I have to come home to a pig sty." It is easy to see in statements like this that some relationship foundation damage has already occurred. This issue can be especially difficult when the spouse does not work outside the home. For the officer, there is often a sense that the other is not keeping up the marriage bargain or "does nothing all day." In this area, the actual circumstances and issues vary, but it places an additional strain on the marriage. Even in relationships where housekeeping is not a major problem, there exists the *sloppy factor*.

Sloppy factors differ for most couples. Spouses with the least tolerance for sloppiness often find themselves doing most of the housework. This is because their tolerance for sloppiness is exceeded before it reaches critical levels for their spouses. Therefore, the spouse with the least tolerance for sloppiness is consistently picking up the house. This may occur with or without resentment. If there is no resentment, there is little problem. If there is resentment, more destructive patterns develop. These patterns are usually characterized by criticism and dysfunction. For example, a husband might say something like, "I can't take this mess." This normally leads the wife to respond, "I'll clean the house, but does it always have to be on your timetable?" Frustrated, the husband begins to clean. The wife, angered by her husband's cleaning because it implies that she is an inadequate housekeeper, yells, "I'm gonna do it. Leave it alone!" To which the husband responds, "When? I told you I can't take this mess! And I'm tired of you never doing anything around here!" (The exchange has now become the housekeeping argument.) The argument goes on until it reaches its predictable end. Exchanges like this are intimacy distancing and do nothing to solve the problem. In situations like this, couples must access a MOB (mindful of blocks) mentality. Only then does the couple have an opportunity to productively address the issue and make the desired changes.

Intentional and Unintentional Harm

Some couples will intentionally harm one another. They do this psychologically, emotionally, and physically. One pattern of intentional harm involves playing the relationship *trump card*. The relationship trump card is played when a spouse implies or threatens to leave the relationship unless the other person does what is desired. This is different than being dissatisfied with the relationship and honestly discussing the possibility of separation. Playing the trump card is inherently manipulative and dysfunctional. It is intended to hurt, dominate, and control. It is intimacy distancing and risks the relationship. It has several variations including, "If you don't do this, I'll leave" "If you don't like it, there's the door" "I'm not sure I'm coming home" and "Don't let the door hit you on the way out." The use of the relationship trump card is one level below the threatened use of violence, which is one level below actual violence, to obtain what is desired in a relationship.

There are many relationship patterns capable of producing harm. There are also many motivations which maintain these patterns, including anger, intimidation, hatred, revenge, punishment, and control.

Fortunately, most couples would not intentionally harm one another. Even if they become angry, frustrated, or disappointed with their spouses, most persons would not look to harm them in any real manner. This is an important characteristic of most marriages. It has clinical significance for couples in counseling. *If a couple would not intentionally harm one another, then it makes sense to believe that any harm experienced must be unintentional.* This realization can move a couple forward not only in counseling, but also in everyday life.

When considering unintentional harm, two points should always be kept in mind: (1) you do not have to intend harm to do harm (this is the very definition of unintentional harm), and (2) if you feel harmed, you should talk about it. Do not let the feeling of being harmed, even unintentionally, build resentment or lead you to unfounded conclusions.

It is reasonable to assume good faith and good intention on the part of your spouse. If you feel harmed, tell your spouse that you believe the harmful behavior was either unintentional or had a motivation other than harm (many jokes or attempts at humor can unintentionally harm others). Open the discussion in an appropriate manner. Choose where, when, and how you will initiate the discussion. Confront the issue gently and work for resolution.

If you are advised that your behavior has caused harm, even though you did not intend harm, try to remain open minded and listen non-defensively. Once you know that some part of your behavior unintentionally harmed your spouse, it is incumbent upon you to alter the behavior. In functional relationships, one spouse would not continue to engage in behavior that he or she now knows harms the other.

Silent Treatment

There are few patterns of couple's behavior that are as destructive to intimacy as the *silent treatment*. It is often used to punish someone for behavior deemed inappropriate. Remaining silent allows the other person to project their worst fears into the silence. Becoming upset, taking a break, and remaining quiet for a short period of time will not normally damage a relationship, especially when the couple reengages to resolve the issue. However, long periods of silence, days or weeks of silence, place the relationship on a very undesirable course. When there is an issue to address, it is better to confront it than to bury it in silence.

Change

People do not change easily (think about what happened to your last dieting effort). In order for persons to bring about consistent change, effort must be applied throughout the change process. Initial effort must be applied to achieve what is desired; secondary effort must be applied to maintain the result. It is effort for change and effort for consistency.

The process for change involves (1) accepting responsibility for your behavior, (2) identifying what you want to change, (3) developing a plan for change, (4) implementing the plan, (5) evaluating for success, and (6) altering the plan or means of implementation if not successful.

As it pertains to couples, a plan for change can involve skills to be learned. Spouses can learn to be better mates, fathers, mothers, and partners. For individuals, persons can learn how to alter their thoughts, feelings, and behaviors. Most importantly, when it comes to change, keep in mind that good intentions and plans, while necessary, are not sufficient for change. Like a blueprint for construction, even the best intentions and the most detailed of plans must be put into action before any results are observed.

Healthy Marriages and Gottman's Marriage Tips

Couples researcher, psychologist John Gottman identified seven tips for keeping marriages healthy. In combination with the Foundation Blocks of Functional Relationships and Some Things to Remember, they provide an excellent framework for those wishing to maintain or enhance their marriage.

- *Seek help early.* The average couple waits six years before seeking help for marital problems (and keep in mind, half of all marriages that end do so in the first seven years). This means the average couple lives with unhappiness for far too long.
- *Edit yourself.* Couples who avoid saying every critical thought when discussing touchy topics are consistently the happiest.
- *Soften your "start up."* Arguments first "start up" because a spouse sometimes escalates the conflict from the get-go by making a critical or contemptuous remark in a confrontational tone. Bring up problems gently and without blame.
- *Accept influence.* A marriage succeeds to the extent that the husband can accept influence from his wife. If a woman says, "Do you have to work Thursday night? My mother is coming that weekend, and I need your help getting ready," and her husband replies, "My plans are set, and I'm not changing them". This guy is in a shaky marriage. A husband's ability to be influenced by his wife (rather than vice-versa) is crucial because research shows women are already well practiced at accepting influence from men, and a true partnership only occurs when a husband can do so as well.
- *Have high standards.* Happy couples have high standards for each other even as newlyweds. The most successful couples are those who, even as newlyweds, refused to accept hurtful behavior from one another. The lower the level of tolerance for bad behavior in the beginning of a relationship, the happier the couple is down the road.
- *Learn to repair and exit the argument.* Successful couples know how to exit an argument. Happy couples know how to repair the situation before an argument gets completely out of control. Successful repair attempts include: changing the topic to something completely unrelated; using humor; stroking your partner with a caring remark ("I understand that this is hard for you"); making it clear you're on common ground ("This is our problem"); backing down (in marriage,

as in the martial art Aikido, you have to yield to win); and, in general, offering signs of appreciation for your partner and his or her feelings along the way ("I really appreciate and want to thank you for . . . ."). If an argument gets too heated, take a 20-minute break, and agree to approach the topic again when you are both calm.

- *Focus on the bright side.* In a happy marriage, while discussing problems, couples make at least five times as many positive statements to and about each other and their relationship as negative ones. For example, "We laugh a lot;" not, "We never have any fun". A good marriage must have a rich climate of positivity. Make deposits to your emotional bank account. (Copyright 2000-2010 by John M. Gottman. Reprinted with permission from the website of the Gottman Institute at www.gottman.com)

In summary, a good marriage is like a traditional mechanical clock. Wind it up, input positive energy to keep it going, and it ticks away faithfully for years.

Law Enforcement Marriage and Relationship Guidebook

The Law Enforcement Marriage and Relationship Guidebook is comprised of this chapter and additional relationship information, including a Marriage and Couples Exercise. To download a copy of the Law Enforcement Marriage and Relationship Guidebook at no cost visit *www.jackdigliani.com*

Chapter 8

Coping with Death and Mourning

In general, America is a death denying society. Cemeteries are "memorial gardens" and "burial parks." Most Americans "pass on" or "pass away" instead of dying. This is because most of us are uncomfortable thinking about or discussing death. Want to be a hit at your next party? Initiate a discussion about death. The popularity of this topic will soon reveal itself.

In most technological societies, even the death of food animals is uncomfortable. We are familiar only with neatly packaged animal body parts enclosed in plastic wrap. We do not care to see or become familiar with the living animal that will end up on our dinner plate. It is fortunate for those who enjoy the consumption of meat that there are some persons who are capable of working in slaughterhouses and the meat industry.

When thinking about death, we occasionally think about those in the funeral business. Our thoughts often include wondering how they do it. It certainly takes a special kind of person to deal with death on a regular basis. Funeral directors, coroners, medical examiners, and certain physicians seem to be among those special kinds of persons. They provide services that many people would find unpleasant. It may be possible for nearly everyone to develop a greater tolerance for death exposure if circumstances required. Nonetheless, if given a choice, most of us are content to keep a healthy distance from the reality of death.

Humans are probably the only species that knows it will die. This knowledge has led to the development of a number of religious, philosophical, and psychological belief systems. All societies, whether considered primitive or advanced, have belief systems and accompanying rituals that help members address and cope with the reality of death.

Grief and Mourning

Grief and mourning are not identical. *Grief* is the personal, emotional response to loss. *Mourning* represents the public, culture-specific way of expressing loss. There are varied mourning rituals that are characteristic of various cultures. For example, it is not uncommon for deceased Italian-Americans to have items that were important to them during life placed in their casket prior to burial. My grandfather was buried with a bottle of whiskey, among other things. My father was buried with a cigar.

Grief

There are many expressions of grief. A person's grief can be somewhat unique, and therefore difficult for others to understand. Upon a loss, some persons may express little outward sentiment, while others will be consumed by uncontrollable bouts of expressed emotion.

It is difficult to predict how a person will respond to death; and more difficult to predict how a person will respond to the death of loved one. I once followed a case of a woman who expediently cleared the entire house of everything owned by her deceased husband. This included clothes, bedding, tools, and so on. She accomplished this within one week of his death. I have also known persons to keep a house, or a room in the house, intact, just as the deceased left it, for years after the death. This included cigarette butts in the ashtray.

There are varying lengths of time needed to grieve. It depends on the person. One thing seems certain. For any specific person, grieving cannot be rushed. Grieving appears to have a timeline of its own.

In several ways, loss can be viewed as an injury. It is an emotional and psychological injury. Much like a physical wound, these injuries need time to heal. If you broke a bone in your arm yesterday, you would not expect it to be healed today. So it is with loss and grief. The loss of yesterday is not likely to be healed today.

Tasks of Grieving and Mourning

After the death of a loved one, survivors are confronted with the completion of at least four tasks before they can once again fully engage life. (1) The first task is to fully accept the reality of the loss. To complete this task, survivors must accept the loss emotionally. The disbelief which often accompanies the denial of the loss must be processed. Accepting the loss involves confronting the vacuum left in your life by the person's death. (2) The second task of grieving is to experience the pain of the loss. This means that persons must accept and work through their feelings, and avoid conscious efforts to suppress their sadness. (3) The third task is to adjust to the environment in which the deceased is missing. This involves adjusting to even the simplest of tasks, such as who will now take out the trash. I have often heard survivors say that they did not realize how much the deceased did until they had to assume their everyday responsibilities. (4) The fourth task is to withdraw the emotional investment in the deceased and recover the ability to reinvest in other relationships (Worden, 1982). This is sometimes referred to as "learning to love again." It can be especially difficult for widows, widowers, and partners.

Upon the death of a loved one, some persons act out in various dysfunctional ways. This behavior is frequently an attempt to manage the powerful emotions associated with the loss. For example, sexual promiscuity is sometimes observed upon the death of a spouse; and the inappropriate coddling of another's child may be seen upon the death of a child.

Isolation, the opposite of acting out, is also observed in grief. Even after an extended period of time, some people will continue to socially and emotionally isolate themselves. This is most often seen in persons who have lost a beloved spouse. In their isolation, becoming platonically involved with another person is avoided (for a number of possible reasons). Becoming romantically involved with another person is unimaginable. This causes a suspension of any relationship-developing behavior. If this situation remains unchanged, task four is never completed. This has significant implications for the remainder of the survivor's life.

Death and Guilt

The experience of guilt is common for human beings. There are two types of guilt normally associated with death, *real guilt* and *survivor guilt*. Real guilt is based in (1) behavior and/or (2) thoughts. Real guilt for behavior involves something done or not done. For instance, real guilt for something done might involve a recent conversation with the deceased wherein there was an angry exchange of words. Real guilt for something not done might involve a failure to visit a sick relative in the hospital who suddenly died. Real guilt for thoughts involves current or past thinking. For example, a person might feel guilty about having thought that the deceased feigned symptoms for attention or exaggerated the sickness that eventually caused death. Real guilt is associated with a perceived violation of personal values, a standard of behavior, or some moral code. Because individual morals and values differ, one person may experience guilt in circumstances where another does not. It is important to remember that real guilt is relative. It describes only the fact that a person is feeling guilty for some perceived reason. It has little to do with whether anyone else believes that there are justifiable reasons for the person's guilty feeling. Additionally, it is possible to feel guilty and not understand why. Have you ever said to yourself, or heard someone else say, "I shouldn't feel guilty, but I do," or "I don't know why I'm feeling guilty. I didn't do anything wrong." Such circumstances normally represent an internal unaddressed or unresolved issue.

Survivor guilt is different than real guilt. Survivor guilt is the term used to describe the feeling of guilt associated with surviving while others died. It is common among soldiers who have returned from combat where comrades were killed. The question often asked is, "Why did I live and not them?" Pursuing an answer to this question can lead to a lifelong quest and, unfortunately in some cases, lifelong difficulty.

Real and survivor guilt can occur in combination. A combination of real and survivor guilt might be observed in the following hypothetical situation: a father, driving while accompanied by his infant daughter, is late for an appointment. He is driving faster than the speed limit. As he approaches a curve in the road, he loses control of the vehicle and strikes a highway abutment. The crash kills his daughter while he walks away without injury. In this imagined tragic scenario, it is very likely that the father would experience real and survivor guilt.

Guilt is often unwanted, uncontrollable, and difficult to understand. Because guilt can be punishing, it can cause significant problems. It can drive abnormal dysfunctional behavior and generate destructive thoughts.

To outside observers, a person's guilt may seem out of proportion to the circumstances. No matter, such guilt often leads to or is a component of depression. If serious enough, thoughts of suicide develop. The father in the aforementioned hypothetical car crash represents a significant risk for intense guilt, depression, and suicide. Persons suffering from this degree of guilt require immediate intervention and professional treatment.

Life happens. Even good relationships have occasional unpleasant or regrettable transactions. This is normal. Punishing yourself with guilt for things that are part of practically every relationship is to treat yourself unfairly. Move past these incidents and focus on what was good in the relationship.

Guilt and Connection

Guilt is an emotion that can help us to feel we are still connected to the person that has died. By feeling guilty, the connection remains prominent. Many persons unconsciously fear that losing the guilt will cause them to lose the connection. Actually, guilt and the feeling of connection are quite independent. Healthy grieving involves letting go of guilt while maintaining the connection through an understanding of the person's legacy.

Guilt as a Positive Force

The feeling of guilt can be used as a behavioral guide. It can be seen as a factor in developing a person's morals and values. If morals and values are developed by design, the experience of guilt can be a signal that there is deviation from the selected path. Make the appropriate amends or corrections, and the guilt feelings subside. Death, and the guilt that can follow the loss of those important to us, serves as a reminder to conduct ourselves in an appropriate manner while loved ones are still with us.

Healing from Loss

Healing from loss involves feeling good again. After the death of a loved one, many persons feel that it is disrespectful to the deceased to again have fun, enjoy life, and move forward. This feeling is normal and usually diminishes over time. To heal, survivors must acknowledge that it is not disrespectful to once again enjoy life. To accomplish this, it is sometimes comforting to remember that the deceased also confronted the death of loved ones and also had to move forward.

Healing, Legacy, and Psychological Legacy

Honoring the legacy of the deceased is also necessary for healing. Legacies are complex, multifaceted, and unique to each survivor. Simply stated, a legacy is what you feel the deceased has contributed to your life. There are several types of legacies. One of the most important for survivors is the psychological legacy. Psychological legacies have nothing to do with financial legacies which involve wills, houses, money, and other property.

Psychological legacies are unique because they are developed out of the particular relationship a person had with the deceased. This is why the psychological legacy experienced by one person can be very different from that experienced by another.

Like photographs, psychological legacies come *in-the-positive* and *in-the-negative*. Both contribute positively to our lives.

Psychological legacies in-the-positive are what you perceive as the valued contributions the person made to your life. They involve what you consider "good lessons learned" and those things about the deceased that you wish to emulate. For example, you may have admired how the person treated family members and resolved to do likewise. In this way, you want to be like the person.

Psychological legacies in-the-negative contribute positively to our lives by teaching us what not to do. For example, you may not have admired how the person treated family members and resolved to do better. In this way, you want to be different than the person but the lesson is valuable nonetheless.

Psychological legacies are not considered inherently good or bad. Psychological legacies in-the-positive and in-the-negative teach you something valuable relative to your value system. Psychological legacies become good or bad only when evaluated against an external value system.

If finding or understanding the psychological legacy of the deceased is difficult or confusing for you, consider looking at pictures of the person. You can do this alone or with someone you trust. Talk about the pictures and the memories they represent. In this way, the psychological legacy is discovered. Ask yourself how the person contributed to your life. The answer(s) to this question will help clarify their psychological legacy.

For a personal journey, consider writing a journal about what the deceased meant to you. Start with your earliest memory of the person. Include the good and the not so good. No one is perfect. There is no disrespect in understanding and expressing your feelings.

If you have unfinished business with the deceased, finish it in your journal. As part of your journey, consider writing your thoughts on a separate paper. Write down what you feel is unfinished. Include your feelings and things that you wished you said while the person was alive. Say goodbye. When completed, burn the paper. This keeps your thoughts and feelings private and sends smoke upward. Some persons feel that this also sends the message upward. For most, this is a healing activity. For some it is a spiritual experience. For nearly all, it helps to provide closure.

Your journey is complete when you can think of the deceased, accept the good and the not so good, appreciate the psychological legacy, and smile through the tears. This is the highest honor that you can bestow.

Death, Loss, and Survivorship

The following is a summary of issues involved in death, loss, and survivorship.

1. *Learning of the death*. Shock and denial are common initial responses to death, especially if the death is sudden and unexpected. Disbelief and confusion are frequently experienced.
2. *Reactions to death*. Many factors influence how intensely we feel the loss. Among these are the nature of attachment, spiritual views, the age of the deceased, how the person died, the similarity of the deceased to those we love, and the extent of the void that the person's absence leaves in our life. The death of another can also trigger our own fears of death and memories of previous traumatic events or losses.
3. *Grief and mourning*. Grieving takes time. This is important to remember because American culture is not readily accepting of lengthy grieving or mourning periods. Instead, there is the idea that a person needs to put the loss behind them and get on with life. There is no correct way to grieve. People deal with loss in different ways for different periods of time.
4. *Coping with loss*. It is common to experience powerful emotions. Confront emotions openly. Strong emotion may feel overwhelming. Breathe through it. Remember the "ocean wave" (chapter 4).
5. *Specific reactions to loss*. There are many possible reactions to loss. Common and normal reactions include sadness, crying, numbness, loss of appetite, inability to sleep, fatigue, anger, frustration, finding it difficult to be alone, or wanting to be alone. Utilizing your support system is the best way to deal with the pain of grieving.
6. *Stages of grief*. Many clinicians have identified what they refer to as stages of grief. Although such stages differ in terminology, the basic structure of the stages involve (1) an initial shock and denial, (2) a subsequent impact and suffering period, followed by (3) some adjustment and degree of recovery (similar to exposure to any

Reflections of a Police Psychologist

traumatic event). However, grieving is a complex process; it does not progress clearly from one stage to another. It is normal to once again have feelings long thought to have disappeared.

7. *Healing.* Acknowledge and accept your feelings. You may experience seemingly contradictory feelings such as relief and sadness (for example, relief that a burden of care or the person's suffering has ended, and sadness due to the loss). This is normal. Keep in mind that your emotional attachment does not end upon the death of someone you care about. Remember, bereavement is the normal process by which human beings deal with loss.

8. *Surviving the loss.* Surviving the death of someone you care about involves honoring the memory of the person by acknowledging what the person contributed to your life. From here, you can further honor the person by reengaging life.

It is important to remember that similar feelings can follow the death or loss of pets, non pet animals, and even plants and inanimate objects that have acquired some special meaning (like losing a family heirloom). Brain studies show that the same neural pathways of grief are activated regardless of the loss.

Uncomplicated Bereavement and Depression

If a person seeks the support of a clinician for issues involved in grief, *uncomplicated bereavement* (V62.82, DSM-5) is specified. Uncomplicated bereavement is not a mental disorder. It is the experiences associated with the normal process of grieving.

If a person becomes significantly depressed in response to someone's death and meets the criteria of a major depressive episode, *major depressive disorder* (296.00, DSM-5) may be diagnosed.

Memorials and Legacy

Memorials are common in America and throughout the world. Some memorials start as recognition of the achievements of the living. For example, America was named for the then living Italian explorer Amerigo Vespucci (1454-1512) in 1507. Others are dedicated after death. Memorials are present in our street names (Eisenhower Blvd), waterways (Hudson River), and government structures (Kennedy Space Center). Memorials honor the dead and keep their legacy connected to the living. They may be public and grand (like the Washington Monument) or private and personal (like the planting of a backyard tree).

Personal memorials help to fill the void left by the death of a loved one. They serve to ameliorate the pain of the loss. One type of personal memorial seen more frequently today is the tattoo. Due to the current sophistication of tattooing, actual photographs of the deceased can be reproduced in ink on human skin. These images, as well as dates of birth and death, reproduced signatures, and special designs and symbols comprise many of these very personal memorials.

Personal memorials can be just about anything. Regardless of the form of any personal memorial, all have one thing in common: all personal memorials feel special to the survivor - and therein lies their power.

Chapter 9

Interacting with Persons that are Mentally Ill

The conception of mental illness varies widely in human belief systems. From ancient cultures to modern societies, humans have struggled to define, understand, and treat illnesses of the mind. Ancient explanations for today's mental disorders included the influence of spirits and demons, punishment or influences from the gods, or the results of witchcraft spells and magic. (There are 21st century cultures where these remain the primary explanatory factors of mental illness.) Later theories were based on a developing understanding of the brain. As part of this theoretical advancement, mental illnesses came to be understood as primarily organic or functional.

Organic mental illnesses were characterized as: (1) a defect in brain structure, (2) chemical intoxication or withdrawal, (3) medical conditions, or (4) brain injury. This class of mental illness represented those cases wherein the cause of the disorder was traced to the brain — the organ of the mind (hence *organic*). These were the diseases of the so-called "psychobiologic unit" (APA, 1952, 1).

Functional mental illnesses were those in which there was a mental disturbance; however, based on the science of the day the brain appeared to be intact. In this class of mental illness the structure of the brain appeared normal but the brain did not appear to be working normally. These illnesses were thought to be caused by impairment in brain function (hence *functional*). The conception of functional mental illness generated various theories to account for, explain, and treat the conditions associated with impairment in brain function.

Although the organic and functional terminology is seldom used today, many of the most serious mental disorders once thought to be functional are now known to be brain disorders.

The Concept of Mental Illness

The concept of mental illness has normative features and is culturally relative. It changes as cultural norms evolve. The clearest example of how cultural changes effect what is considered a mental illness is homosexuality; and its evolution from a mental disorder to a non-mental disorder can be traced through the various editions of our current diagnostic manual.

In America, the Diagnostic and Statistical Manual of Mental Disorders (DSM), published by the American Psychiatric Association, has been the primary text for the classification, statistical data, and diagnosis of mental disorders. The DSM was first published in 1952, and since then has undergone several revisions. The original DSM included the diagnosis *sexual deviation* and specified homosexuality as a mental disorder. This conception and diagnosis was carried into the first revision of the DSM, DSM-II, published in 1968.

The 1960's and 1970's characterized a period of change in America. There was Vietnam and all it entailed, and the civil rights movement. The previous standards and acceptances of American society were being challenged; societal norms were changing. With these changes, the perspective on homosexuality also changed. In the beginning of 1973, the DSM-II continued to specify homosexuality as a mental disorder. However, in December of 1973, upon the seventh printing of the DSM-II, the trustees of the American Psychiatric Association voted to eliminate homosexuality *per se* as a mental disorder. In its stead was placed the diagnosis *sexual orientation disturbance*. Sexual orientation disturbance described "individuals whose sexual interests are directed primarily toward people of the same sex and who are either disturbed by, in conflict with, or wish to change their sexual orientation. This diagnostic category is distinguished from homosexuality, which by itself does not constitute a psychiatric disorder" (44). This represented a significant change in the clinical conception of homosexuality.

The third revision of the DSM, DSM-III (1980) eliminated sexual orientation disturbance as a diagnosis. It was replaced by *ego-dystonic homosexuality*. The diagnostic criteria of ego-dystonic homosexuality consisted of two elements: "The individual complains that heterosexual arousal is persistently absent or weak and significantly interferes with initiating or maintaining wanted heterosexual relationships" and "There is a sustained pattern of homosexual arousal that the individual explicitly states has been unwanted and a persistent source of distress" (282).

The diagnosis of ego-dystonic homosexuality was never widely accepted by clinicians, likely because it lacked adequately descriptive criteria. It was also determined that many homosexual persons were distressed by their homosexual arousal, at least at first. In 1987, with the publication of the DSM-III-R (revised), the diagnosis *ego-dystonic homosexuality* was eliminated. Since that time, there has been no specific diagnosis categorizing homosexuality in any form as a mental disorder.

Today, if a person sought treatment for unwanted or distressing homosexual orientation, there would not be a mental disorder diagnosis. Instead, clinicians would specify: *focus of clinical attention; encounter for counseling - sex counseling* (V65.49, DSM-5, 2013).

Types of Mental Disorders

There are several major categories used to specify the various types of mental disorders. Contemporary classification of mental disorders include neurodevelopmental disorders; schizophrenia spectrum and other psychotic disorders; bipolar and related disorders; depressive disorders; anxiety disorders; obsessive-compulsive and related disorders; trauma and stressor related disorders; dissociative disorders; somatic symptom and related disorders; feeding and eating disorders; elimination disorders; sleep-wake disorders; sexual dysfunctions; gender dysphoria; disruptive, impulse-control, and conduct disorders; substance-related and addictive disorders; neurocognitive disorders; personality disorders; and paraphilic disorders (DSM-5).

Diagnoses

Diagnoses are made when the diagnostic criteria for a specific condition are met. Clinicians use *signs* and *symptoms* to assess diagnostic criteria. Signs are things that you can perceive in others. They include another person's behavior, dress, appearance, odor, activity in context, and so forth. For example, grimacing, jaw clenching, and head holding are signs of a headache. Symptoms are conditions reported by the person. For example, a person holding his head and saying "My head really hurts" is reporting a symptom (pain). Many persons will speak of symptoms and include both signs and symptoms within their description.

Most mental disorders have as diagnostic criteria:

1. specific elements of the diagnosis,
2. a specified length of time that elements must be present (e.g., "minimum of three days," "for one month," etc),
3. a particular level of impairment or distress (the condition causes clinically significant impairment or distress),
4. positive or negative symptoms (positive symptoms are those that are not present in healthy persons—such as hallucinations, while negative symptoms are those conditions that are present in healthy persons but are lacking in the diagnosis of some mental disorders—such as the ability to experience pleasure) and
5. the condition is not caused by substance intoxication, medical condition, or better accounted for by another mental diagnosis.

The classifications and specific conceptions of mental disorders serve purposes other than diagnosis. They also assist in the gathering of statistical data and in the development of effective treatments.

Although the current DSM (DSM-5) is written in a manner that can be understood by many, self-diagnosis or diagnosis by unqualified persons must be avoided.

Mental Disorders, Insanity, and Nervous Breakdown

Mental disorders are specific clinical conditions defined by specific diagnostic criteria. Mental disorders do not include insanity. Insanity is a legal concept, not a clinical condition. Therefore, a person may be adjudicated insane, but not diagnosed insane.

In most states, when persons are adjudicated insane, they are not held criminally liable for their behavior. They are not held criminally liable because of the determination that at the time of the offense, the person was mentally ill and due to the mental illness was either incapable of distinguishing right from wrong, incapable of understanding the consequences of their actions, or incapable of controlling their behavior.

Attorneys representing clients charged with criminal offenses sometimes enter pleas of *not guilty by reason of insanity* (NGRI). In America, attorneys for serial killers are the most likely to proffer the NGRI defense. During the years from 1992 to 2007, 474 serial killers are known

Reflections of a Police Psychologist

to have been criminally charged in the U.S. Of these, 85 (17.6 percent) entered a plea of NGRI. Of the 85, 15 (16.5 percent) were found NGRI (Moberg and Aamodt, 2007).

Although not a serial killer, John Hinckley, the man who attempted to assassinate President Ronald Reagan in 1981 in an attempt to impress actress Jodie Foster, was determined to be not guilty by reason of insanity. During the incident, President Reagan was shot and his press secretary James Brady was seriously wounded. Police officer Thomas Delahanty and secret service agent Timothy McCarthy were also shot. The public outrage at the NGRI verdict led to the passage of the Insanity Defense Reform Act of 1984. This Act revised the standards of the NGRI defense in the federal court system. Although NGRI remains available in the federal court system, several states have abolished the plea defense of NGRI.

Most persons judged NGRI are committed to mental hospitals for treatment (as was John Hinckley). Being "not guilty" they are not sentenced to prison.

Some people facing criminal charges are determined to have been temporarily insane. This means that the person was mentally ill and not responsible for personal behavior at the time the crime was committed, but is not now mentally ill. Most persons determined to have been temporarily insane are released immediately after trial.

Like insanity, nervous breakdown is not a clinical diagnosis. It is a generic term used by non-clinicians to describe various depressive, anxiety, and stress disorders. The term reached a pinnacle of popularity in 1965 when it became part of the lyrics of a number one song by the English rock band Rolling Stones. The song was titled "19th Nervous Breakdown."

Recognizing Mental Illness

Person suffering from serious mental disorders such as schizophrenia, major depression, and bipolar disorder (manic and depressive episodes), when severe, are easily recognized. When the intensity of these disorders is less than severe, impairment becomes less obvious. Generally speaking, the more moderate the person's impairment, the more difficult it is to recognize.

When assessing for mental illness, the person's behavior should always be evaluated within context. It is not difficult to imagine that a particular behavior which might indicate mental illness in one situation may not be so indicative in another.

Defining Mental Illness

Every state provides a legal definition of mental illness. In Colorado:

> '*Person with a mental illness*' means a person with one or more substantial disorders of the cognitive, volitional, or emotional processes that grossly impairs judgment or capacity to recognize reality or to control behavior. Developmental disability is insufficient to either justify or exclude a finding of mental illness within the provisions of this article (C.R.S.27-65-102 (14) Definitions).

Under the law and in clinical conceptualizations, developmental disability is different than mental illness. This difference is especially important in the distinctions that must be made in emergency situations where Colorado police officers might act under the authority granted in C.R.S. 27-65-105, *Emergency procedure* (involuntary custody due to mental illness when specific conditions are also present). It is important for police officers to understand the legal definition of developmental disability as well as that of mental illness.

Voluntary and Involuntary Compliance

The goal of all police interactions is voluntary compliance. Police officers seek, desire, and should be trained in methods of interpersonal communication which improve the probability of voluntary compliance. During police interactions, when there is voluntary compliance, the interaction moves in the direction desired by the officer (for example, when an officer asks a man to move along and he leaves the area). When there is noncompliance, and depending upon the circumstances, officers may be justified in using force to compel compliance. This type of compliance is involuntary. In cases of involuntary compliance, persons do not willingly follow the directions of officers, but have been made to comply. During involuntary compliance, the police ethic for the use of force is to engage only the degree necessary to accomplish the task. Depending on the circumstances, it can include deadly force.

Human behavior is ultimately unpredictable. This is true because all we can really do is to predict the behavior of others in terms of probability. No matter how high the probability that persons will behave in a particular way, they can always act against the odds. This is true even under the best of circumstances.

The predictability of human behavior is confounded by mental illness. In practical terms, this means that when officers are interacting with a mentally ill person, they must always engage appropriate officer safety measures. Officers must avoid a false sense of security due to initially cooperative behavior. Behavior can change in an instant. This is true even though research shows that statistically, mentally ill persons represent about the same level of threat to police officers than those not mentally ill. Having said this, keep in mind that based upon the actual symptoms of particular mental illnesses, *some mentally ill persons may represent a significant threat to the safety of police officers (and others)*.

In summary, police officers should never bet their lives on the probability that any person, mentally ill or otherwise, will act as expected.

Field Assessments for Mental Illness

Police officers must be capable of conducting accurate field assessments for mental illness. As you might expect, the standards for police officer field assessments are different from those assessments conducted by mental health professionals. In field assessments, police officers need only to determine (1) whether reasonable cause exists to believe that a person is mentally ill, and (2) due to the mental illness, does the person represents a danger to self, others, or is gravely disabled. To accomplish this task, officers rely on their personal observations, information gathered from reliable others, and information obtained from the person. The ability of officers to conduct accurate field assessments leads to better decisions and improved resolutions.

The more police officers understand the behavioral expressions and symptoms of mental disorders, the more likely they are to make accurate field assessments. Of the more serious mental disorders, persons suffering from a psychotic disorder, major depression, and bipolar disorder are most likely to come to the attention of police. When officers are interacting with persons suffering from a mental illness, they must always remember that serious mental illness is a disease and that *it is not against the law to be mentally ill.*

Psychotic Disorders

Psychotic disorders are some of the most debilitating of the mental disorders. Schizophrenia is the most widely known psychotic disorder. It is characterized by impairment in several critical areas of normal functioning.

Schizophrenia represents a condition wherein the person experiences odd and sometimes bizarre hallucinations, delusions, and emotional disturbances. These cause the person to behave in very strange and unusual ways. Historically, persons experiencing a psychotic disorder were considered as having "lost contact with reality." This continues to be an apt description, as a person suffering from schizophrenia will often appear to be lost in the aberrant world of hallucination, delusion, and emotional distress.

Hallucination

Hallucination is a disorder of perception. Persons experiencing hallucinations may see things that are not there, hear things that no one else can hear, and often respond to these stimuli in ways that are confusing or frightening to others. Hallucinations can occur in all five senses. In schizophrenia the most common type of hallucination is auditory. Persons afflicted with schizophrenia most often hear voices. The voices can be perceived as coming from the environment or from inside the head. They can be the perceived voices of strangers, dead relatives, or deities. "You're shit" and "You want to f—k your mother" are two actual auditory hallucinations reported by schizophrenic patients. The first patient also experienced olfactory hallucinations and constantly smelled manure. The latter patient was a man in his 30s and lived with his mother. For him, this unwanted and uncontrollable voice was very disturbing. In a small percentage of cases, the voices of auditory hallucinations are at least partly flattering or complementary. Some persons report that the voices they hear tell them they are beautiful, should be made king or queen, and so forth.

Auditory hallucinations can order persons to do things. These are known as *command hallucinations* and, depending on their content, can cause persons to engage in violent behaviors; including killing themselves or harming others. The first thing police officers should do if they suspect a person is experiencing auditory voice hallucinations is to determine what the voices are saying. This is because officers can interact with a hallucinating mentally ill person quite differently if the person informs the officer that the voice is saying, "You'll never amount to anything" as opposed to "Cops are dangerous and should be hurt." Command hallucinations in schizophrenia are more common than previously thought. In one group of schizophrenic patients, auditory hallucinations commanding harm to others was reported by 30 percent of those assessed. Twenty-two percent of these patients reported that they had complied with the commands (McNiel et al., 2000). In another study, command hallucinations were documented in 50 percent of schizophrenic outpatients; however, not all of the commands were violent in content (Zisook et al., 1995). Complying with commands, violent or otherwise, is more likely if the hallucinated voice is recognized and if the commands are related to a specific delusion (Hersh and Borum, 1998).

A lethal combination of hallucination and delusion was seen in the well publicized Son of Sam serial killings in New York City during 1976 and 1977. During this time, six people were murdered and seven others were wounded. The crimes were carried out by David Berkowitz (born Richard David Falco) who claimed that he acted on command of his neighbor's (Sam Carr) demon-possessed dog, a Labrador retriever named Harvey.

As indicated, hallucinations can occur in sense combination. A person with schizophrenia might hear voices and taste poison in their food, smell noxious odors, or see strange, frightening, or morphing faces. As part of a treatment team, I once worked with a patient who heard voices and also suffered from tactile hallucinations. She consistently felt insects crawling under the skin of her forearms, a hallucination known as *formication*. She needed to be restrained as she continually attempted to tear her skin in an effort to remove the bugs. This patient eventually responded to antipsychotic medication and the hallucinations disappeared.

Hallucinations are different from *illusions*. Illusions involve misinterpretations of actual visual stimuli. Illusions are relatively common in human experience and are not considered a feature of psychotic disorders (nearly everyone is familiar with the idea of "optical illusion"). In fact, police officers are very familiar with the illusion phenomenon. Most officers, tired on a midnight shift, have experienced the late night perception of a "crouching man," which upon closer inspection turns out to be a fire hydrant or a small shrub. Illusions are different from vivid images (chapter 4) in their etiology. They are not considered a high-stress, critical incident response visual phenomenon.

The visual hallucinations sometimes seen in schizophrenia must be distinguished from the visions associated with *Charles Bonnet syndrome* (CBS). In CBS, mentally healthy persons with significant vision loss experience complex visual phenomena. (There are no auditory hallucinations in CBS.) The visions of CBS are most frequently comprised of lines and color patterns, vague and nondescript faces, people and animals, plants and trees, and inanimate objects. The visions can be animated and move about the person's visual field, such as small people running about tipping their hats and waving their arms. CBS is predominately observed in the elderly suffering from macular degeneration and glaucoma, but can appear in others who are visually impaired (Vukicevic and Fitzmaurice, 2008). Many persons experiencing CBS know nothing about it. They may become frightened by the visions or feel that they are going crazy. For the latter reason, they often keep their experiences secret. Although there are no known effective treatments for CBS, intentional blinking can sometimes help. Remaining in stimulating social environments and well-lit areas may also produce some improvement. Police officers can help those with CBS by referring them to their physician. Write down "Charles Bonnet syndrome" for the person so that he may bring the note to his doctor—this should be done because many physicians are unfamiliar with CBS. Once the causes of CBS are understood by those afflicted, any associated anxiety normally diminishes. Keep in mind that the symptoms of CBS are not indicative of schizophrenia or any other mental illness.

Delusion

Delusion is a disorder of thinking. Delusions differ from thoughts or beliefs that are simply incorrect. When a non-delusional person maintains a thought that is shown to be incorrect, the thought is changed. For instance, if you believed there was a wolf in a closet and I arranged for you to look in the closet and you did not see a wolf, you would change your belief. This is not the case for those experiencing delusions.

The case of Miss M demonstrates delusional thinking. Miss M was a psychiatric patient diagnosed with paranoid schizophrenia. She was being treated with medications and psychotherapy. Her delusional system involved the belief that wild animals seeking to harm her were hiding in various spaces. There was one particular closet of the psychiatric unit that caused her great dismay. She was fearful of a wolf which she believed was hiding there. One day, upon encouragement from hospital staff, she chose to confront her fear and examine the closet. She slowly walked up to the closet. Upon her permission and with staff support, the closet door was slowly opened. With great courage, she looked into the closet. When asked about her observations, she said that she did not see a wolf. When asked if she now felt safer, she quickly answered, "No! The wolf disappears when anyone looks at it, and it comes back as soon as you look away!" Such is the power of delusional thinking.

Delusions cannot be altered by reality testing. They have a magical quality that resists all information to the contrary. The most common types of delusion are paranoid, grandiose, and bizarre. Paranoid delusions involve thoughts of being persecuted, singled-out, and marked for harm. Grandiose delusions are thoughts and beliefs of self-importance, greatness, and superiority. Bizarre delusions are characterized by strange and odd beliefs such as thinking that your home attic is occupied by invisible interstellar aliens. Delusional thinking can include a combination of the major types, or represent something altogether different.

Just what constitutes a delusion is not always easy to determine. As stated in the DSM-5, "The distinction between delusion and a strongly held idea is sometimes difficult to make and depends in part on the degree of conviction with which the belief is held despite clear or reasonable contradictory evidence regarding its veracity" (87).

Of the more interesting specific features of delusional thinking are *thought insertion* - the belief that others are inserting thoughts in your head; *thoughts of reference* - where it is believed that everything perceived relates or refers directly to you; *thought broadcasting* - where it is believed your thoughts are being broadcast to others; and *thoughts of influence* - where you believe that you can influence the external world by the mere act of thinking.

Incidentally, Miss M responded well to treatment and her delusion of concealed wild animals looking to harm her eventually vanished. Once in remission, she discussed her delusions and remembered everything about her closet confrontation. It is common for recovered patients to remember their hallucinations and delusions. Most patients will retain full recall of their experiences during psychotic episodes, including how they were treated by police officers. These memories endure long after the symptoms disappear.

Delusions can exist in the absence or non-prominence of hallucination. In cases where delusions are present and there is no history of schizophrenia, *delusional disorder* (297.1, DSM-5) is diagnosed.

Emotional Disturbance and Behavior

The emotional and behavioral disturbances associated with schizophrenia and other psychotic disorders include the negative symptom of anhedonia (an inability to experience pleasure), emotional lability (lack of emotional stability), depression, anxiety, unusual behaviors, and poor impulse control.

Speech is a form of behavior that can provide significant information during field assessments for a psychotic disorder. During psychotic episodes, speech can be marked by several unusual phenomena. *Loose associations* are the most common. Loose associations are verbal responses which do not follow any logical sequence (sometimes referred to as *word salad*). They are reflective of disorganized thinking and a deficit in the ability to form continuing coherent thoughts. *Clanging* may also be present. Clanging is a condition wherein the person responds more to the sound of a word than to its meaning. *Echolalia* is sometimes observed. This is indicated by repetition of a word, phrase, or sentence spoken by someone else. For example, to the inquiry, "Are you ok?" the person responds, "Are you ok, are you ok, are you ok." *Perseveration* also involves repetition. Perseveration is repeating words in an unusual manner such as "*I like candy, candy, candy.*" Such responses can also be expressed in answer to different questions, "What is your name? *I like candy.* Are you ok? *I like candy.* How did you get here? *I like candy.*" *Neologisms* or invented words are sometimes seen. For example, "I need to find my *timshhoker.*" Strings of nonsense words or meaningless mumblings may also be present.

The speech abnormalities of schizophrenia are frequently accompanied by odd or unusual behaviors such as inappropriate clothing for the context or temperature, eating odd substances, fascination with feces, a failure to maintain personal hygiene, assuming unusual postures, and behaviors consistent with responding to internal voices or delusional beliefs.

Diagnosis of Psychotic Disorders

The diagnoses of specific psychotic disorders are dependent upon symptoms and their duration. As an example of how duration impacts diagnoses, consider that all three of the following can be comprised of identical symptoms. It is only the duration of symptoms that differentiate these disorders:

Brief psychotic disorder—symptoms for at least one day but less than one month
Schizophreniform disorder—symptoms for at least one month but less than six months
Schizophrenia—symptoms for at least six months

Summary of Field Assessment for Psychotic Disorders

In a field assessment to determine if a person is experiencing the symptoms associated with schizophrenia or another psychotic disorder, police officers should observe the person and engage in discussion.

Observe the person's behavior and appearance to determine:

1. if behavior is appropriate for context.
2. if clothing is appropriate for temperature.
3. if behavior is strange, bizarre, or otherwise odd.
4. if there are issues of personal hygiene.

Engage in discussion to:

1. determine the presence of hallucinations and delusions. Rule out command hallucination.
2. determine the presence of loose associations, odd verbal communication patterns, and any accompanying bizarre thoughts.
3. assess emotional disturbance.
4. assess if the person is a danger to self, others, or gravely disabled.
5. rule out the possibility of a medical condition. If medical concerns are present, initiate an EMS response.
6. determine degree of impairment in social, occupational, and personal settings.
7. assess if the person requires emergency intervention.

Suggestions for Police Officers Interacting with Persons who are Psychotic or Otherwise Mentally Ill

Always be cautious and remain alert. Be mindful of your level of awareness. Keep in mind that human behavior is ultimately unpredictable. Assessment of mental illness and threat level is complicated by alcohol and other drug intoxication.

Take time to consider the situation. Request backup. Interacting with a mentally ill person is not the time to go it alone. Another officer may better relate to the person for reasons that are not immediately apparent. Also, a team approach offers a greater margin of officer safety. Unless *duty bound,* proceed slowly and thoughtfully.

Communication. Talk to the person in a way that encourages communication. Speak in simple language but do not talk down to the person. Try to develop rapport and trust. Consider deemphasizing your authority. Use first names if appropriate. State your purpose: "I am here to help." Avoid abusive language and threatening behavior. If appropriate, explain what you are going to do before you do it. This normally decreases anxiety and lessens the probability that the person will act out. Avoid insults, challenges, and profanity. Try to communicate with whatever remains rational. Keep providing rational verbal stimuli until you achieve voluntary compliance or you assess that the person is too ill to be influenced in this manner.

Interaction. Many mentally ill persons are or become frightened, especially upon arrival of the police. Most will respond positively to a caring attitude. Ask for the person's help to accomplish your goals. Build upon the time that you are in contact. For example, "We have been talking for ten minutes. We have done well together. Let's keep working as a team. How about . . . (specify your request)." Consider the *short order* if necessary or if rapport fails. (A short order is a brief, authoritative order aimed at gaining compliance or interrupting dangerous or undesirable behaviors. *STOP! SHOW ME YOUR HANDS!* and *DO IT NOW!* are examples of short orders. Compliance with short orders is founded upon a presumed history of the person complying with authority figures.)

Appropriate supportive touch. Some mentally ill persons respond well to appropriate supportive touch such as a pat on the back or a handshake. Apply an appropriate supportive touch only if you assess that it is safe to do so. If you use an appropriate supportive touch to calm or reassure a mentally ill person, be certain that the person cannot easily access your police equipment. Appropriate supportive touch is best used when there is more than one officer on scene.

Mentally ill does not mean unintelligent. Never assume that the person cannot understand you. Be careful of what you say during side conversations with other officers.

Do not allow yourself to be angered. Try to remain calm. The person may be very adept at provoking anger (name calling, threats, etc). For many mentally ill persons, anger directed at others is often displaced. The person's anger responses are frequently the result of frustration, anxiety, or fear. If you remain calm, you increase the probability that the person will be voluntarily compliant. Some persons will mildly resist to a point and cooperate after a degree of rapport is established.

Avoid excitement. As a general rule, limit outside stimulation. A quiet, more stable environment tends to decrease anxiety. Lessened anxiety increases the probability of compliance.

Avoid deception. It is sometimes tempting to lie to bring about a resolution; however, deception is often unnecessary and may be harmful. Exception: when life is at risk, any strategy or technique that you reasonably think might accomplish your goal is justified.

Disposition. Contact relatives or friends of the person if necessary. Leave him in place if there is no reason to do otherwise. If, due to mental illness, the person is a threat to self or others, or is gravely disabled, ask for his cooperation and initiate voluntary intervention. If the person will not consent to voluntary intervention, initiate the procedure for involuntary evaluation and treatment (Reiser, 1982).

Officer safety. Never deemphasize officer safety.

Mood Disorders: Depression and Bipolar Disorder

Mood disorders are mental illnesses that are characterized by disturbances in *affect*. Affect refers to emotions and feelings. For example, the profound sadness in depression and the feelings of euphoria in mania are disorders of affect. Disturbances of sleep, appetite, concentration, cognitive ability, sexual interest, and behavior are often observed in the mood disorders. *Major depressive disorder* and *bipolar disorder* are two of the more well known mood disorders.

Major Depressive Disorder

Major depressive disorder is characterized by feelings of sadness, flat affect, loss of interest in previously enjoyed activities, sleep disturbances (either no sleep or hypersomnia), appetite disturbances (either no appetite or overeating), loss of interest in sex, impairment in memory and concentration, unintended weight loss or gain, feelings of guilt or worthlessness, thoughts of death, suicidal thinking, suicidal behavior, and psychomotor retardation. The severity and course specifiers for major depressive disorder are: mild, moderate, severe, with psychotic features, in partial remission, in full remission, and unspecified.

Research into the causes of major depressive disorder and other mood disorders has implicated imbalances in at least one of three primary neurotransmitters: norepinephrine dopamine, and serotonin.

Bipolar Disorder

Bipolar disorder evolved out of the former *manic-depressive disorder*. This diagnosis involves mania and depression. As a diagnosis, bipolar disorder first appeared in DSM-III (1980). Today, there are two primary bipolar diagnoses, *bipolar I disorder* and *bipolar II disorder*. Some researchers and theoreticians speculate that there may be as many as six discernible bipolar disorders.

To be diagnosed with bipolar I disorder, persons have to be experiencing, or have at some previous time experienced, a manic episode. The person may or may not have experienced a major depressive episode or a hypomanic episode. A manic episode in the absence of a depressive episode or hypomanic episode is sufficient to diagnose bipolar I. Bipolar II disorder is comprised of at least one hypomanic episode and a major depressive episode.

A person needs only to have experienced one manic episode to be diagnosed bipolar I; and only one hypomanic episode and major depressive disorder to be diagnosed bipolar II. This is true even if only major depressive episodes are experienced from the time of the manic or hypomanic episode onward. *Mixed features,* as well as several other specifiers, may be present in bipolar I and II. Mixed features are characterized by the simultaneous presence of symptoms associated with a manic or hypomanic episode and a major depressive episode.

Manic episodes cause marked impairment in normal functioning and can include all or several of the following: feelings of euphoria, loss of need to sleep, expansive thinking, increased interest in sex, poor impulse control (travel, spending, etc), pressured speech, racing thoughts, irritability, distractibility, grandiose delusions, loss of judgment, high energy levels, behaving in uncharacteristic ways, the presence of psychotic features, and the need for hospitalization. Overall, the person appears "revved up" and unable to effectively manage life's demands. Manic episodes may be mild, moderate, or severe.

Hypomanic episodes are similar to manic episodes, but do not cause marked impairment; they do not include psychotic features or the need for hospitalization. Like manic episodes, hypomanic episodes may be mild, moderate or severe.

Bipolar disorders may cycle. That is, the person may experience recurring, alternating manic or hypomanic episodes and major depressive episodes. If there are four or more manic, hypomanic, mixed, or major depressive episodes within a year, *rapid-cycling* is specified.

While the major depressive episodes involved in bipolar disorder and in major depressive disorder appear similar, some of the medications which successfully treat major depressive disorder will trigger a manic or hypomanic episode in those with bipolar disorder. This is also true of steroids, cocaine, and cannabis (Williams, 2006). The underlying mechanism by which this occurs is not yet fully understood.

Bipolar II disorder is considered an independent diagnosis and not a milder form of bipolar I disorder.

Mental Illness, Alcohol, and Drugs

Some persons with mental illness abuse alcohol and other drugs. Some persons that are mentally ill are also substance addicted. The intake of alcohol and other drugs may be an attempt to cope with the symptoms of the underlying mental disorder (especially in cases of psychotic and anxiety disorders). Regardless of the reason for substance use, if continued, it is not long before substance abuse becomes a problem and an independent focus for treatment. In such cases, the person is said to have a *dual diagnosis* (mental illness and substance abuse or addiction). Abuse of or addiction to alcohol or other drugs significantly complicates the treatment of mental illness.

There is a major controversy within the field of alcohol and drug addiction today. This controversy is expressed by those experts who (1) feel that substance addiction is a disease and out of the control of the person and (2) those who conceptualize the substance addiction as a choice. The fact that some persons are able to stop using their substance of addiction is seen by choice supporters as evidence for their position. They oppose the disease hypothesis by arguing that with substance addiction a person can choose not to be substance addicted, whereas in a true disease, like diabetes, a person cannot choose not to be diabetic.

Mental Illness and Medical Conditions

There are many medical conditions that can produce psychiatric symptoms. Police officers must remain aware that some persons who appear mentally ill or intoxicated may be suffering from a medical condition requiring immediate medical attention.

Mental Illness and Medication

Great advances in the pharmacological treatment of mental disorders have been made since the synthesis of chlorpromazine in 1950 (sold in America under the brand name Thorazine). The success of Thorazine in the treatment of schizophrenia and other mental disorders revolutionized the practice of psychiatry. Today, much more is known about the neurobiology of the brain, the physiology of mental illness, and the medications that best treat mental illnesses.

Like all medications, psychoactive medications have *main effects* and *side effects*. The main effect of a medication is that which treats or ameliorates the disorder or symptom. Main effects are useful and desirable. Side effects are unintended and may produce undesirable outcomes.

The side effects of some medications may be used to treat other conditions. The common aspirin is a good example. Aspirin is an effective analgesic; its main effect being that of pain reduction. It has long been known that a side effect of aspirin is stopping blood platelets from forming clots. This side effect of aspirin is used as a modern day main effect to prevent and treat coronary blockages.

The side effects of some psychoactive medications are serious enough that other medications are needed to manage them. Without these ancillary medications, the person might not be able to continue taking the primary medication.

Sometimes the side effects of a medication are so severe or undesirable that the medication must be discontinued. If the medication is stopped, the side effects normally subside, however the symptoms for which the medication was prescribed usually reappear. Some symptoms worsen significantly when primary medications are discontinued.

For police officers, knowing something about psychoactive medications can greatly aid field assessments. Knowledge of the more widely prescribed antipsychotics, antidepressants, and anxiolytics is especially useful. This is because knowledge of a person's past or present medications provides a short-cut source of information about their condition and likely diagnosis. A list of medications used to treat various mental disorders has been published by the National Institute of Mental Health. It can be accessed at *www.nimh.nih.gov.*

Treatments for Mental Illness

There are many treatments for mental illness. Treatments for mental illness have changed dramatically since the days of chained confinement, spinning chairs, ice baths, and strait jackets. Modern conceptions of mental illness and a greater understanding of the causes of mental disorders have improved therapies and therapeutic outcomes for millions of people. Today, there are two primary treatments for mental disorders: psychotherapy (counseling and a myriad of specific treatment protocols) and psychopharmacology (medication and biochemical interventions).

Psychotherapy

There are several orientations or schools of psychotherapy. They include therapies based upon the theories of psychoanalysis, behaviorism, cognitive-behaviorism, gestalt, brief intervention, systems intervention, humanism, existentialism, spiritualism, and transpersonalism. Most specific counseling interventions are based upon one or more of the main schools of psychotherapy. Many psychologists and other mental health professionals practice eclectic psychotherapy, a combination and blending of several therapies and techniques originating from various schools of intervention. Comprehensive psychotherapy programs often include elements of proper nutrition (diet) and appropriate physical activity (exercise).

Psychopharmacology

Psychopharmacology has a long history. The use of substances to influence consciousness, mood, mental conditions, and psychological ailments has been known since ancient times. Various societies have made use of the over four thousand plants known to include psychoactive substances. At least sixty of these plants or plant derived substances have been in common use for millennia, including cannabis, opium, coca, tea, coffee, tobacco, and alcohol (Malcolm, 1972).

Modern psychopharmacology is directed at treating various mental disorders. The development of psychoactive drugs with high efficacy and low or no side effects is the primary goal of psychoactive drug research laboratories. Their efforts have proven beneficial. There is little doubt that modern psychoactive medications make it possible for many persons to live a better life. In many cases of mental illness, the symptom improvements brought about by psychopharmacological treatment is remarkable.

Some psychoactive medications seem to have staying power, such as the *selective serotonin reuptake inhibitor* Prozac (FDA approved in 1987). Prozac remains one the most prescribed antidepressant medications in America. Others seem to come and go. Of these medications, some are removed from the market following unanticipated health risks (Serzone), some remain unpopular because of troubling side effects (Remeron), and some simply never seem to catch on. For instance, when was the last time you saw a television commercial for *Ludiomil*?

What of psychotherapeutic approaches that combine psychotherapy and psychopharmacology? Interestingly, research outcome studies have shown that psychotherapy is at least as effective as medication in the treatment of depression. However, research indicates that neither psychotherapy nor antidepressant medication alone appears to be as effective as both combined (Keller et al., 2000). Psychotherapy has also been shown to enhance the treatment outcomes of medication regimens for psychotic and other mental disorders (Smith, 2003).

Several recent studies have called the chemical efficacy of antidepressant medication into question. These studies concluded that although depressed persons improved on antidepressant medication, the improvement was statistically similar to that reported by depressed persons that received pills which were chemically benign (Kirsch, 2009). Their improvement was attributed to the *placebo effect*, the ability of expectation and hope to change the way persons feel. The placebo effect may be due to the body's ability to respond to its own naturally occurring substances. For this to occur, it seems necessary for the person to believe the medication may help. If this is true, it represents an interesting explanation of how antidepressants work.

The placebo effect for antidepressants was stronger in cases of mild to moderate depression than severe depression. In severe cases, the chemical effects of antidepressants may yield an actual benefit although that effect was reportedly slight (Begley, 2010). There remains much controversy and some confusion in this area. Certainly, more research is needed. In the meantime, debate over whether antidepressants work due to placebo effect, brain chemical alteration, or a combination of both, continues.

A disturbing finding involving antidepressant medication is that in some children, adolescents, and young adults, treatment with antidepressants *increases* suicidal thinking and behavior. This finding has prompted the FDA to require antidepressant drug manufacturers to provide appropriate "black box" label warnings.

St. John's Wort

There is evidence that the popular mood-enhancing botanical, St. John's wort (an extract from the flowering plant *Hypericum perforatum*), may dangerously interact or interfere with several classes of prescribed medications. Persons taking prescribed medications and/or oral contraceptives should consult with their physicians before initiating a course of St. John's wort or any herbal remedy. Research conducted into the efficacy of St. John's wort for the treatment of mild to moderate depression has produced conflicting results (NIMH, 2010).

Electroconvulsive and New Age Therapy

Other psychotherapeutic interventions include electroconvulsive therapy (ECT) (formerly called *electroshock*) and what might be considered the *new age* therapies.

Electroconvulsive therapy consists of an electrical stimulus applied to the brain to produce a convulsion. It was first used as a stimulus for convulsive therapy in 1938 by Ugo Cerletti and his colleague Lucio Bini. ECT is used primarily to treat life threatening depression and select other conditions when medications and additional therapies have failed. It can also be used as a first-line intervention, in place of medication and other treatment. Critics of ECT maintain that real ECT is only marginally more effective than placebo ECT, and that the possible side effects of ECT outweigh its benefits (Ross, 2006). Despite this criticism, ECT continues to be used when deemed appropriate by supporters of convulsive therapy.

A milder and more recently developed electro-treatment for depression is *transcranial direct current stimulation* (tDCS). This treatment involves the application of a very weak electrical current to specific areas of the brain via electrodes placed on the scalp. Unlike traditional ECT, tCDS does not produce convulsions. The early experimental results of tDCS have been promising.

New age therapies are comprised of those interventions that lie outside the currently accepted norms of psychotherapeutic intervention. Certain energy and technique therapies might fall into this category.

Psychosurgery

Psychosurgery is a type of neurosurgery. Psychosurgery is surgery performed on the brain which has as its goal the treatment of a diagnosed mental disorder. This is different from other forms of neurosurgery, which have as their goal the treatment of various other brain and neurological conditions.

The oldest known form of psychosurgery, *trepanning*, was practiced as early as 6500 BCE (Restak, 2000). Trepanation is the act of drilling a hole in the skull. Historically it was used to treat headache, seizures, and mental illness. In modern times, trepanation is used to treat subdural hematomas and several other medical conditions. There are some groups that believe there is benefit in "venting" the brain and continue to practice trepanation; however there is no modern application of trepanation for the treatment of mental illness.

During the heyday of psychosurgery, the most often performed procedure was the pre-frontal lobotomy. A significant figure in the American history of lobotomy was Walter Freeman (1895-1972). Although Freeman did not invent the lobotomy, he developed the transorbital lobotomy - a procedure wherein an ice pick-type instrument (called an orbitoclast) was inserted under each eyelid and pounded through the thin bone of the eye socket. Once the instruments entered the braincase, they were pushed into the brain about one and one-half inches and moved in a pre-planned manner. This motion severed the fibers of the pre-frontal lobes, separating them from the rest of the brain. Once this was accomplished, the instruments were withdrawn. The lobotomy was completed.

Of the estimated 40-50,000 lobotomies performed in the United States from the 1940s through the 1960s, Freeman recorded performing 3,439 of them; most by using the "ice pick" method. His fee for performing an ice pick lobotomy: $25.00; his anesthesia: electroconvulsive shock (Cordingly, 2005). Freeman performed his last lobotomy in 1967 on long-time patient, 52 year old Helen Mortensen. She died of a cerebral hemorrhage following the procedure. It was her third Freeman lobotomy (NPR, 2005).

Modern and more recently developed psychosurgery includes the capsulotomy, cingulotomy, subcaudate tractotomy, and limbic leucotomy.

Dementia and Delirium

Dementia is a neurocognitive disorder which causes impairment in brain function. It has multiple causes and results in generalized cognitive deterioration. The primary symptoms of dementia are memory loss, moodiness, communication problems, and confusion. In dementia, executive function is impaired. *Executive function* is the term used to describe the highest cognitive abilities of the human being, including information processing and reasoning. If the impairment is significant, the person may not be able to safely live independently. Dementia normally worsens over time. There are many types of dementia. Alzheimer's disease is likely the most well-known (Geldmacher, 2003).

Delirium is also a neurocognitive disorder, but different from dementia. Delirium is an impairment of consciousness characterized by reduced awareness of the environment. It normally has a rapid onset. Persons with delirium are disoriented (confused about date, time, and place), have difficulties paying attention, confused, and may experience hallucinations (mostly visual and tactile). Delirium is often temporary and reversible. Its most likely cause is drugs, prescription or otherwise. Delirium is common after surgery, due to anesthesia and pain control medications. Delirium is sometimes observed in the elderly without a drug etiology, often as part of an underlying health condition such as a urinary tract infection. Some deliriums are irreversible. Irreversible delirium may be caused by brain injury, stroke, or other physical trauma. Delirium is a serious condition and requires immediate medical assessment and treatment.

Dementia and delirium are not mutually exclusive. Persons with dementia may also experience delirium. For some persons with delirium, the condition evolves into a chronic brain dysfunction similar to dementia (Anton et al., 2006).

Tourette's Disorder and Munchausen Syndrome

Police officers must know something about *Tourette's disorder* and *Munchausen syndrome*. Tourette's is a neurodevelopmental brain disorder which produces multiple involuntary motor tics and one or more verbal tics, with onset before the age of eighteen. The verbal tics can be comprised of throat-clearing sounds, grunts, screams, and words. Sometimes the word vocalizations of a person with Tourette's include profanity. A person suffering from Tourette's and engaging in outbursts of profanity due to the disorder must be distinguished from a person simply behaving badly.

Munchausen syndrome is not a diagnosis. It is a commonly used term to describe the falsification, faking, or otherwise intentionally producing medical or psychiatric signs and symptoms for the assumed goal of being a patient. Persons with Munchausen syndrome present themselves to care providers as ill, impaired, or injured. They may inflict harm upon themselves and "doctor shop" in order to continue to receive medical attention. They willingly undergo invasive medical procedures and in the most serious cases, have multiple surgical scars as a result. This behavior can continue even in the absence of obvious external rewards. *Munchausen by proxy* occurs when a caregiver falsely presents another as ill, impaired, or injured. Persons with Munchausen by proxy may cause harm to someone else, most often a child, to satisfy their needs or to receive the attention of care providers. This can be a factor in certain child abuse investigations.

The formal diagnoses for the various forms of Munchausen syndrome are *factitious disorder imposed on self* and *factitious disorder imposed on another* (300.19, DSM-5).

Myths of Mental Illness

The American Psychiatric Association published the following information in an effort to dispel the myths associated with mental illness.

1. *Mental illness doesn't affect the average person.*
   - Fact: No one is immune to mental illness.

2. *Children do not get mental illnesses.*
   - Fact: In reality, over 12 million children—from infants through 18-year-olds suffer from diagnosable mental disorders such as depression, attention deficit disorder, and pervasive development disorders.

3. *All people suffering from mental illness receive treatment.*
   - Fact: Only about one in five people dealing with a diagnosable mental disorder seek treatment.

4. *All mentally Ill people are dangerous.*
   - Fact: People suffering from mental illness are statistically about as dangerous as those people without mental illness.

5. *If you have a mental illness, you are crazy all the time.*
   - Fact: The course of serious mental illness such as schizophrenia, bi-polar disorder, depression and other mental disorders often "wax and wane" and are influenced by several factors including life circumstances, severity of the illness, and type of treatment (if any) that a person is receiving.

6. *If I am diagnosed with a mental illness, I will have to take drugs or electroshock.*
   - Fact: There are various treatments for mental illness. The recommended type and course of treatment varies with the type and severity of the particular disorder.

Reflections of a Police Psychologist

7. *If I go to see a mental health professional, people will look down on me or think I'm crazy, strange, or weird.*
   - Fact: Great strides have been made in public education about the nature of mental illness. As people have begun to understand more about mental illness, the past stigma of visiting with a mental health professional has significantly declined. The fact is that most of us will need some help at some point in our lives.

8. *People never recover from mental illnesses.*
   - Fact: As many as eight in ten people suffering from mental illness can effectively return to normal, productive lives with appropriate treatment.

Intellectual Disability and Mental Illness

Intellectual disability (formerly called *mental retardation*) is different from mental illness. Whereas mental illness is characterized by signs, symptoms, and additional criteria, the essential feature of intellectual disability is subaverage intellectual functioning (specified as *intelligence quotient*) (IQ) accompanied by limitations in several life skill areas.

Intellectual disability and mental illness are not mutually exclusive. It is possible for a person to have an intellectual disability and one or more mental illnesses.

Modern History of Intellectual Disability

In the early 1900s, American psychologist Henry Goddard (1866-1957) proposed and popularized the following classifications of those assessed to be "feeble-minded": *moron* (IQ 70-51), *imbecile* (IQ 50-26), and *idiot* (IQ 25-0). This nomenclature was first presented on May 18, 1910, at a meeting of the American Association for the Study of the Feeble Minded. These diagnostic categories were used for several decades.

The notion of feeble-mindedness and the classifications of moron, imbecile, and idiot fell out of favor toward the end of the 1940s. They were not included in the first DSM (1952). Instead, the DSM utilized a new diagnosis, *mental deficiency*. Mental deficiency was defined as "primarily a defect of intelligence existing since birth, without demonstrated organic brain disease or known prenatal cause" (23). Mental deficiency could be mild, moderate, or severe.

The diagnosis of mental deficiency was replaced by the diagnosis of *mental retardation* in the DSM-II (1968). In DSM-II, mental retardation could be borderline, mild, moderate, severe, or profound, depending upon assessed IQ. In the DSM-III (1980) the "borderline" specifier was eliminated. The DSM-IV (1994) and DSM-IV-TR (2000) retained mental retardation as a diagnosis. Mild retardation was diagnosed at IQ levels of 50-55 to approximately 70. Moderate mental retardation was specified at IQ levels of 35-40 to 50-55. Severe mental retardation was characterized by IQ levels of 20-25 to 35-40, and profound mental retardation was diagnosed at IQ levels below 20-25. In DSM-5 (2013), the diagnosis of mental retardation was replaced by *intellectual disability* (also called *intellectual developmental disorder*). Intellectual disability is defined as "a disorder with onset during the developmental period that includes both intellectual and adaptive functioning deficits in conceptual, social, and practical domains" (33).

Although standardized intelligence tests continue to be used in the diagnosis of intellectual disability, the severity of intellectual disability (mild, moderate, severe, and profound) is now determined by the level of adaptive functioning and not IQ. This represents a significant departure from the traditional way in which the degree of intellectual impairment was assessed.

When the focus of clinical attention is intellectual functioning but the diagnostic criteria of intellectual disability are not present, *borderline intellectual functioning* (V62.89, DSM-5) may be specified.

Recognizing Intellectual Disability

The ability to appropriately interact with persons with an intellectual disability is an important skill for police officers. This is because some intellectually impaired persons may look adult but cannot act in the manner suggested by their appearance.

Adults who are intellectually impaired:

- may dress, communicate, and comprehend as a child.
- may dress and appear as an adult but be incapable of responding or processing information as an adult.
- may not comply with police commands because they cannot fully understand them or appreciate the gravity of noncompliance. There have been incidents where intellectually impaired persons have

attacked police out a sense of anger, fear, or frustration. In several such circumstances, officers have had to defend themselves with deadly force.

- may be easily influenced by others. When this happens, they may get into trouble due to a lack of judgment or wanting to belong.
- may be sensitive to their perceived deficits. As compensation, some may become street toughs or thugs. Those persons with abilities closest to average are most likely to come to the attention of police for this reason.
- may wander around the community watching or otherwise interacting with children. This may be because children can be better understood by the person and the person feels better understood by them.
- may come to attention of other adults because of their preference to be in the company of children, especially around playgrounds and parks. Others may become frightened and call the police.
- may struggle with adult emotional and sexual drives while having only a limited cognitive ability to express them in appropriate ways.
- may be able to live independently with proper assistance.

Police Stress and Exposure to Persons Who are Mentally Ill and/or Intellectually Impaired

Interacting with persons who are mentally ill and/or intellectually impaired can be stressful. Sadly, during these interactions, there is the potential for tragic outcomes (similar to interactions with non-mentally ill and/or non-intellectually impaired persons). If officers find themselves traumatized or struggling with an issue arising out of an experience with a person who is mentally ill and/or intellectually impaired they should:

- talk it out with a trusted person
- contact a member of the Peer Support Team or the agency chaplain
- contact the police psychologist or other support clinician
- contact the Employee Assistance Program
- not go it alone

Chapter 10

Suicide and Police Officers

Suicide is the intentional act of self killing. Although persons suffering from mental illness (especially mood disorders) commit suicide, not all suicidal people are mentally ill. Throughout human history there have been those who have intentionally sacrificed themselves for religious beliefs, for comrades, for family, and for political purposes.

Some persons are committed to killing themselves. If they are knowledgeable and have the opportunity, they will choose a means that nearly assures the outcome of death. For this type of suicidal person, the usual end is death. The means they choose frequently involves the use of a firearm, or potent drugs or poisons (history records that Adolf Hitler used both, cyanide and a gunshot). Recent statistical information shows that over half of all completed suicides involve the use of firearms. The muzzle of a firearm placed over a vital organ of the body in a suicide effort leaves little room for resuscitation, thereby increasing the probability of death.

Most suicidal persons are not committed to killing themselves. They are ambivalent about dying. They may think about death, but are unsure about killing themselves.

In some cases, persons act out in a suicidal way to influence others. This is usually to compel others to behave in some desired manner. In other cases, persons will make a suicidal gesture to send the proverbial cry for help. In both of these circumstances, death is not the underlying goal.

Most suicidal thinking and suicide attempts are not really about dying. They are about stopping the pain. Help the person stop the pain, and the reason for self-destruction diminishes or disappears.

Suicidal acting out is a sign of serious difficulty and a signal of significant distress. Appropriate intervention is required. Appropriate intervention offers suicidal persons realistic hope. With realistic hope, most persons that are suicidal will not remain suicidal. This is true even for those who have survived a previous suicide attempt - although a previous suicide attempt increases the risk that a person will again attempt suicide.

All suicidal ideation, gestures, and attempts should be taken seriously.

Incidentally, dying at one's own hand by the failure of a fail-safe device designed for autoerotic purposes is not a suicide. Such a self-caused death is accidental.

Suicide Intent and Means

Suicide attempts must be evaluated in terms of *intent* and *means*. Some people are intent on dying but due to inadequate knowledge they select a means that proves non lethal. These survivors remain a significant danger to themselves. Conversely, some people do not intend to die. They wish to accomplish something else with their "suicidal" behavior. However, because they did not recognize that the means selected was lethal, they kill themselves. Both of these circumstances involve a misunderstanding of the potentially lethal effects of the chosen means. In the first case, the person is very suicidal, even if the suicide attempt appears frivolous (like ingesting four aspirin). In the second case, the completed suicide is more accurately described as an accidental death. However, because the person is dead, this can only be determined upon psychological autopsy.

Suicide Prone

Suicidal thinking varies along a continuum. On one end, there are passing suicidal thoughts. On the other end, there are obsessive thoughts of death. Suicidal thinking is more common than might be expected. Many people at some point in their life have thought about suicide. Suicidal thoughts occur most frequently when persons cannot see a way to resolve a significant problem, cope with a significant loss, or are overwhelmed by negative emotions. Thankfully, most persons eventually find a way to manage these difficulties and the suicidal thoughts disappear. As strange as it may seem, suicidal thoughts can also be triggered by certain medications, even in non-depressed people with no history of suicidal thinking.

In those prone to suicidal thinking, suicidal thoughts often co-vary with environmental stressors. For these people, when things are perceived as going well, suicidal thinking is absent or minimal. As stressors increase or things begin to go badly, suicidal thinking becomes more prominent.

Death is sometimes passively desired. This is known as *passive suicidality*. Passive suicidality may be conscious or unconscious. When persons are passively suicidal, they do not plan to kill themselves. Instead, they wish their death through other means. One passively suicidal person reported praying that the airplane in which she was a passenger would crash. This is an example of *conscious passive suicidality*. Interestingly, there were no thoughts or concerns for the lives of the other passengers. This was not because she was an uncaring person or that she wished others would die. It is because persons in this state of mind cannot see or think past their anguish and despair. This is an example of *tunnel thinking*, a type of thinking that has become so focused that consequences other than that desired simply do not enter personal awareness.

Another person struggled with thoughts of suicide as part of a major depression. After his depression lifted, he became anorexic and would not eat. This is an example of *unconscious passive suicidality*. Although he reported feeling better and was no longer actively suicidal, he was slowly, unconsciously starving himself to death. In cases of unconscious passive suicidality the person often consciously fights or resists the unconscious desires, but has little insight into their existence or origin.

All passively suicidal persons retain some energy for life but they are usually apathetic and emotionally exhausted. As they work in therapy to address the prevailing issues, their zest for life frequently returns and they can once again experience life's pleasures.

Perspectives, Suicidal Thinking, and Psychological Buffers

There are some perspectives that seem to encourage suicidal thinking. Persons that see themselves as inadequate and powerless to change undesirable circumstances are more likely to consider suicide. This is because they have very little confidence in their ability to make difficult situations better. When they look into the future, they see more of the same, or worse. This perspective is one of the most significant differences between persons who are likely to consider suicide and those who are not.

When most people find themselves at a low point in their lives, they have thoughts like "Well it's so bad now. It can't do anything but get better" (This is the "no place to go but up" idea). Thoughts like this are hopeful and optimistic. They act as a buffer against thoughts of suicide. However, optimistic thoughts are not present in persons more likely to consider suicide. Instead, they experience ideas similar to, "It's so bad now. It will never get better, it will just get worse" and "I can't bear this pain anymore and there's nothing

I can do about it." Thoughts like these encourage further negative thinking and contribute to feelings of despair. Now, feeling helpless and powerless to change anything, the person becomes hopeless: "There's no point to living." The situation can worsen to the point where death is viewed as a relief. In these unfortunate cases, death becomes an escape and is viewed as the only way out (This is the "I'm trapped and I can't take this anymore" idea). This state of mind can be the result of years of consideration or it can develop quite rapidly upon a change in life circumstances.

At this point, the psychological buffers against suicide begin to fail. There are several predominant psychological buffers against suicide including: (1) the ability to experience pleasure - many people that are "tired of living" report that they do not attempt suicide because they continue to experience pleasure in at least some portion of their lives; (2) some meaning in life - there is something to live for; (3) concerns about family - worry about how their suicide would affect family members; and (4) religious/philosophical beliefs - suicide is prohibited by religious or philosophical beliefs.

All of these are excellent buffers against suicide. But when these buffers begin to fail, the person begins to think about themselves, family, and their beliefs in a different way. Thoughts like:

- *Things are bad but at least I still have and enjoy X* become *I do not enjoy anything anymore,*
- *I live because ...* become *There is no point to living,*
- *I cannot kill myself because it would devastate my family* become *My family would be better off without me,* and
- *I cannot kill myself because it is a sin* become *God has forsaken me.*

The weakening or failure of any or all of these psychological buffers increases the probability that the person will consider suicide. As the buffers deteriorate and the tunnel of thinking narrows, suicidal thinking becomes more prominent. At the end of the tunnel is suicide.

Family and Suicide

Survivors often struggle with the suicide of a family member. Common issues include, "Why didn't I see it coming?" "Why didn't he reach out to me?" and "Why couldn't I prevent it?" Sometimes there are reasonable answers to these questions, most times there are not.

Family members can experience a tremendous amount of guilt over the act of suicide. It is not unusual for family survivors to feel some degree of guilt, blame themselves, or blame other family members for the death. Feeling guilty and blaming oneself or others is common. Blaming may be expressed explicitly or implicitly as family members struggle to answer the question, "Why?"

Family members must remain aware that there may be little they could have done to prevent the suicide. This is because: (1) some persons are committed to dying, at least at the time they attempt suicide (2) not everyone exhibits suicidal warning signs. Suicidal intentions can be kept secret, (3) if warning signs are present, they may be difficult to recognize. (For example, a person who says "I'm giving away my stuff because I'm tired of it" may actually be tired of it. Another person might say "I'm giving away my stuff because I'm tired of it" as part of a suicidal plan. The true meaning of these identical statements may be difficult to discern), and (4) family members may be emotionally numbed by past suicidal threats and behaviors. (This can occur even in families that care and have tried their best to help.) Emotional numbness is a normal process that can occur following months or years of trying to help a suicidal person. The development of emotional numbness is facilitated by the difficulty inherent in sustaining a relationship with someone that is consistently pre-occupied with thoughts of suicide (especially prevalent in persons with mood disturbances and some personality disorders).

Emotional numbness on the part of family members and others is characterized in statements like: "He'll either do it or he won't. I can't deal with him anymore. I have no more to give and I'm exhausted from worrying about it. He is responsible for what he does. I have done all I can."

For family members, emotional numbing involves the feeling of not knowing what more can be done. It is sometimes the only remaining way to cope with the suicidal behaviors of others. This is not to say that family members (or others) have no ability to successfully identify and assist a suicidal relative. Many successful family suicide interventions are accomplished each year.

Suicide, Family, and Cause of Death

Many families are in anguish following the suicide of a family member. It is not only the anguish caused by the loss of a loved one, but also the anguish caused by the thought that their loved one would choose to leave them. In an attempt to deny this psychological feature of suicide, family members sometimes beseech the office of the coroner to change the determined cause of death. They insist that the cause of death be changed from "suicide" or "self-inflicted" to "accidental" or even "homicide." This has occurred even in cases where comprehensive investigation can conclude nothing but suicide. Indeed, the idea that a son, daughter, mother, father, or other relative would make the decision to abandon the family by killing themselves is a very difficult thought for many families to accept.

Families must keep in mind that their loved one was not thinking rationally at the time of suicide and that their buffers against suicide had likely failed. They may not have "chosen" to leave the family. Instead, they may not have been able to see that other viable options existed.

Suicide and Family Responses

Some family members may not be disturbed by the suicide. Some may be neutral or actually pleased that the person is dead, a fact that Hollywood has incorporated into many of its productions. The expression, observation, or perception of these reactions can create major difficulties within a family system.

A confounding factor in some instances of suicide involves life insurance. Some life insurance policies restrict or deny payment in cases of suicide, at least for a period of time. Others will pay. If there is an insurance payment, what should a family do with the money? Some family members describe the life insurance payoff as "tainted" or "blood money," and are uncomfortable living the good life on the funds provided to them by a loved one's suicide.

For some family members there is embarrassment for the suicide. They may see suicide as a "cop out" and weakness which shames or casts a shadow over the entire family. They feel that the suicide reflects poorly upon them. This is why many families maintain the secret of suicide. In such families, no one is permitted to speak of the person or the death, either within or outside the family. Other family members may view the suicide as permission to carry out their own suicidal impulses. There have been numerous cases wherein the suicide of one family member was followed by the suicide of another. Any or all of this can be present as part of the maelstrom following a suicide.

Suicide Information

The National Institute of Mental Health (2010) identified the following risk factors for suicide:

- depression and other mental disorders, or a substance-abuse disorder in combination with other mental disorders (over 90% of people who die by suicide are suffering from depression and other mental disorders, or a substance-abuse disorder in combination with other mental disorders)
- prior suicide attempt
- family history of mental disorder or substance abuse
- family history of suicide
- family violence, including physical or sexual abuse
- firearms in the home
- incarceration
- exposure to the suicidal behavior of others such as family members, peers, or media figures

Annually in America, suicides have consistently outnumber homicides by approximately two to one. Men complete suicide about three times more often than women; women make about four times as many suicide attempts as men. Firearms, suffocation, and poisoning are the most common means used to complete suicide. Suicide is the 10th leading cause of death.

On average, in the world, it is estimated that a person completes suicide about every forty seconds; in the United States, about every seventeen minutes. The idea that most suicides occur around the winter holidays is a myth. Although suicides do occur during the holiday season, suicide rates are normally lowest in winter and highest in the spring.

Some research indicates that suicide notes are left in less than one-third of suicide cases (NIMH, 2010). This seems to differ for police officers. Police officers who complete suicide almost always leave a suicide note. Some police officer suicide notes are lengthy, including funeral arrangements, financial information, final thoughts, and final messages. Some are brief. Below is the entire text of an actual police officer suicide note. Unusual for a police officer, the suicide did not involve a firearm.

I'm sorry for any pain this may cause anyone. I'm just tired of fighting.
I am now at peace.

Most people who become suicidal give some warning of their thoughts and intentions (estimates are about 80%). This number is not 100% because, as mentioned previously, human beings have an ability to maintain a secret inner life. They may look one way, but feel another. In a poem first published in 1923, Maine poet Edwin Arlington Robinson (1869-1935) skillfully expressed this component of human experience in his portrayal of *Richard Cory*:

Whenever Richard Cory went downtown,
We people on the pavement looked at him:
He was a gentleman from sole to crown,
Clean-favored, and imperially slim.

And he was always quietly arrayed,
And he was always human when he talked;
But still he fluttered pulses when he said,
"Good morning," and he glittered when he walked.

And he was rich—yes, richer than a king-
And admirably schooled in every grace:
In fine, we thought that he was everything
To make us wish that we were in his place.

So on we worked, and waited for the light,
And went without the meat, and cursed the bread;
And Richard Cory, one calm summer night,
Went home and put a bullet through his head.

Suicide Warnings

Behaviors indicative of suicidal thinking range from subtle to apparent. The subtle signs of mounting suicidality include increasingly poor hygiene, greater isolation, less concern with appearance, less verbal communication, less energy and activity, lower standards for house and car maintenance, and behaviors that appear uncharacteristic of the person. These are signs of depression and may indicate a developing mood disorder.

The more apparent and well known signs of suicidal thinking include the giving away of treasured items, assigning caretakers for pets, and verbal communication of veiled or explicit suicidal thinking.

Those who are the closest to the person are in the best position to assess and evaluate suicidal behaviors. Statements such as, "They'll see something tomorrow" "I can't take this much longer" "I know what I have to do" "Give this to X" "I want you to have . . ." and "When I'm gone . . ." should never go unchallenged. Responses such as "What do you mean . . ." "Tell me more about that . . ." "What are you thinking?" and other exploratory inquiries are appropriate in such instances. Many times, persons considering suicide will readily communicate their thoughts or plans if asked. This is especially true if they lack a family or other functional support system.

Suicide and Alcohol

Alcohol, like all drugs, is dose dependent. In small body concentrations, alcohol is a thought and behavioral disinhibitor. This is why after a few drinks, you are more likely to have thoughts you would not have when sober, and engage in behavior you would not consider when sober. In larger quantities, alcohol depresses central nervous system activity. This results in the lethargy and the cognitive impairment seen in alcohol intoxication. If dosing continues, this latter effect will render the person unconsciousness. If enough alcohol has been consumed prior to unconsciousness, death will ensue.

Some persons who are mildly suicidal become more suicidal when intoxicated. This is due to alcohol's disinhibiting effect. With this, impulsivity increases - never a good thing for depressed or suicidal persons.

Some suicidal persons will anesthetize themselves with alcohol before attempting suicide. In such cases alcohol may function in several ways, (1) reduced inhibition of suicidal thoughts, (2) reduced inhibition of suicidal behavior, (3) psychological numbing, and (4) physical numbing.

Most persons that are suicidal when intoxicated are not suicidal (or not as suicidal) when sober. This makes detoxification the first and primary intervention of intoxicated suicidal persons.

Suicide Plan

Many persons who become suicidal develop a plan for death. Suicide plans may be simple or elaborate. The mere existence of a suicide plan increases the probability of suicide. The more thought out and detailed the plan, the more likely it is that the person will attempt suicide.

Various Motivations and Types of Suicide

There are various motivations for suicide. The particular motivation for suicide appears to be correlated with a specific type of suicide. Some types of suicide and likely motivations are:

- blaze of glory—to be remembered or to make a statement
- fate suicide—let another or circumstances decide
- suicide by cop—suicide by provoking a police officer
- protest suicide—political, social, or other cause
- cause suicide—political or military objective
- psychotic suicide—delusion/command hallucination
- medical suicide—terminal illness or health issues
- hopelessness suicide—depression, loss, mood disorder
- revenge suicide—punish someone
- honor suicide—avoid disgrace
- shame suicide—exposure of secret activity, embarrassment
- guilt suicide—sense of responsibility
- anger suicide—anger at self or others
- hate suicide—self hatred
- life change suicide—overwhelmed by change

There can be combined motivations for suicide. Within the motivation for suicide lies the *rationale*. The rationale for suicide seldom appears *rational* to outside observers.

Suicide by Cop

There are those who seek to be killed by the police. *Suicide by cop (SBC)*, *victim-precipitated suicide*, and *decedent-precipitated suicide* are current terms for this too frequently observed phenomenon. Persons intending to be killed by police officers will act in ways that compel officers to defend themselves. In the majority of cases, persons so disposed will point a firearm at police officers.

Some persons intending to be killed by police officers are armed with functioning, loaded weapons. A proportion of these persons will not hesitate to kill others in their effort to die at the hands of the police. Others use air, pellet, BB, toy, or authentic looking replica weapons to threaten police. Still others draw and point non-firearm objects, like flashlights, wallets, or cell phones in a way that a firearm would be drawn and pointed, in their attempt to get police officers to fire.

In some cases, a person indifferent to dying will engage in threatening behavior or point a weapon at an officer and let fate decide the outcome. This circumstance combines the *fate suicide* with *suicide by cop*. Persons in this frame of mind are incapable of caring whether they live or die, at least at the time. They do not comply with officers' orders, threaten officers, and may compel officers to defend themselves. Many of those seeking to be killed by the police are suffering from depression or other mental disorders.

The well publicized Long Island, New York, case of Moshe Pergament is illustrative of how far a person might go to be killed by the police. This case is representative of many tragic intentional suicide-by-cop incidents:

On November 15, 1997, 19-year old Moshe Pergament, known as Moe to his friends, was intentionally driving recklessly on the Long Island Expressway, planning to be contacted by police. He sideswiped several cars. It was not long before his dangerous driving was reported. A short time after the reports, he was located and stopped by police. Once stopped, Moe exited his car. He pulled out a handgun. Officers ordered him to drop the weapon. He did not comply. He began to walk toward officers with his gun pointed at them. When Moe again failed to comply with the officers' orders, they fired, killing him. In Moe's vehicle, investigators found ten notes. Nine were addressed to family members and friends. One was addressed "To the officer that shot me." It read,

> Officer, It was a plan. I'm sorry to get you involved. I just needed to die.
> Please remember that this was all my doing. You had no way of knowing.
> Moe Pergament

Pergament was holding and pointing a realistic-looking plastic replica of a silver .38 caliber revolver. He had purchased it earlier the same day. Investigation later determined that Moe owed $6,000 in gambling debts. The *New York Daily News* (News) reported it this way, "A Nassau County teenager with a death wish and $6,000 in World Series gambling debts was gunned down by Long Island police Friday night after he pointed a fake gun at them, authorities said" (November 16, 1997). The next day, The News reported, "The well-off and well-liked 19-year-old college student gunned down by Long

Island police in an apparent 'suicide-by-cop,' took his secrets to the grave yesterday" (November 17, 1997).

It appears that the phrase *gunned down* was popular with News staff writers in the 1990s. Sensational terms used in sad and tragic cases are sometimes used to increase newspaper sales. However, this phrase, when used in the context of a forced suicide by cop, demonstrates a general insensitivity on the part of reporters for the officers involved. This type of reporting can have a traumatizing effect on involved officers and can become a major component of police officer second injury (chapter 4). Unfortunately, this poor standard of sensationalistic news reporting continues today.

Officer-involved Shootings and Suicide

Researchers recently studied 707 cases of officer-involved shootings in North America from 1998 to 2006. Results revealed that 36 percent of all the police shootings studied met the criteria for suicide by cop. This was in contrast to several older studies which estimated the suicide by cop rate from 10 percent to 26 percent of all police shootings (Mohandie et al., 2009).

Of the persons that attempt suicide by cop, a proportion of them are in possession of functional and loaded weapons. The question arises, why do they not shoot themselves? Why force a police officer to shoot in self-defense? Several factors are suspected in these cases, including:

1. Social concerns. There is still a social taboo against suicide.
2. Suicide by cop allows suicidal persons to die without actually killing themselves.
3. Fear or other inability to follow through with suicide.
4. Religious prohibitions against suicide (SBC as a religion "loophole"?)
5. Concerns over life insurance policies.
6. Wanting to go out in a blaze, make the news.
7. Psychological inability to kill oneself.

Clinton Van Zandt, a former FBI hostage negotiator, commented that persons prone to suicide by cop are those that fear other attempts at death. They are afraid that if they drive into a bridge abutment, cut their wrists, and so forth, they may not die. Provoking a police officer to shoot increases the probability that they will accomplish their goal (1993).

Suicidal Persons and the Police

Police officers may encounter persons who are suicidal in a number of ways. They can be dispatched to assist the person, they can come upon the person during patrol or other duties, they can be on a call that starts out as something else and evolves into a suicidal person interaction (e.g., welfare check, disturbance, etc), or they may conduct a field assessment in any circumstance and determine that the person is suicidal. Persons who are suicidal may be mildly or severely suicidal, cooperative or uncooperative, dangerous or represent little threat to others, alone and in the open, barricaded with or without other people, armed or unarmed, and so on. The possible variables are too numerous to mention. Because police officers may encounter a person who is suicidal at any time and under varied circumstances, it is helpful to consider some basic guidelines for interaction. Of course, what is possible during any contact with a person who is suicidal is determined by the actual state of affairs.

Suggestions for Police Officers Interacting with Persons who are Suicidal

Suggestions for police officers interacting with persons who are suicidal necessarily overlap the "Suggestions for Police Officers Interacting with Persons who are Psychotic or Otherwise Mentally Ill" (SIPPOMI) (chapter 9). Several suggestions specified in SIPPOMI which are not repeated here, are equally applicable.

Several of these suggestions are intended to be engaged simultaneously. Some, like officer safety assessment, should be engaged throughout the interaction.

1. *Gather information.* Officers should gather as much information as is practical prior to contacting a suicidal person. This will help you determine your approach. Arrange for additional police units. Do not go it alone. Although in some cases you may be duty-bound to take solo action, it is safer for you and the person to have adequate assistance.
2. *Determine environment and person variables.* Is the person accessible or barricaded, intoxicated or sober, armed or unarmed, alone or accompanied, angry or cooperative, etc.

3. *Officer safety assessment and contact*. Interacting with a suicidal person requires an immediate and *ongoing* assessment of threat to officers. *Most suicidal persons are not homicidal—but do not bet your life on this probability*. Some suicidal persons will harm others. Utilize all pertinent officer safety procedures. When contact is made, you may have to act rapidly and decisively. More likely, you will have ample time to initiate contact and open discussion. If the situation is chaotic, prioritize your intervention. Try to slow things down. Slowing things down tends to reduce impulsivity, which makes the situation safer.

4. *Remain calm*. Interacting with a suicidal person is stressful. Take a deep breath. Try to relax. Speak in a clear, calm voice. Avoid profanity, excitement, and abusive language. These tend to increase instability. Provide an emotionally stable influence during the interaction. Proceed thoughtfully unless duty-bound to intervene. You will better help the person and increase the probability of a desired outcome if you can remain calm.

5. *Establish rapport*. Obtain and utilize the person's name. You can use first name or title (Mr., Dr., etc) as deemed appropriate. Identify yourself by first name if you wish to deemphasize authority. Tell the person that you are there to help. Keep in mind that most people are ambivalent about dying and will readily talk to you.

6. *Obtain some information quickly*. Ask or otherwise attempt to determine if the person is concealing a weapon, has weapons available, has recently ingested street drugs or medication, has been drinking alcohol, or has just made a suicide attempt (ingestion of substances and some injuries are not easily observed). This information increases officer safety, allows for appropriate intervention, and contributes to your field assessment.

7. *Remove lethal means*. The priority is to have the person distance himself from any possessed weapon or weapon within reach. If the person is communicative and compliant, tell him what you want him to do in a step by step manner. For example, if the person is pointing a handgun to his head with his right hand, avoid statements like "drop the gun." Instead use statements like "remove your finger from the trigger, point the gun toward the sky, with your left hand grab the barrel of the gun, release the gun from your right hand, move the gun slowly to the floor" and so on. This is much better than watching the gun bounce off the floor in compliance with your order to "drop

the gun." It also lowers the probability of an accidental discharge. Additionally, you do not want to be so mentally prepared to see the gun move quickly that your reflexes have to compensate for an unexpected dangerous gun movement. What are your options if the person is not compliant? Remain in a tactical cover position and keep working to establish rapport. As long as the person is not an active threat to you or others, you may continue your efforts for voluntary compliance.

8   *Request additional emergency personnel as needed.* Request specialized police units, paramedics, fire, and so on as necessary. *Tactical considerations.* If you are in contact with the person and feel exposed, threatened, or otherwise unsafe, and immediate apprehension is not possible, withdraw from the environment as rapidly and safely as possible. Once safely out, proceed as outlined in department policy for such circumstances.

9.   *Continue conversation.* Keep talking. Ask open-ended questions about recent events in the person's life, such as "What happened today?" "What's happening in your life?" and the always reliable "Tell me more." Ask about how the person arrived at this point. Discuss the person's history to strengthen rapport and gain information for your field assessment.

10. *Acknowledge the person's stated or implied difficulties.* Tell the person that you understand this is a difficult time. Avoid being judgmental, "You're suicidal over that? You're wasting my time!" is never a good intervention strategy. Watch for *either/or* thinking. This is seen most often in a crisis and is represented by "either X must happen or I'm going to kill myself" (a false dichotomy). In cases of either/or, you must present the person with realistic and viable options. For example, "Either my girlfriend has to come here or I'm going to kill myself!" Officer: "Your girlfriend is in the emergency room being treated for her injuries. She cannot come here. Here are some things that are possible . . ."

11. *Do not be afraid to bring the issue of suicide into the open.* Ask about the length of time that the person has felt like killing himself, whether he has had previous thoughts of suicide, whether he has attempted suicide in the past (if so, by what means), his substance use, and whether he has a suicide plan: "Have you thought about how you might kill yourself?"

12. *Avoid deception whenever possible.* Unless necessary or you are directed to provide deceptive information for tactical reasons, avoid deception. It is often difficult to recall previously made untrue statements during the course of conversation. Nearly every issue can be discussed honestly. Do not hesitate to say "I don't know" or "I'm uncertain about that" if the person asks a question you cannot answer. What circumstances would justify providing deceptive information? If life is at stake and no other option exists.
13. *Avoid challenges.* "You don't have the guts to kill yourself!" has never been a very successful intervention when interacting with a suicidal person.
14. *Use authority when appropriate.* An order to "put the gun down now!" may stop a person from following through on a suicidal intention and engaging behavior (like pulling the trigger) when rapport has failed. Consider using a *short order* when appropriate (chapter 9).
15. *Personal inquiries and self-disclosure.* If the person begins to ask you questions that become too personal, such as *where do you live*, *where do your kids go to school*, and so on, advise the person that you are interested in him. This redirects the conversation. Is it ever appropriate to discuss your experiences? Yes, but keep it limited and refocus on the person. For example, a person who is suicidal because his business failed may respond well to you sharing information that your father once had a business that failed. You can inform the person that your dad struggled for a time, but things improved. Follow-up with something like "Let's talk about how this might happen for you." Build upon the discussion.
16. *Provide realistic hope.* Throughout your discussion, talk about the person's issues, views, and when appropriate, introduce alternatives, "I'm wondering if you've thought about . . ." Inform the person that you can arrange for him to meet people who will work with him to address his problems. Assure him that you have arranged assistance for others in similar situations. Realistic hope involves helping the person see beyond the current circumstances. It explores the *possible* and the *potential*. Inform the person that (1) even if he believes there is no way out, others can help, (2) specially trained people may be able to help in ways not yet imagined, and (3) the future could be very different from the current circumstances.

17. *Do not argue.* Arguing is seldom helpful and it can lead to angry exchanges and impulsive behavior. It is frequently better to ameliorate any disagreements, maintain rapport, and provide realistic hope.

18. *Maintain your psychological boundary.* Do not allow yourself to become angry. It's easy to become tired, tense, and frustrated, especially if the interaction endures for a lengthy period of time. If you begin to have thoughts like "either accept help or kill yourself, I just want this over" it is time to take a deep breath and try to relax. If successful, reengage the person. If this does not work, bring another person into the interaction and take a break. You can introduce another police officer or negotiator by informing the person that you need a little time to refresh yourself. Appropriately introduce the person taking over for you. You can return to the interaction when you are ready.

19. *Psychological boundary.* Human beings have killed themselves for as long as there is recorded history. When interacting with persons who are suicidal, keep in mind that all you can do is to support them and help them explore options. You cannot read minds or control behaviors. Persons who are suicidal will eventually decide their course of action. This is because by the time persons who are suicidal come to the attention of the police, officers may have no or little ability to control the situation. Instead, officers can only attempt to influence the person and thereby hope to increase the probability of a positive outcome. There are no guarantees. You cannot assume responsibility for the life of the person, even if the rescuer part of you might like to. What is your responsibility to a suicidal person?...to do your best.

20. *Resolution.* By far, most police interactions with persons who are suicidal end in a desirable way, with the person cooperating and receiving treatment by mental health professionals. Many persons that are feeling suicidal readily accept the help of police officers. Some do not. Some will be taken into custody by forceful action. Most times the force needed is minimal. Other times it may involve the use of less than lethal weapons and the SWAT team. Some will compel suicide by cop. Others will, in spite of your best efforts, attempt or complete suicide during your interaction and in your presence.

For police officers, interacting with persons who are suicidal is an unavoidable occupational stressor. Officers should think about the likely psychological issues that can arise after a suicidal person call. How would you cope with the aftermath of a person who completes suicide in your presence? What are the possible short and long term effects of witnessing a suicide? These are questions that should be considered by all officers.

Suicidal Call Resolution

In cases where the person is at least somewhat cooperative, there are a number of resolutions possible. After your interaction and field assessment,

1. if you determine that no imminent threat of suicide exists, you may leave the person as you found him, contact family or friends, provide referrals, transport him to a support or mental health agency, or arrange for another appropriate disposition;
2. if you are uncertain whether an imminent threat of suicide exists, you should contact someone who can assist you, such as an officer specially trained in mental illness crisis intervention or your supervisor;
3. if you conclude that an imminent threat of suicide exists, ask the person if he will accept assistance. If yes, follow your department policy for transport. In this case, even though the person represents an imminent threat for suicide, you do not need to take the person into involuntary custody;
4. if you conclude that an imminent threat of suicide exists and the person will not accept assistance, you must initiate the emergency procedure.

C.R.S. 27-65-105 *Emergency Procedure*

Every state has a provision for the emergency involuntary detention, evaluation, and treatment of a person who is mentally ill and meets certain criteria. In Colorado, this provision is C.R.S. 27-65-105, *Emergency procedure* (formerly C.R.S. 27-10-105, repealed April 29, 2010). There are two ways in which the emergency procedure can be initiated: (1) through an affidavit sworn or affirmed before a judge and (2) by a police officer or other authorized person. The statutory criteria for initiation of the emergency procedure is specified below:

(a) (I) When any person appears to have a mental illness and, as a result of such mental illness, appears to be an imminent danger to others or to himself or herself or appears to be gravely disabled, then a person specified in subparagraph (II) of this paragraph (a), each of whom is referred to in this section as the 'intervening professional,' upon probable cause and with such assistance as may be required, may take the person into custody, or cause the person to be taken into custody, and placed in a facility designated or approved by the executive director for a seventy-two-hour treatment and evaluation.

(II) The following persons may effect a seventy-two-hour hold as provided in subparagraph (I) of this paragraph (a):

(A) A certified peace officer; . . ." (C.R.S. 27-65-105)

The statutory definition of *gravely disabled* is comprehensive and too lengthy to be reproduced here. Primarily, it represents a condition wherein a person, as a result of mental illness, is endangered by being incapable of appropriate self care. All officers should take the time to acquaint themselves with the statutory definition of this condition.

Once the emergency procedure is initiated, police officers should follow their department policy outlining security, transportation, and destination options. *All police agencies should have a policy outlining the implementation of the emergency procedure.*

The emergency procedure is sometimes erroneously thought of as a *seventy-two hour hold*. It is erroneous because those detained under this statute will not necessarily be held for seventy-two hours. A person detained under the emergency procedure will be released prior to seventy-two hours if he or she is assessed to no longer present a danger to self or others, or is no longer considered gravely disabled. The release prior to the seventy-two hour provision authorized under C.R.S. 27-65-105 corresponds with the reigning treatment ethic in the field of mental health: *least amount of medication* in the *least restrictive environment.*

Short and Long Term Involuntary Treatment

What if a person is held for seventy-two hours, receives emergency treatment and evaluation, and continues to present a danger to self or others, or remains gravely disabled? In Colorado, if a person detained under the emergency procedure remains a danger to self or others, or gravely disabled after seventy-two hours, and refuses voluntary treatment, he may be certified for involuntary short-term treatment for no longer than an additional three months. If necessary, this certification can be extended for another three months. If this period of treatment proves insufficient, involuntary long-term treatment can be initiated after at least five consecutive months of involuntary short-term treatment.

Every state has provisions for the involuntary short and long term care of persons who are mentally ill and present a danger to self or others, or are gravely mentally ill.

Police Officer Suicide

Some police officers kill themselves. They kill themselves mostly by firearms. This is no surprise as police officers have ready access to firearms.

Police suicide rates in America have traditionally been reported as being two to three times that of the general population. This estimate was based upon the belief that between 400 to 450 police officers completed suicide each year. These numbers have never been confirmed and they are not supported by recent research. Specialized studies conducted from 2008 through 2012 concluded that there were 141 police officer suicides in 2008, 143 in 2009, 147 in 2010, 146 in 2011, and 126 in 2012 (O'Hara and Violanti, 2013). Although every suicide is a tragedy, and a police officer suicide is especially painful to those in policing, these numbers are significantly lower than some earlier estimates.

Some research suggests that when certain variables such as State of residence, age, gender, race, and marital status are taken into consideration, suicide rates for police officers may be as much as 26 percent lower than the general population (Aamodt and Werlick, 2001). If this is accurate, the fact that most police officer candidates are psychologically assessed for emotional stability may prove to be a factor. Other research suggests that the police officer suicide rate is higher than the general population.

The diverse conclusions of past police-suicide research highlight the difficulty inherent in conducting such research. A major problem is data collection. There is no requirement on the part of police agencies to report officer suicides to a central database. There is no governmental agency or private organization responsible for recording police suicides. Therefore, researchers must rely on various sources for data including police organization websites, news reports, social media systems, individual police agencies, and police officers themselves. For a comprehensive discussion of police suicide and police suicide-related issues see Violanti, et al (2011).

Police officers should not avoid other officers that they think might be suicidal. If officers feel another officer may be suicidal, contact should be initiated. During the contact, discuss your observations. *Do not hesitate to bring the subject of suicide into the open.* Conduct a field assessment and follow through on your observations. If you feel that the officer is imminently suicidal, do not leave the officer alone. Arrange for professional help (including involuntary treatment and evaluation if necessary). If the officer is not imminently suicidal, spend some time together. Listen and provide emotional support. Contact or encourage the officer to contact the police psychologist, the peer support team, the employee assistance program, clergy, or a family member. The point is, *do not hesitate to do something.* You may save a life.

Police Officer Suicide Risk Factors

There are certain factors that increase the probability that a police officer will suicide (most of these factors apply to all persons). The greater the number of risk factors present, the greater the risk of suicide. Police officer suicide risk factors include:

- A diagnosis of depression, bipolar, anxiety, or psychotic disorder
- Veiled or outright threats of suicide.
- Development of a suicidal plan.
- Marital, money, and/or family problems.
- Recent or pending discipline, including possible termination.
- Over-developed sense of responsibility. Responsibility absorption.
- Frustration or embarrassment by some work-related event.
- Internal or criminal investigations.
- Allegations of wrongdoing; criminal charges.
- Assaults on an officer's integrity, reputation, or professionalism.
- Recent loss, such as divorce, relationship breakup, financial, etc.
- Little or no social support system.
- Uncharacteristic dramatic mood changes. Angry much of the time.
- Increased aggression toward the public. Citizen complaints.
- Feeling "down" or "trapped" with no way out.
- Feelings of hopelessness and helplessness.
- Feeling anxious, unable to sleep or sleeping all the time.
- History of problems with work or family stress.

- Making permanent alternative arrangements for pets or livestock.
- Increased alcohol use or other substance abuse/addiction.
- Family history of suicide and/or childhood maltreatment.
- Uncharacteristic acting out; increased impulsive tendencies.
- Diagnosis of physical illness or long-term effects of physical illness.
- Recent injury which causes chronic pain; overuse of medications.
- Disability that forces retirement or leaving the job.
- Self isolation: withdrawing from family, friends, and social events.
- Giving away treasured items. Saying "goodbye" in unusual manner.
- Easy access to firearms (a constant for police officers).
- Sudden sense of calm while circumstances have not changed.
- Unwillingness to seek help because of perceived stigma.

By knowing some of the risk factors involved in police officer suicide, you can help other officers, and help other officers to help themselves. You can also help yourself. Keep in mind that if you become suicidal, it is more likely that you are already acquainted with those most likely to assist you.

If you are feeling suicidal, whether this is a new feeling for you or you have been struggling with such feelings for some time, help yourself - *reach out now!* There are people who care. There are people that can help.

Police Officer Suicide: Primary and Secondary Danger

The primary danger of policing is comprised of the inherent risks of the job, such as working in motor vehicle traffic, confronting violent persons, and exposure to critical incidents. Sadly, there is an insidious and lesser known *secondary danger* in policing. This danger is often unspecified and seldom discussed. It is an artifact of the police culture and is frequently reinforced by police officers themselves. Secondary danger is the idea that equates "asking for help" with "personal and professional weakness." How serious is police secondary danger? So serious that some officers will choose suicide over asking for help.

For the years in which there is reasonably reliable data, the number of police officer suicides has consistently exceeded the number of officers killed by felonious assault or by accident. In most of these years, the number of police suicides has exceeded the number of officer deaths from felonious assault and accidents *combined*. This makes secondary danger and the accompanying propensity for suicide the number one killer of police officers.

The "Make it Safe" Police Officer Initiative

The "Make it Safe" Police Officer Initiative was developed in 2013. It is comprised of 12 elements designed to address the frequency of police officer suicide by changing the police culture, engaging proactive programs, removing perceived stigma in asking for help, and reducing secondary danger.

The "Make it Safe" Police Officer Initiative encourages:

(1) every officer to "self-monitor" and to take personal responsibility for his or her mental wellness.

(2) every officer to seek psychological support when confronting potentially overwhelming difficulties (officers do not have to "go it alone").

(3) every officer to diminish the sometimes deadly effects of secondary danger by reaching out to other officers known to be facing difficult circumstances.

(4) veteran and ranking officers to use their status to help reduce secondary danger (veteran and ranking officers can reduce secondary danger by openly discussing it, appropriately sharing selected personal experiences, avoiding the use of pejorative terms to describe officers seeking or engaging psychological support, and talking about the acceptability of seeking psychological support when confronting stressful circumstances).

(5) law enforcement administrators to better educate themselves about the nature of secondary danger and to take the lead in secondary danger reduction.

(6) law enforcement administrators to issue a departmental memo encouraging officers to engage psychological support services when confronting potentially overwhelming stress (the memo should include information about confidentiality and available support resources).

(7) basic training in stress management, stress inoculation, critical incidents, posttraumatic stress, police family dynamics, substance use and addiction, and the warning signs of depression and suicide.

(8) the development of programs that engage pre-emptive, early-warning, and periodic department-wide officer support interventions (for example, proactive annual check in, "early warning" policies designed to support officers displaying signs of stress, and regularly scheduled stress inoculation and critical incident stressor management training).

(9) agencies to initiate incident-specific protocols to support officers and their families when officers are involved in critical incidents.

(10) agencies to create appropriately structured, properly trained, and clinically supervised peer support teams.

(11) agencies to provide easy and confidential access to counseling and specialized police psychological support services.

(12) officers at all levels of the organization to enhance the agency climate so that others are encouraged to ask for help when experiencing psychological or emotional difficulties instead of keeping and acting out a deadly secret.

If law enforcement officers wish to do the best for themselves and other officers, it's time to make a change. It's time to make a difference.

For more information about the "Make it Safe" Police Officer Initiative visit *www.jackdigliani.com*

Chapter 11

Life After a Police Career

Unless officers die during their police career, they will again become civilians. Like entering policing, leaving policing involves a psychological transition.

There are two ways in which police officers transition to civilian life: involuntarily and voluntarily. Involuntary departure from police service includes: (1) termination of employment for cause and (2) separation due to a developed disability.

When officers are terminated for cause, it usually involves a prior *due process*. Within due process, officers have an opportunity to address the circumstances for which they may be terminated. Once terminated, due process often includes a termination-appeal procedure. However, there are still some police agencies where due process is not required. In these agencies, officers serve at the discretion of the chief or sheriff, and they can be terminated at will. Termination from agencies without a due process requirement can occur for any reason.

Disability, either total or occupational, can result from illness or injury, including psychological injury caused by traumatic exposure. In cases of disability, officers often struggle with the premature ending of their career.

Depression and grief are frequently observed when disability ends an officer's career. The grief experienced in such cases is twofold: grief for the loss of career and all that goes with it (status, income, benefits, comradeship, etc), and grief for the loss of the "healthy self." The experience of grief in response to the loss of health is somewhat unique. Some officers experience mild sadness, while others develop major depression. Much depends upon the disability, stage of the officer's career, age of the officer, personality factors, family situation, financial circumstances, and other variables. The intensity of grief following the disability may or may not correspond with an outside assessment of the degree of disability. It is possible to experience a severe psychological disorder in response to what appears to others as a mild disability. Separately, the loss of a career or the loss of health can cause significant psychological distress. The loss of both simultaneously can be devastating.

Voluntary departure involves leaving policing on one's own accord. There are many reasons why officers choose to leave policing, including to pursue other interests, retirement, and even to avoid being fired. Whatever the reason for departure, officers must consider the future. Everyone has heard the old adage, "You should retire to something, not from something." This is excellent advice, and it is as applicable to any reason for leaving policing as it is for retirement.

Many officers have successfully moved beyond policing careers. Yes, there is life after policing. Some officers find fulfillment in new career challenges. Officers in this category transition to become politicians, lawyers, real estate agents, business owners, school bus drivers, and even psychologists.

Some officers transition into full retirement. These officers are not interested in launching new careers. Instead, they find fulfillment in family, friends, travel, community service, and other endeavors. The important thing in retirement is to do something. It should be something that is personally fulfilling and meaningful. For many former officers, volunteering for favorite charities, organizations, or worthy causes fills the bill.

Role Transition

Regardless of the type of departure from policing, successfully managing the transition means dealing with the loss of the police role. For some officers, leaving policing is a welcomed change. For most, it is a challenge. Even officers that welcome the transition to civilian life will acknowledge missing at least part of the job.

Many officers have lived the "cop life" for so long that they do not know how to live any other way. This is reflected in their continued practice of carrying a concealed firearm, meeting with the "boys" and the "sisters," and hanging around the police station. Normally, as the length of time increases from the date of departure, these behaviors decrease. Slowly, for most officers, the "ownership" of the police agency is given over to the next generation of officers and the attachment to the police role diminishes.

The loss of the officer's role can also affect spouses. Some wives of retired police officers talk about their husbands as if they were still police officers. There seems to be a vicarious social status enjoyed by these women; many find the status difficult to relinquish. For example, one wife consistently referred to her retired officer husband as "the lieutenant." This was interesting because she would do this only in public. Another wife of a former police officer, upon his transition to new car salesman, complained, "I used to be somebody. I was the wife of a police officer." Evidently, she did not derive similar satisfaction from being the wife of a car salesman. Although the husband's job change was not the only factor, this couple divorced about a year after he left the police department. Clearly, wives, like officers, sometimes struggle with the idea that the lost police role is tantamount to not being a "big shot" (as one officer put it) any longer. Children of police officers can have similar experiences.

Many officers struggle with the timing of retirement. Although there are no strict rules for when an officer should retire, the retirement system of an officer's agency often influences this decision. There are still some police departments with a fixed-benefit retirement system. In these agencies, if officers work for a specified number of years (usually twenty or twenty-five), they receive a percentage of their active duty salary upon retirement. For most, this is collectable immediately upon retirement and is a lifetime benefit. It is unusual to see officers work much past twenty to twenty-five years in these departments. This is because after the retirement-eligible years of service, officers are effectively working for a portion of their salary (the amount difference between their salary and what they would receive in retirement). Some officers with a fixed-benefit retirement will retire from their original agency and start a new career with another police or sheriff's department.

In agencies that provide a contributory benefit for retirement, such as the 401K system, it is not unusual to see officers with more than thirty-five years of service. This system encourages longevity because the longer that officers work, the more money is accumulated. Unlike a fixed benefit retirement, when 401K money is exhausted, there is no further retirement benefit. Add this to the fact that most police officers do not pay into social security (so they lack that benefit), and it is easy to see why some officers will work for many years in the same agency with this type of retirement system.

Successful Retirement

For successful retirement from policing, officers need to prepare. Although having sufficient funds is important, this preparation should go beyond financial considerations. Officers need to prepare psychologically. This is best accomplished by life-by-design considerations and should begin years before actual departure. To better decide when you should retire and to psychologically prepare for the transition out of policing, officers should consider the following Retirement Checklist:

1. Have you planned your financial circumstances to meet your retirement needs?
2. Have you discussed your retirement with your family? How will it affect their lives?
3. Have you arranged for medical insurance benefits?
4. Is it time for a change? Have you given all that you reasonably can to policing?
5. Are you still connected to policing or have you checked out years ago? If you are still connected and it is not time for a change, continue your career. If you have checked out and it is not time for a change, reclaim your career. If it is time for a change, pursue retirement. *Do not end your successful police career as a ROD (Retired on Duty) officer.*
6. Are you prepared to lose the status and prestige associated with being a police officer?
7. Have you thought about who you are without the badge? What will be your personal identification after retirement? Will "retiree" or "retired police officer" work for you? If not, what will you put in its place? For some officers, being a retired police officer is enough. For others, it is not. For the latter, the identity of functioning in a new role can be helpful, such as business owner, volunteer, sports enthusiast, grandparent, hiker, and so on. It can be just about anything, as long as it feels right.
8. How will you occupy the time normally spent at work? Hopefully, not with food, alcohol, or computer games. Many officers that have never had a serious problem with overeating, drinking too much, and spending unproductive days in front of a computer, develop these problems following retirement.
9. Following retirement, there is frequently some measure of boredom. Most officers will deny this. They say things like "I'm busier now than when I was working." It is seldom true. I am uncertain why it is so difficult for retired officers to admit that their lives have slowed down.

After all, isn't that part of the reason for retirement? Of course, this may not be true for all former officers. It is likely that some retired officers are busier retired than when working. But for most of them, things slow down. Newly retired officers frequently report feeling as if a great weight has been removed from their shoulders (even if they are busier, what is keeping them busy is often less stressful than policing). The stress reduction experienced by most officers upon retirement is often remarkable.

10. Time structuring and time management is important in retirement. Even the pleasure of travel, sports, activities, and not having to work eventually wears off. This is especially true if many of the officer's friends are still working. Managing time and making it meaningful is a major challenge of retirement.

11. Have you prepared yourself for other activities? Will you begin another career, pursue a hobby, or pursue a dream? Will it be meaningful?

12. How will you continue to contribute to your community? After a career of public service, many officers enjoy continuing community service.

Responding to these questions and thinking about these issues will better prepare officers for retirement. As mentioned, retirement is a transition. Transitions take time. Once retired, be patient. It may take some time to find your retirement rhythm.

Retirement and Emotional Abandonment

Upon retirement, some officers report feeling emotionally abandoned by the department staff and former coworkers. They express these feelings in statements such as "My department has forgotten me" and "I guess when you're gone, you're gone!" For these retired officers, it seems that once the retirement ceremony ended, so did the years of work-group camaraderie and support. This can be especially distressing for officers who feel that they have given decades of honorable service to the agency, only to be swiftly forgotten.

To address this issue, some police agencies have developed programs which actively involve retired officers. These programs include volunteer services and assignments, social events, alumni associations, and ongoing access to the police building (which encourages ongoing transaction with working police personnel). However, as desirable as these programs have proven to be, most departments lack them.

Retired officers that feel emotionally abandoned and have a desire to reconnect with their agency or former coworkers have at least two options: (1) wait for someone to reach out to them or (2) initiate behavior that is designed to maintain or reestablish the supportive relationships which once existed. As you might guess, pursuing option two significantly increases the probability of reconnection. The actual behaviors initiated under option two would depend upon the desired outcome. Therefore, a desire to stay in contact with specific former coworkers might involve arranging a breakfast meeting at a favorite restaurant. Such a meeting might evolve into a standing coffee gathering . . . an excellent way to stay connected with friends. Planning and inviting others to common interest activities is another great way to keep in touch. The point is, as a retired officer, if you feel emotionally abandoned, do not suffer in silence or wait for others to remedy the situation. Instead, take the initiative and do something about it. Your efforts may not result in exactly the outcome you want, but it is likely that it will be good. Remember, the outcome does not have to be perfect to be ok. Try again if things do not first turn out as you hoped.

If you are a working officer and have had close ties with a now retired officer, you should consider reaching out. The reach out does not have to be anything elaborate, an occasional telephone conversation or invitation for coffee will do. Even if the retired officer does not feel emotionally abandoned, your efforts will almost certainly be appreciated. Keep in mind that when you reach out, you honor the service and contributions of a retired officer who made some difference in your life and police career. Reaching out to a retired officer that meant something special to you is a very good thing to do, for both of you.

Retirement and Marriage

If married, retirement will normally bring the couple back to the beginning. The kids, if any, are usually out of the house. The couple, as when first married, is back to living as a couple. The difference this time is that there is no job to go to. This means a lot of unprecedented couples time. In 1984, psychologist John Stratton said that for police marriages, retirement can be a "time of friction or a time of rediscovery" (284). This is as true today as it was then. As Stratton reported, one police wife put it this way when asked how it felt to have her husband home. She answered, "Great, I went out and got a job." Another said, "I took him for better or for worse, but not for lunch" (284).

Following retirement, couples should expect an adjustment period. Work to make retirement a couple bonding experience and a new phase of your lives together. Do not allow the golden years of retirement to distance the intimacy in your relationship.

My FCPS Retirement

I retired from FCPS in August, 2001. When I decided to leave, I knew that I was leaving my police career behind. Although as the FCPS Director of Human Services I had not been in a field assignment for the past eleven years, I could dress in uniform at any time and work a patrol district. I did just that on New Years' Eve of the 1999-2000 millennia. I thought this was a good idea in the event that some of the dire predictions of the time came to pass. However, with retirement, I would never be able to do this again. I would no longer be a police officer. Leaving FCPS would mean a life transition.

My transition from police officer to civilian was likely made easier by my last police assignment. For over a decade prior to retirement, I was serving as the FCPS police psychologist, working in civilian clothes and driving an unmarked police car. Still, after retirement, I missed being part of FCPS. I expected these feelings to diminish over time, and as life would have it, they did. I remained retired for about eighteen months. It was an excellent respite. In 2004, I decided to return to work. I am now in another phase of my career, a police psychologist in contract and private practice.

I continue to maintain contact with many of my former coworkers and working-officer friends.

Chapter 12

Reflections of a Police Psychologist

I have been fortunate to have had the opportunity to combine two of my most significant interests, police work and psychology, into a single career. I am uncertain whether most people have such an opportunity. The following reflections are the result of working in these combined professions. They are not presented in any particular order. They are simply a collection of thoughts that I feel bear some significance to those in policing. Similar to many ideas and issues expressed in this book, they may have relevance to those working outside of policing.

Police Officer-Husband Modes of Transaction

Have you ever tried to assist your wife with a problem that *she* brought to *you*, only to have her become upset when you provided problem solutions? Did it seem like she became more frustrated each time you told her how to solve the problem? If you answered "yes" to either of these questions, it is most likely that you have unwittingly violated the *mode zone*.

Police officers have at least two possible transactional modes when it comes to discussing problems presented by their wives. There is the *cop mode* and the *husband mode*.

In the cop mode the officer transacts with his wife in a manner similar to that involving any citizen: when she presents a problem, he fixes the problem, tells her how to fix the problem, or advises that he cannot help.

In the husband mode the officer listens to his wife as she describes the problem. He tries to understand her and supports her efforts to explore, discuss, and address the problem. He does not try to fix things. He helps her to work through it in her own way. This may include a request from her for further husband involvement.

Over the years, I have learned that for the most part when wives bring up a problem for discussion, they are seeking their husbands and not a police officer . . . good to know.

When your wife is looking for her husband, and finds only the cop, you can rest assured that she will leave the conversation feeling frustrated, disappointed, and maybe angry. Too frequently, wives of police officers have reported feeling minimized and "treated like a child" when spoken to in the cop mode by their husbands. In essence, the wives responses are the result of transacting with a somewhat emotionally uninvolved police officer instead of a supportive and empathetic husband. To avoid an unintentional excursion into the cop mode, keep in mind that most wives want and need their husbands when they are confronting difficulties. In such circumstances, cop mode will fall short and produce less than desirable outcomes.

The next time your wife comes to you with a problem, turn the transaction into something positive (regardless of the problem). You can strengthen your marriage and enhance intimacy by remaining in husband mode.

The characteristics of the "cop" and the "husband" transactional modes apply equally to unmarried police couples, female officers and their husbands, and gay and lesbian police couples. They can also be seen in other personal relationships, such as parent-child and friendships.

The development of cop mode is related to the defense mechanism *emotional insulation* (chapter 7) and appears to be an occupational hazard for police officers.

Counseling

Little is guaranteed in life. The same is true of counseling. In counseling, a psychologist can guarantee only effort. Effort is not result. The result of counseling is dependent upon several things, not the least of which is the person seeking assistance.

Accepting responsibility for change is one of the first challenges for persons entering counseling. When confronting a problem or seeking changes, persons must ask themselves, "What role am I playing in the maintenance of this problem?" The path for improvement becomes clearer when this question is honestly addressed.

Counseling is founded upon the premise that people can do something other than what they do. Without this premise, there would be no reason to enter counseling - there would be no hope for change. Change can be difficult. Although change can be difficult, change is possible. The difficulty of change should never be confused with the possibility of change. I like to think of it this way, *change may be difficult but it is not impossible*. Even the remnants of an undesirable childhood can be altered. This is also true for the seeming enduring effects of traumatic life experiences.

Perception and Insight

Many of us can readily perceive the changes needed in the lives of our friends, family members, and others. It is easy to see that others should stop drinking, stop bullying, start treating others more kindly, and so on. So why do we have such a difficult time seeing these things in ourselves? There are many reasons. The self-centered perspective is one of the most important. The self-centered perspective is characterized by seeing things only from your point of view. Why is this so important? It is important because our perspective drives our behavior.

While it is normal to see things from a personal point of view, most of us have a degree of self-insight and at least some ability to see things from the view of others. These abilities help us to see and understand the effects of our behavior. They allow us to continually assess ourselves and change things when necessary to make desired improvements. In this way, we learn from our experiences and develop wisdom as we move through life.

But this is not true of everyone. Some people lack insight and an ability to see things from other points of view. They consistently repeat behaviors that are harmful to themselves and others. They do not seem to learn from life experiences. They gain little wisdom. They are blinded by internalized dysfunctional principles such as, "A real man wins every argument" "Children should be seen and not heard," and "What kind of man (or woman) would I be if I did X."

Confronting and evaluating internalized principles and the behaviors founded upon them is a primary task of self-examination and personal growth. It is a fundamental goal of most counseling and self-help programs. The bottom line is, *avoid being blinded by a dysfunctional principle*. Blindly following some principle learned early in life that does little but cause trouble will make your adult life more difficult. It is much better to think about what is possible, instead of being locked into what has always been.

Confronting What You Fear

There is an old saying, "If you see a ghost and run, it will chase you. If you stop and look at it, it will disappear." This adage captures the essence of *confronting what you fear*. Although fear is normal and serves as a warning of impending danger, unreasonable fears limit and diminish life experiences. If you hope to overcome a fear and the associated anxiety, you must confront it (like our swimmer in chapter 2). To do otherwise allows the fear to continue.

In situations that produce fear, we have three fundamental choices: avoidance (stay away from what we fear), withdrawal (get away from what we fear), and confrontation (engage what we fear).

Avoidance and Withdrawal

Most of us deal with fear by avoidance or withdrawal. Avoidance or withdrawal are functional options and are excellent choices in many situations - avoiding a dark alley in a crime ridden neighborhood or withdrawing from a burning building are certainly wise choices. However, there are circumstances in which avoidance or withdrawal might not work as well - for a worker whose office is located on the 35th floor of a high-rise building, avoiding or withdrawing from the elevator due to a fear of confined spaces would undoubtedly make going to work more difficult.

When we avoid, we do not experience fear but the underlying fear remains. When we withdraw, the fear terminates in the present time but the underlying fear remains. Because the fear terminates following the withdrawal, the act of withdrawal is *negatively reinforced*. Negative reinforcement occurs whenever an uncomfortable feeling is terminated by some action. If withdrawal terminated the fear, the act of withdrawal is reinforced and thereby more likely to be repeated in fearful situations. Another way of saying this is that the act of withdrawal has become stronger.

Incidentally, negative reinforcement should not be confused with *punishment*. Punishment is the presentation of an aversive stimulus, such as spanking (positive punishment) or the removal of something desirable (negative punishment). When applied immediately following a behavior, punishment tends to suppress that behavior. When applied later, as in the popularized maternal admonishment to a child behaving badly, "Just wait until your father gets home!" the mom is relying upon the fact that the child will make the connection between the punishment and the act being punished. As punishment does not increase the likelihood of any particular behavior, it is not considered a reinforcer. One last word on negative reinforcement and punishment: as a parent, if you spank a child that is behaving badly and the child's undesirable behavior stops, you have been negatively reinforced for spanking. Therefore, *spanking is punishment for the child and negatively reinforcing for the parent.*

You may have to think about this for a while. However, it helps to explain why parents that spank are more likely to continue spanking. For reasons too complex to be specified here, spanking or any form of corporal punishment for child discipline is strongly discouraged.

Confrontation

If we confront what we fear in a manner that enhances our ability to cope with or overcome it, we become stronger and the fear subsides.

There are several ways to confront what you fear. The exposure therapies of *systematic desensitization, flooding*, and *response prevention* comprise one category of confrontation intervention.

Systematic desensitization (Wolpe, 1969) involves incremental exposure to the feared object or circumstance. It utilizes relaxation, reciprocal inhibition, and a stressor hierarchy. Briefly, it works like this. Persons wishing to confront their fears construct a fear hierarchy. At bottom of the list is the item least problematic; at the top, the most problematic. They learn relaxation techniques. In a relaxed state, they confront the items listed on the hierarchy from least to most problematic. When the least problematic item no longer produces fear or the associated anxiety, the next item is addressed. This continues until the top item is addressed and no longer produces fear. Systematic desensitization is based upon the theory that a person can overcome fear by mastering incremental exposure to the feared object or circumstance. This is accomplished through the principle of reciprocal inhibition, the idea that a person cannot be relaxed and fearful simultaneously (relaxation inhibits the experience of fear and vice versa). An actual hierarchy might start with imagining the feared object or situation, then looking at pictures, and finally moving on to real-world exposures. Recently, and with great promise, virtual reality devices have been employed in systematic desensitization.

Another way to confront what you fear is by flooding. Flooding involves intense exposure to the feared object or circumstance. The exposure is maintained until the fear subsides. Securing persons fearful of tight spaces in an elevator until fear is no longer experienced is an example of flooding. Flooding is more traumatic than systematic desensitization and is not always the best way to confront fear. Flooding may be more appropriate in cases of mild fear and anxiety.

Flooding and systematic desensitization have been successful in the treatment of phobias, conditioned fear and anxiety responses, acute stress disorder, posttraumatic stress disorder, generalized anxiety, and other anxiety-related psychological disorders.

Like flooding and systematic desensitization, response prevention has demonstrated efficacy in the treatment of anxiety. Response prevention has a primary application in the treatment of the anxiety associated with obsessive-compulsive disorder (OCD). Obsessive-compulsive disorder is comprised of two basic elements; obsession (thought) and compulsion (behavior). In OCD, irrational thoughts create anxiety, while directed behaviors reduce it. For example, persons who cannot stop thinking of germs are driven by the thought to wash excessively (directed behavior). In this example of OCD, the thoughts of germs are the obsession, while the washing is the compulsion. A complicating factor in OCD is that the compulsion is negatively reinforced by the reduction of anxiety associated with the irrational obsessional thought.

In response prevention, the person is prevented from engaging the compulsive behavior. Therefore, the person is compelled to cope with the obsession without the compulsion. Eventually, the person comes to understand that the obsession represents no real danger. This results in a reduction of obsessional thought and a realization that the compulsive behavior is unnecessary.

You can think of it this way: if obsessional anxiety is relieved by engaging the compulsion, the compulsive behavior gains strength (it is negatively reinforced). If obsessional anxiety is successfully confronted, the person gains strength. As the person becomes stronger, the intensity of the obsession diminishes. The power of the obsession to drive the compulsion is weakened, and neither the obsession nor the compulsion remains dominant in the person's life.

It is possible to experience obsessions without overt compulsions. In such cases, the obsession may drive mental exercises or mental rituals which function to reduce the anxiety produced by the obsession (Null, 2006).

Fear and Behavior

Fear has an interesting relationship with behavior. Most of us have, at some times in our lives, acted out of fear. At other times, we have acted in spite of fear. This is as true for police officers as it is for anyone else.

Some police officers struggle with the emotion of fear. They have an idea that once they become police officers, they should never experience fear. This is irrational. There is no badge that will keep anyone from ever experiencing fear. For officers, being fearful at times is normal. Experienced officers cope with fear by learning to act while fearful. If the actions of officers are reasonable and appropriate, they should not punish themselves for sometimes feeling afraid. No one is immune from fear. Even seemingly fearless persons will experience fear in certain circumstances. Police officers should accept this fact and move forward with their careers.

Don't Have to Like It, Just Have to Do It

In life there are many things that are easy to dislike. Consider the colonoscopy. This procedure is not something most people look forward to. So why do we undergo the procedure? We do it because we value the outcome. *We do it, but we don't like it.* Flu shots, same thing. We do it because we value the outcome. Imagine if we had to like having a colonoscopy before consenting to have one. It seems a bit too much to ask.

The same is true for things outside of colonoscopies and flu shots. For example, we don't have to like all the classes required to obtain a degree but if we wish to graduate, we have to take them. We don't have to like vegetables but if we desire their nutritional benefits, we have to eat them.

People sometimes get confused about having to *like* something in order to *do* something. They think that in order to bring about positive change, they have to learn to like something they dislike. This is not true. We can do things solely because we desire the outcome; we can work through something we dislike in order to achieve something we like. Understanding this makes doing things once thought of as impossible, possible (like quitting smoking).

When tempered with positive values and a sense of social responsibility, doing something you dislike to achieve something desirable can produce very good outcomes. To reap the benefits of doing something for a desirable outcome, *you don't have to like it; you just have to do it.*

Possibility, Probability, and Contingency

Have you ever walked down a country lane in autumn and looked up just in time to see a leaf falling gently to the ground? Or walked outside in the winter and noticed one specific snowflake on your hand, mitten, or glove? Have you ever wondered about all the things that had to happen to make that particular experience possible?

We live in a world of contingency. The contingencies of everyday life are embedded within possibilities and probabilities. Being so, they are well disguised. This means that the probability of any particular day being much like any other day is quite high. So high in fact, that we sometimes complain about "nothing ever happening" or being "stuck in the same ol' routine." It is only under unusual circumstances that we get to see and come to appreciate the contingent nature of the world. When this happens, we say things like "Who would have ever thought this was possible!" and "What are the odds!"

Take the case of Ann Elizabeth Hodges (1923-1972). Ann was napping inside her home in Sylacauga (Oak Grove), Alabama, on November 30, 1954. Around 6:46 p.m., she was awakened by a loud noise and shortly thereafter felt a pain on her left side. It took a while, but she soon realized that a meteorite fragment had crashed through the roof of her home. It bounced off a wooden radio in the living room and struck her in the left hip. The meteorite weighted about 8.5 pounds. Ann's case was the first well-authenticated injury to a person caused by an extraterrestrial object (Povenmire, 1995). As far as contingencies go, can you imagine all that had to happen for Ann to be struck by this particular fragment of meteorite? The contingencies involved in observing a leaf falling from a tree pale in comparison (although the falling leaf is no less contingent). Considering that the Hodges meteorite, as it came to be known, is *billions* of years old (Taylor, 2001) and that it had been zooming around the universe for all that time, makes the odds of it striking Ann incalculable. Still, it happened.

Understanding contingencies helps to answer the question, "Why me?" The answer to this question becomes clearer as our understanding of the universe deepens. The answer to "why me?" is that we live in a contingent universe. In a contingent universe, it makes just as much sense to ask, "Why not me?" In a contingent universe, it's not always the other guy, sometimes it's us - and consider, it's never the "other guy" to the other guy.

The human perception of, and emotional responses to, life's probability is relative. For example, imagine that ten thousand people are gathered in an arena. Each person holds a piece of paper. On the paper is a number ranging from one to ten thousand. A person not included in the group has a bin that contains ten thousand pieces of paper. Each piece of paper in the bin is numbered from one to ten thousand. The person not included in the group will draw a single piece of paper from the bin. The person in the group holding the number indicated on the piece of paper drawn from the bin will win one million dollars. This seems simple enough. It is nothing more than a raffle with the odds of winning being one in ten thousand. Now think of the experience of the person who will draw the number. For him, it is "Well, someone has to win. It will be one of these ten thousand people. Ho hum." He knows that the probability of someone winning the one million dollars is 100 percent. Contrast this to the experience of the person whose number is drawn. For that person, it can be life changing. It is "Wow, me? Why me!?" In fact, the odds of winning this raffle were so small that the winner will likely need to answer the "why me" question. Depending upon his or her personal beliefs, the answer will range from *pure chance* or *dumb luck* (after all, someone had to win) to divine intervention. For those who did not win, the question "Why not me?" will likely be answered in terms of the probability; "Well, look at the odds. What chance did I have?" No matter. Each of the ten thousand and one people involved in the drawing will have had some personal experience. The point is this: life's experiences look and feel different depending on one's perspective, position, and involvement.

The *relativity principle* underlies everyday human experiences. There is such a high probability that today will be like most others that we come to rely on and expect what is normal. When events, whether good or bad, defy the probability, we are exposed and unprotected from perceptions of contingency. This is likely the only meaningful way that the contingent nature of the universe is truly experienced. This exposure is a consistent component of the experiences encountered in critical incidents.

To the universe, all events are neutral. It is only how events relate to human endeavors that values are assigned. This is why we can have *good* weather and *bad* weather. Really, isn't weather just weather? Weather is perceived as good or bad depending upon how it affects individuals. So, the same rainstorm that is good for the farmer can be bad for the camper; but in the universal scheme of things it is just a rainstorm.

Many persons recognize contingent events by saying things like "I guess I was just in the right place at the right time." Interestingly, such events seem to be equally well explained by any combination of the right-wrong and place-time dichotomies: *the wrong place at the right time, the right place at the wrong time,* and *the wrong place at the wrong time.*

Sometimes contingencies come together to create the perfect storm. When this happens, the result can be tragic. This is because despite our best efforts, contingencies cannot be entirely anticipated or controlled. Even with complete life-by-design, the unanticipated can occur. This means that life involves unavoidable risk. *Risk* is as good as it gets for living organisms.

Recognizing the risk feature of human existence helps persons to maintain a more appropriate life perspective. Every person everyday lives within life's contingencies. Many of our everyday experiences are the result of colliding contingencies. We do not notice or indentify them as such due to their frequency of occurrence or lack of personal importance. It is only when the consequences are noticeably and relatively good or bad that we are forced to acknowledge the contingent nature of life.

The fact that some contingencies may result in undesirable outcomes should not discourage participation in life. To become obsessed with thoughts of negative outcomes due to fears of what might happen is to limit life. If your life feels restricted, bound, or otherwise stunted, you can enhance it by assuming reasonable and calculated risk. This idea is summarized in the often stated anthem "Go for it!"

Decision Making

Most persons find it difficult to decide some things some of the time. This is normal and part of everyday life. Some persons find it difficult to decide most things most of the time. This can become problematic and it can interfere with a normal life.

Difficulty in making decisions is frequently correlated with anxiety: the greater the anxiety, the more difficult the decision making. As journalist Daniel Smith, a long time sufferer of elevated anxiety put it, "(anxiety) is a petty monster able to work such humdrum tricks as paralyzing you over salad, convincing you that a choice between blue cheese and vinaigrette is as dire as that between life and death" (2012).

Even in cases where elevated anxiety is not an issue, some persons have difficulty making decisions. Reasons for this include: a desire to avoid responsibility for consequences, the experience of lower levels of anxiety, some or all other options may be lost once a decision is made, and the attractiveness of available options (making it difficult to choose any one).

The attractiveness of available options can literally paralyze decision making, but it is not the only cause of selection indecisiveness. Frequently, the attractiveness of any available option is offset by some real or imagined undesirable component that accompanies the attractive option. For example, the attractiveness of an evening out with friends is normally accompanied by increased monetary expenditure. Most attractive options are like this. Once selected, they come with the good and the not so good. This makes most options imperfect. It is the reason why most decisions involve *selecting from imperfect options*.

Decision Making and Conflict

If a person has to select from two equally attractive options, an *approach-approach* conflict exists. In an approach-approach conflict, decision making is difficult because selecting one desirable option locks out the other desirable option.

If a single option includes desirable and undesirable components, an *approach-avoidance* conflict ensues. In this type of conflict, a person might consider selecting (approach) the option due to its attractiveness, only to be repulsed by its undesirable aspects (avoidance). Approach-approach and approach-avoidance conflicts exist in all areas of life.

It is also possible to experience an *avoidance-avoidance* and a *double approach-avoidance* conflict (Lewin, 1935). All variations of approach and avoidance conflicts frequently result in a state of decision deadlock.

The Right Decision

Searching for the "right decision" is often frustrating and sometimes stifling. This is because in most cases, there is no one right decision. There are only decisions that lead to various outcomes; and the outcomes may include undesirable and unanticipated consequences.

In major life decisions, no matter what is decided, persons should prepare themselves to question their decision at some future time. Self-questioning a decision of some magnitude does not always happen, but it should not be a surprise if it does. For example, a person who spends an entire career in an unsatisfying job, might, upon retirement, question the decision to remain in the job for so many years. Correspondingly, a person that quit a job early in a career might wonder what life would have been like had he decided to stay. The same is true for marriages. Many married persons live with the idea that "I should have left years ago" while many divorced persons wonder if "maybe I should have tried harder to make my marriage work." Interestingly, the degree of self-questioning seems to be negatively correlated with the perceived desirability of the results produced by the decision; the more desirable the actual outcomes - the less degree of self-questioning.

It is normal to wonder about the probable results of the roads not taken. But be careful, such speculation frequently takes on a hue of fantasy. That is, it is often imagined that the roads not taken would have been much better than they likely would have been if actually chosen.

Not Perfect, But Ok

The outcome of most decisions will not be perfect (depending upon your definition), but is it ok? If it is ok, we can move forward to consider additional options. Sometimes, regardless of effort, ok is the best we can achieve. For some things, *not perfect, but ok* may be as good as it gets. Life by design (chapter 3) involves not getting stalled or stuck by an unreasonable expectation or pursuit of perfection.

Magic 8-Ball

When confronting difficult circumstances, many officers have come to my office and asked, "What should I do?" In my effort to never be without an answer, I have a Magic 8-Ball. If you shake it and turn it upside down, it provides a response to any question. The Magic 8-Ball was a gift from my wife. She must have recognized the daily dilemmas inherent in a psychologist's professional life. At times, in appropriate circumstances and with appropriate humor, I consult the Magic 8-Ball to answer officers' questions. It *always* comes up the same, *outlook unclear*. After a well earned laugh, the officer and I begin the real work. I explain that in nearly everyone's life, there are those who would be happy to tell us what to do. I then ask if there are people like this in their lives. I have never had a person say "no." I ask how helpful these people have been. As you might guess (after all, they are in my office) their response is always something like "not very helpful." I am never surprised by this response. Most of us cannot simply follow advice that usually comes in the form of "Well, you should..." or "If I were you, I would...." We like to decide for ourselves. We like to decide for ourselves because there is something personally gratifying in making our own decisions.

When officers are unsure about what to do, I often encourage them to think backward until they are sure about something. It is from this point that we can reliably move forward. For example, one thing that most officers are sure of when they think backward is that the circumstances that brought them to my office are no longer acceptable.

Mandated Counseling and Fitness-for-duty Evaluations

At times, it becomes necessary to mandate officers into counseling. If a police agency does not have a staff psychologist, a mental health professional outside the agency is often utilized. Mandating officers to counseling is appropriate when significant concerns for their mental health arise and they refuse to seek counseling voluntarily. Ordering officers to counseling is different than ordering officers to undergo a psychological fitness-for-duty evaluation (FFDE).

A psychological FFDE is ordered in cases where the agency has a genuine concern pertaining to officers' ability to appropriately perform their duties due to their current state of mental health. In mandated psychological FFDEs, the privilege of confidentiality is held by the police agency. The evaluating psychologist completes the evaluation and reports the findings to the department. Three determinations are possible: (1) the officer is fit for duty, (2) the officer is not fit for duty, or (3) the officer is not fit for full duty but capable of modified duty. If officers are found fit for duty, they return to work. This finding may include a recommendation for ongoing counseling.

If officers are found unfit for duty, they are placed on leave and psychological intervention is initiated. Following treatment, they are reevaluated. If found fit for duty on reevaluation, they return to work. If reevaluated as unfit for duty, other options must be considered. Other options include additional therapy and subsequent reevaluation, additional therapy with modified duty and reevaluation, and occupational or total disability.

Fitness for duty circumstances can become complex. They can involve retirement administrators, risk management, city personnel departments, second opinions from other clinicians, police union representatives, property rights, attorneys, and the court system. The same is true if officers are found unfit for full duty but capable of working modified duty.

It is possible for officers to be mandated into counseling *and* ordered to undergo a fitness for duty evaluation (see #7 below).

Mandated Counseling

Officers may be ordered to counseling for a variety of reasons including poor performance, poor attitude, violation of agency policy, and so on. Procedures for mandating a counseling program differ among agencies. Regardless of the specific differences among police agencies, when supervisors order a person to counseling, some general rules should be observed.

Suggestions for Supervisors Mandating Personnel to the Police Psychologist

Supervisors should consider ordering a subordinate into counseling only after attempts to encourage voluntary participation have failed. Voluntary participation in counseling normally increases the probability of a successful outcome. If an order becomes necessary, a written document must be submitted to the police psychologist. In the document the supervisor should:

1. *Avoid referring to mandated counseling as discipline.* Although ordering an officer to meet with the police psychologist may be the result of a corrective action which includes discipline, describing a psychological intervention program as discipline characterizes it as punishment. This places the psychologist in an untenable position and makes successful intervention more difficult. If the intervention program is thought of as an element of punishment by the person being ordered, this mindset becomes the first obstacle to overcome in the therapeutic effort. Supervisors can assist the goals of the police psychologist by keeping identified discipline separate from the mandated intervention program.

2. *Identify the reason(s) for the mandated intervention program.* When supervisors order someone to counseling it is usually because they have observed or learned of behaviors, attitudes, emotional responses, events, and so on which concern them enough to conclude that intervention is necessary. Specify this information and include it in your document. This information identifies the problem and helps focus the therapeutic effort.

3. *Specify how you have tried to address the problem.* This information assists the psychologist in assessment and intervention program design. Advise if a performance improvement plan has been initiated. If so, include a copy.

4. *State your order in a manner that facilitates motivation.* For example, "In an effort to assist you to better manage your anger, you are ordered (directed, mandated, required) to contact psychologist Dr. (name) prior to (date) and to participate in a counseling support program. The design and duration of the program will be determined by Dr. (name)." *Note*: Avoid designing intervention programs. Do not specify "You will meet with the police psychologist weekly for a period of

six weeks" or something similar. This was once included in a police department document and it was the first item impeached by the officer's attorneys who successfully argued that police supervisors were not qualified to design psychological intervention programs.

5. *Clearly specify the privilege of confidentiality.* When an officer voluntarily becomes a client of the police psychologist, the privilege of confidentiality within the limits specified by law, rests with the officer. However, similar to FFDEs, when an officer is ordered to counseling, the confidentiality privilege rests with the department. Like individuals, law enforcement agencies have the option of waiving the confidentiality privilege:

   A. If the department is interested in having the officer receive assistance but is not interested in receiving any information about the intervention, supervisors may order the person to the police psychologist and specify "As you are being ordered (mandated, directed) to counseling, the department has the privilege of confidentiality. The department waives this privilege to the extent specified - your support program and any communication, oral or in writing, between you and Dr. (name) shall remain confidential as prescribed by law. Dr (name) will only be required to confirm your compliance with this order and your continued participation in the support program." *Note:* To confirm the officer's compliance with the order and his continued participation, the ordering supervisor must contact the psychologist. The psychologist should never be placed in the role of "snitch" by being asked to periodically inform the department of the officer's compliance.

   B. In the event that the department wishes to receive information regarding the officer's program and progress, it helps the psychologist if you include something similar to "As you are being ordered (mandated, directed) to the police psychologist, you have no privilege of confidentiality. Dr. (name) will be required to report on your program design, your program compliance, and your progress within the program. He (she) will also be required to provide to staff any other pertinent data, including but not limited to information relating to assessment, opinion, prognosis, and outcome."

6. *Specify off-duty compensation.* It is not always possible or feasible to meet during duty hours (assuming the employee remains in some work capacity). When an officer is ordered to counseling, like any mandated activity, most departments must compensate the employee. Your document should state your department's policy.

7. *Fitness for Duty Evaluation (FFDE).* Many times there are no questions regarding fitness for duty. Other times, this is not the case. FFDEs, if needed:

    A. Must be independent of the mandated counseling program (completed by a professional other than the psychologist providing counseling).

    B. Must be appropriately sequenced with the mandatory counseling program. The placement of a FFDE associated with a mandatory counseling program will depend upon actual circumstances and the assessment of the primary counseling clinician.

8. *Casual orders.* Casually ordering an officer to meet with the police psychologist or with a member of the Peer Support Team (PST) is ethically unsustainable and must be avoided. If you are concerned about a subordinate, contact the police psychologist or a member of the PST. A *reach out* or other appropriate intervention will be initiated (chapter 5). Supervisory suggestions or recommendations to contact the police psychologist or PST are acceptable and encouraged. Be careful not to turn supervisory suggestions into unofficial orders.

Police Psychologists and Training

The training role of the police psychologist has been widely accepted in policing. As early as the 1960s, police administrators recognized the value of having psychologists involved in the officer training process. Traditionally, psychologists have provided training on such topics as human relations, interpersonal communication, conflict resolution, interacting with persons that are mentally ill, alcoholism and other addictions, peer counseling, and stress management.

More recently, police psychologists have been called upon to provide an ever expanding array of services. These services range from the well established practice of psychological evaluation of police candidates to the development of new and innovative programs (see COMPASS, p. 66).

One of the most important of these programs is stress inoculation training (SIT) (Meichenbaum, 1993). SIT, or similar stressor management programs, are ideally presented during the police pre-service skills academy (chapter 2). Such programs are comprised of specialized training in the characteristics, effects, and management of everyday and traumatic stressors. They are normally the first exposure of new officers to the complexities of unavoidable police stressors and critical incidents.

The Trauma Intervention Program (TIP) (chapter 4) is constructed to incorporate the advantages of pre-service stressor management training. Because stress management programs are designed to provide officers with a psychological buffer (inoculation) against the negative effects of occupational stress, they comprise the first element of the TIP. The remainder of the TIP enhances the original goal of the stressor management programs—the continued psychological health of police officers exposed to the stressors of policing.

Psychologists and Lawyers

"The first thing we do, let's kill all the lawyers" (Shakespeare, 1591). Although historically there is no love lost between defense attorneys and police officers, police officers and police psychologists would never seriously agree with this line from Shakespeare's *King Henry the Sixth*. Lawyers serve a vital role in complex modern societies. Without their expertise, many issues would not be resolved and many injustices would go without redress.

There are two interesting circumstances that can arise among clients, psychologists, and attorneys: *therapeutic outcome versus claim standing* and *stress inherent in litigation*.

Therapeutic outcome versus claim standing involves a situation wherein a psychologist and an attorney have the same client. Both the psychologist and the attorney are professionally obligated to act in the client's best interest. At times these goals seem to clash, especially if the client is involved in an injury claim for enduring psychological decompensation. The psychologist and the client work to eliminate psychological difficulties. The attorney and the client have a stronger case if the psychological difficulties remain. This is because in most disability litigation, the more disabling the symptoms, the greater the monetary reward. This circumstance was once summed up by a client who reported, "The better my symptoms get, the more money I lose." In situations like this, clients have to set a priority. Most choose good mental health. Regardless, consciously or unconsciously, pending litigation involving psychological decompensation supports ongoing psychological difficulties.

The second circumstance is the stress inherent in litigation. Whatever the reason for attorney involvement, confronting legal issues is stressful. It draws energy from the client and creates anxiety. It almost always complicates the clinical condition. The psychological condition of clients will generally improve, sometimes remarkably, once existing legal processes are concluded. This is likely because (1) the stressor of pending litigation is terminated and (2) the unconscious (or conscious) need to maintain symptomology is eliminated.

Similar to psychological difficulties, improvement in reported physical symptoms such as headache, fatigue, general pain, mobility, and overall functioning have been reported upon conclusion of legal matters. *Therapeutic outcome versus claim standing* and *stress inherent in litigation* is not the same as feigning psychological or physical symptoms in an effort to obtain monetary or other rewards.

Alcohol and the Police Officer

The consumption of alcoholic beverages is common throughout the world. In moderation, alcohol seems to represent no significant health or career risk. In higher quantities of prolonged consumption, alcohol can lead to loss of career, loss of marriage and family, addiction, poor health, and devastating disease.

Some police officers experience difficulties with alcohol. Even one night of abusive drinking can lead to behaviors that are *unbecoming a police officer*. Getting drunk, dancing on a table in a bar, falling down, getting into a fight, getting arrested and convicted might not get you fired from some jobs; but it is nearly a guarantee of employment termination for a police officer. Police officers are held to higher standard of conduct, even off duty, than many other workers. This standard is made explicit in the Law Enforcement Code of Ethics (appendix A) and in the values statement of most police agencies.

Police officers, like those in all occupations, abuse and become addicted to alcohol. If the abuse or addiction is addressed in a timely manner and the officer has been fortunate enough to have avoided behavior resulting in termination, police officers can salvage their careers. Unfortunately for some officers, their drinking destroys their career. It has been painful to watch the careers of once respected and outstanding police officers collapse due to alcoholism. This can occur in spite of the best efforts of family, police agency administrators, addiction specialists, and mental health professionals to prevent it.

There are three primary settings for alcohol and substance use treatment: non-residential treatment, residential treatment, and partial residential treatment. (1) Non-residential treatments include Alcoholic Anonymous, other twelve-step programs, and various individual or group interventions that take place outside of a residential facility. (2) Residential alcohol treatment programs involve living within a facility. They provide twenty-four-hour care and can be short-term or long-term. Many of the short-term interventions were previously called *twenty-eight-day programs*; however, most are now shorter in duration. Long-term residential programs serve those who wish to be treated residentially and those with a history of multiple non-residential treatment relapses. They normally range from four to twelve months and often include individual and group therapy, health education, life management, holistic approaches, and family counseling. (3) Partial residential programs allow persons to remain in a treatment facility for six to eight hours during the day, and return home at night. In partial residential programs, treatment and structure is provided for those persons who are less likely to succeed in non-residential programs, but do not require a residential setting.

Some alcohol treatment programs include the use of medications. Medications used to treat alcoholism discourage alcohol consumption (disulfiram), treat or reduce withdrawal symptoms (chlordiazepoxide), or reduce the craving for alcohol (naltrexone). Even with the best treatment, quitting alcohol appears difficult. The National Institute on Alcohol Abuse and Alcoholism reported that approximately 90 percent of persons trying to quit drinking relapse at least once within four years of initiating treatment (1989). Interestingly, this is similar to the relapse rates of those addicted to nicotine and heroin. This suggests some common underlying bio-psycho-social mechanisms.

Historically, a distinction was made between alcohol *abuse* and alcohol *dependence*. Abuse was described as a maladaptive pattern of drinking that caused a multitude of problems. These included failure to meet primary obligations (absences from work, etc), drinking or intoxicated in situations where it can be hazardous (driving, operating machinery, etc), legal difficulties arising out of intoxication (disorderly conduct, etc), and social problems arising from drinking (arguments with spouse, etc). Alcohol dependence was associated with tolerance (greater amounts needed to achieve the desired effect or lessened effect at same amount), withdrawal (symptoms appear if alcohol is not consumed or is discontinued), lack of control over the amount of alcohol consumed (drinking more than intended before drinking started), unsuccessful efforts to drink less, spending a significant amount of time obtaining alcohol or recovering from its effects, missing important events so that alcohol can be consumed (giving up a child's recital for drinking), and drinking in spite of the fact that it is creating or exacerbating psychological or physical problems (APA, 2000).

Today, the conceptions of abuse and dependence have evolved into an alcohol use spectrum. The spectrum of a "problematic pattern of alcohol use leading to clinically significant impairment or distress" is diagnosed as Alcohol Use Disorder (AUD) (305.00, DSM-5, 490). Alcohol Use Disorder may be mild, moderate, or severe depending upon the number of symptoms present. Tolerance and withdrawal remain components of AUD.

What about *alcohol addiction?* The term *addiction* is not used in the diagnosis of AUD. In fact, it is not used in any of the diagnoses included in the Substance-Related and Addictive Disorders section of the DSM-5. This is because of the difficulty in appropriately defining its meaning and use.

According to a 2002-2004 study by the U.S. Department of Health and Human Services, there is an average 9 percent prevalence of what is now considered alcohol use disorder among police officers. This is lower than the rate found in at least eight other occupations. The idea that 25 to 30 percent of police officers regularly misuse alcohol, first presented during the 1980s, is a modern day myth (Honig, 2007). However, the actual police officer alcohol use disorder prevalence rate may vary widely across various police agencies and jurisdictions.

Medication and Psychoactive Medication for Police Officers

There are millions of persons that take medication: some take medication daily for chronic conditions, while others utilize medication to treat transitory injury or illnesses. Modern medications are the result of years of pharmacological research; they improve the quality of life for countless individuals. It should come as no surprise that some of these individuals are police officers.

Most police agencies have policies that regulate the use of medications. The *Model Policy on Standards of Conduct* published by the International Association of Chiefs of Police specifies officer responsibility in this area, "No officer shall report to work or be on duty as a law enforcement officer when his or her judgment or physical condition has been impaired by alcohol, medication, or other substances" and "Officers must report the use of any substance, prior to reporting for duty, that impairs their ability to perform as a law enforcement officer" (n.d. para.,3).

Medical condition and medication

If the medical condition requiring medication does not prevent the officer from working, the medications used to treat the condition sometimes can. The use of drugs such as muscle relaxants, sedatives, drugs with sedating side effects, and certain analgesics may require that an officer be placed on medical leave. This is because these medications may impair an officer's ability to function normally. Medical leave usually remains in place until (1) the condition is treated and the medication is discontinued, (2) the medications are determined to no longer cause impairment, or (3) the medications are adjusted so as to avoid impairment.

The use of other medications, such as blood thinners may not in themselves require an officer to be placed on medical leave, but because of the dangers associated with the effects of anticoagulants, a modified duty assignment may be necessary. Modified duty assignments for officers taking high dosages of anticoagulants usually involve working on administrative tasks inside the police department. By working inside and not in the field, the probability that an officer will be injured (and bleed uncontrollably) is lessened. Once the medication is discontinued or the effects of the medication no longer pose a risk, the officer can return to full duty.

In all cases of medication-related leave, the agency should require that the medication prescriber complete a written document clearing the officer for full duty prior to actual return.

Psychoactive medication

An issue that sometimes arises for police officers taking medications is the use of psychoactive medications. Psychoactive medications are used primarily to treat psychological conditions. Depression and/or anxiety are the most likely psychological conditions to affect working police officers.

When experiencing clinical levels of depression or anxiety, some officers have no difficulty taking medications. Others are reluctant. They fear that taking antidepressant or anti-anxiety medication will damage their careers.

They fear that others might view them as weak, emotionally unstable, unable to deal with job and personal stress, and un-promotable. Looking to avoid the perceived stigma associated with taking psychoactive medications, some officers choose counseling to address the problem. Some choose medication and counseling. Still others choose neither and continue to struggle with psychological difficulties at home and at work.

Psychoactive medication and police officers: The facts

Working police officers have utilized psychoactive medications for many years without detriment. Like persons in every other occupation, they have benefitted from the appropriate pharmacological treatment of depression and anxiety. This benefit is passed on to the department and the community through the officer's improved quality of service.

From a police administrator's and citizen point of view, think of this: who would you rather have responding to calls - a depressed or anxious police officer, or a police officer that is being successfully treated for depression or anxiety? The choice seems clear.

Intervention outcome studies have demonstrated that psychoactive medications, when used in conjunction with psychological counseling, are more effective than the use of medication alone (especially with depression). When used appropriately, psychoactive medications can be a vital part of an officer's overall psychological health and support program.

For officers, keep in mind that (1) such medications have been proven safe for working police officers over many years and (2) significant progress has been made within the police culture in eliminating the stigma associated with the use of psychoactive medications. While you should not abandon questioning any healthcare provider that suggests you begin a course of psychoactive medication, neither should you dismiss the idea solely out of concerns about agency reprisal or peer ridicule.

Psychoactive medication bias

Want to check your bias regarding psychoactive medications? Consider this. Would you feel differently about your surgeon if you discovered just prior to undergoing surgery that he was being successfully treated with an antidepressant or anti-anxiety medication? Would it surprise you to know that many surgeons and other physicians regularly take such medications?

What about the pilot of your soon to depart flight? Would you feel differently if you knew that your pilot was being successfully treated with medications for depression or anxiety? On April 5, 2010 the Federal Aviation Administration reversed a long-standing ban on allowing commercial pilots to fly while taking antidepressants (many of which also reduce anxiety). On a case by case basis, commercial pilots can now fly if they are being treated with one of four specified antidepressants and the condition has been successfully treated for a year. (Staton, 2010). This change in FAA policy is recognition of the efficacy and safety of such treatment protocols.

The real issue is not that any person is taking psychoactive medication. The real issue is the status of the psychological condition for which the medication is being prescribed. A surgeon is a better surgeon when an underlying depression or anxiety condition is being successfully treated. An airline pilot whose depression is being successfully treated is a safer pilot than when the depression is untreated. The same is true for police officers.

Women and Minority Police Officers

Being a good police officer has nothing to do with race or gender. Minority members and women have distinguished themselves as police officers for many years.

The history of minority police officers in America spans several decades. For the most part, it parallels the issues first brought to light during the civil rights movement of the 1960s and 1970s. Although a comprehensive discussion of minorities in American policing is well beyond the scope of this book, it is fair to say that minority police officers have contributed a great deal to the profession of policing.

Like minorities, women of all ethnic backgrounds have made significant contributions to policing. However, they still comprise only 11 to 14 percent of police officers in America (Horne, 2006). This is despite the fact that women make up about 50.8 percent of the U.S. population (U.S. Census Bureau, 2012). The *Status of Women in Policing: 2000* survey reported that "the gains for women in policing are so slow that, at the current rate of growth (the number of women in policing)...will not reach equal representation or gender balance within the police profession for at least another 70 years, and many experts caution that time alone is not sufficient to substantially increase women's numbers" (Harrington, 2001, 4).

Clearly, women continue to struggle for their place in policing. A 1998 study conducted by the International Association of Chiefs of Police concluded that female officers still confront bias from some male officers. Sexual harassment of female officers still exists in many police agencies (ibid). Although this study was conducted several years ago, it is unlikely that much has changed.

In spite of these unfortunate circumstances, no one would seriously challenge the capabilities of women in policing based on gender. In modern police agencies, women serve honorably at all ranks, including chiefs, sheriffs, commissioners, and directors.

Gay, Lesbian, Bisexual, or Transgender (GLBT) Police Officers

There are thousands of police officers in America and throughout the world. Some of them are GLBT. Many GLBT officers have come out of the policing closet. They have been successful in their careers and report being tired of keeping the secret. Once a taboo, being GLBT and a police officer has gained public acceptance. There are organizations throughout the world supporting GLBT police officers, and several police agencies actively recruit GLBT candidates. It is difficult to estimate the percentage of GLTB police officers in America. Anecdotal guesses average from 2 to 4 percent, with some agencies having no known GLBT officers. This is in contrast to the percentage of GLBT persons in the general population, estimated to be anywhere from 1.2 percent to 10 percent. It is difficult to obtain accurate figures because many GLBT persons, whether or not police officers, maintain their privacy. For police, some GLBT officers remain private because they fear the reactions of their peers, while others feel that their personal life is no one's business.

A gay Boston police officer reported that he believed it was easier for lesbian officers to come out than gay men. He attributed this to the idea that heterosexual male officers are more likely to have problems with homosexual male officers sharing department gymnasiums, locker rooms, and showers. However, in his fifteen years as an openly gay police officer, he had never been threatened or harassed by any of his coworkers (personal communication, March 15, 2010). A local openly lesbian officer agreed that it might be easier for female police officers to come out than their male counterparts. She knew of only one openly gay male officer in northern Colorado (Denver metro area excluded) (personal communication, April 5, 2010). One officer offered an explanation of the lesbian *coming out* phenomenon: "A lesbian officer is seen more manly, more like a traditional cop. A gay guy might be seen as effeminate, less like a traditional cop. So he'll keep it secret." Regardless, experience has shown that many GLBT men and women are excellent officers. Like race and gender, sexual orientation has nothing to do with being a good police officer.

Although the minority status, gender, and sexual orientation of police officers may have social meaning to some individuals, various communities, and particular groups, *all* good police officers share similar characteristics. Good police officers are characterized by integrity, compassion, discretion, judgment, fairness, community-mindedness, positive work ethic, performance, and professionalism. Good police officers Serve and Protect.

Police Biography

My police career began in 1976 when I was hired as a deputy sheriff for the Laramie County Sheriff's Office (LCSO) in Cheyenne, Wyoming. In those days at the LCSO, the common wisdom was that a deputy could get more out of the law enforcement academy if he had some street experience. So, new to the position of deputy sheriff, I was not assigned to attend the academy. Instead, I was assigned to ride with other deputies in order to learn the job. There was no FTO program. I learned some things from several deputies, such as how to write a ticket, how to fill out report forms, where to get free coffee, and so on. After a few weeks, I was working solo in a squad car, responding to emergencies and bar fights, enforcing traffic laws, answering calls for service, and doing pretty much everything that was required of a deputy sheriff.

I still remember my first solo car stop. I also remember my first arrest. It involved a domestic dispute where a man had pushed his girlfriend. In those days, very different from today, officers tried to mediate domestic disputes. After thinking I had successfully mediated the problem, I was walking to my *green and white*, the color of LCSO squad cars in those days. It was parked close to the couple's home. Before I got into the car, I heard the woman yelling from inside the house, "He's doin' it again!" I ran back to the home to witness the man holding the woman against the wall, his hands to her throat. After a brief struggle, I placed him under arrest, handcuffed him, put him in my car, and drove to the jail. Once we arrived, I escorted the man to the booking area. The shift sergeant saw us and asked me, "What's he under arrest for?" I looked at the sergeant and said, "I have no idea." After seeing that facial expression that sergeants often give rookie officers, he helped me to find a charge that best fit the circumstances. Several months later, I attended the then five-week basic training program at the Wyoming Law Enforcement Academy. My police career was truly underway.

After two years at LCSO, I had earned a fairly positive reputation. The chief of the Cheyenne, Wyoming Police Department (CPD) contacted me and asked if I was interested in becoming a Cheyenne police officer. I knew CPD to be a good police department and I was gratified by the chief's inquiry. I completed an application for CPD. After the hiring process, I was offered a position. I resigned from the LCSO and became a CPD officer.

I enjoyed working at CPD. The officers were close-knit. I retain many of the friendships made there to this day. After about two years working as a patrol officer and detective, I was appointed to the staff position of training officer. This was an administrative position that removed me from field assignments, except for *Frontier Days*, when every available police officer worked the street. The training officer position allowed me a great deal of flexibility. As part of my assignment, I was permitted to initiate a somewhat official, somewhat unofficial, officer counseling program. Through this program, I offered counseling services to other officers and employees. It was my first in-house counseling effort.

After about another two years, I left the CPD and the city of Cheyenne. I moved south to Fort Collins, Colorado. Once settled in Fort Collins, I began working as a mental health associate with the Poudre Valley Hospital Psychiatric Unit. This was the first time that I was involved in the treatment of hospitalized mentally ill patients. It was an interesting and eye-opening experience.

I remember one patient who was suffering from a serious brain degenerative disease. Sadly, he had lost most of his ability to reason and to understand verbal communication. He had also lost the ability to control his behavior. The disease had caused him to become impulsive and childlike in his emotional responses. He was on the unit so that his behavior could be stabilized with medication during his final days.

One day, he was determined to leave the hospital. He approached the unit elevator. I saw this and took a position in front of the elevator. I extended my arms out to each side in a nonverbal gesture to signal that he could go no farther. He walked up to me and punched me square on the jaw. I took control of him and walked him back to his room. Due to his weakened condition, I was unharmed. I could not help but smile. Can you imagine a former police officer assuming the open-arms posture when being approached by a person known to have impulse control problems? In my concern for the patient, I had neglected to apply basic personal safety measures. It was a lesson that I did not forget.

As interesting and educational as working on the psychiatric unit was, I missed police work. After about a year on the unit, I decided to return to policing.

I applied for an officer position with the Fort Collins Police Department. On the appointed morning, I drove to the city building and, along with the other police candidates, completed the FCPD written test. After the test, we were instructed to wait in the building lobby where the test results would soon be posted. The candidates who had passed would move forward in the testing process. Those that did not pass would be eliminated from consideration. The test results were posted. My name was not among those who had passed the test.

I was surprised and somewhat confused. The test did not seem difficult. I had taken police candidate tests before and I had always done well. Then, as the human mind would have it, I thought that I must have misinterpreted the test items. This would account for the failing score. I left the city building disappointed.

At home a short time later, I received a telephone call. It was a woman from the City of Fort Collins Personnel Department. She informed me that my police test had initially been incorrectly scored. The scoring template had been improperly placed over my answer sheet. (I can only assume that the score was so low that it prompted a reexamination.) When this was discovered, my test was rescored. I had passed the test. I returned to the city building and continued in the candidate process.

After completing the remainder of the selection process, I optimistically waited for the call. A few weeks passed. One morning, I read in the newspaper that an FCPD officer had resigned under less than ideal circumstances. Later that same day, I received a telephone call from then FCPD chief of police, Ralph Smith. He offered me a position. I accepted. Once hired, I was issued the standard police equipment, including a duty belt, chemical spray, baton, portable radio, handcuffs, and so on. Etched upon my issued handcuffs was the name of the officer who had resigned a few days earlier. I used those handcuffs throughout my FCPS career.

This is how I began my career with the Fort Collins Police Department. The rest, as they say, is history.

Appendix A

Law Enforcement Code of Ethics

A S A LAW ENFORCEMENT OFFICER, my fundamental duty is to serve all persons; to safeguard lives and property; to protect the innocent against deception, the weak against oppression or intimidation, and the peaceful against violence or disorder; and to respect the Constitutional rights of all persons to liberty, equality and justice.

I WILL keep my private life unsullied as an example to all; maintain courageous calm in the face of danger, scorn or ridicule; develop self-restraint; and be constantly mindful of the welfare of others. Honest in thought and deed in both my personal and official life. I will be exemplary in obeying the laws of the land and the regulations of my department. Whatever I see or hear of a confidential nature or that is confided to me in my official capacity will be kept ever secret unless revelation is necessary in the performance of my duty.

I WILL never act officiously or permit personal feelings, prejudices, animosities or friendships to influence my decisions. With no compromise for crime and with relentless prosecution of criminals, I will enforce the law courteously and appropriately without fear or favor, malice or ill will, never employing unnecessary force or violence and never accepting gratuities.

I RECOGNIZE the badge of my office as a symbol of public faith, and I accept it as a public trust to be held as long as I am true to the ethics of the police service. I will constantly strive to achieve these objectives and ideals, dedicating myself before God to my chosen profession . . . . Law Enforcement.

Appendix B

The Imperatives

1. <u>The Communication Imperative</u>: Persons will respond to the message they received and not necessarily the message that you intended to send.

2. <u>The Occupational Imperative</u>: Never forget *why* you do *what* you do.

3. <u>The Relationship Imperative</u>: Make it safe!

Appendix C

<u>C.R.S. 13-90-107(m)</u>:

(1) There are particular relations in which it is the policy of the law to encourage confidence and to preserve it inviolate; therefore, a person shall not be examined as a witness in the following cases:

(m) (I) A law enforcement or firefighter peer support team member shall not be examined without the consent of the person to whom peer support services have been provided as to any communication made by the person to the peer support team member under the circumstances described in subparagraph (III) of this paragraph (m); nor shall a recipient of individual peer support services be examined as to any such communication without the recipient's consent.

(I.5) An emergency medical service provider or rescue unit peer support team member shall not be examined without the consent of the person to whom peer support services have been provided as to any communication made by the person to the peer support team member under the circumstances described in subparagraph (III) of this paragraph (m); nor shall a recipient of individual peer support services be examined as to any such communication without the recipient's consent.

(II) For purposes of this paragraph (m):

(A) "Communication" means an oral statement, written statement, note, record, report, or document, made during, or arising out of, a meeting with a peer support team member.

(A.5) "Emergency medical service provider or rescue unit peer support team member" means an emergency medical service provider, as defined in Section 25-3.5-103 (8), C.R.S., a regular or volunteer member of a rescue unit, as defined in Section 25-3.5-103 (11), C.R.S., or other person who has been trained in peer support skills and who is officially designated by the supervisor of an emergency medical service agency as defined in Section 25-3.5-103 (11.5), C.R.S., or a chief of a rescue unit as a member of an emergency medical service provider's peer support team or rescue unit's peer support team.

(B) "Law enforcement or firefighter peer support team member" means a peace officer, civilian employee, or volunteer member of a law enforcement agency or a regular or volunteer member of a fire department or other person who has been trained in peer support skills and who is officially designated by a police chief, the chief of the Colorado state patrol, a sheriff, or a fire chief as a member of a law enforcement agency's peer support team or a fire department's peer support team.

(III) The provisions of this paragraph (m) shall apply only to communications made during individual interactions conducted by a peer support team member:

(A) Acting in the person's official capacity as a law enforcement or firefighter peer support team member or an emergency medical service provider or rescue unit peer support team member; and

(B) Functioning within the written peer support guidelines that are in effect for the person's respective law enforcement agency, fire department, emergency medical service agency, or rescue unit.

(IV) This paragraph (m) shall not apply in cases in which:

(A) A law enforcement or firefighter peer support team member or emergency medical service provider or rescue unit peer support team member was a witness or a party to an incident which prompted the delivery of peer support services;

(B) Information received by a peer support team member is indicative of actual or suspected child abuse, as described in section 18-6-401, C.R.S., or actual or suspected child neglect, as described in section 19-3-102, C.R.S.;

(C) Due to alcohol or other substance intoxication or abuse, as described in sections 27-81-111 and 27-82-107, C.R.S., the person receiving peer support is a clear and immediate danger to the person's self or others;

Reflections of a Police Psychologist

(D) There is reasonable cause to believe that the person receiving peer support has a mental illness and, due to the mental illness, is an imminent threat to himself or herself or others or is gravely disabled as defined in <u>section 27-65-102</u>, C.R.S.; or

(E) There is information indicative of any criminal conduct

Appendix D

Diagnostic Criteria
for Posttraumatic Stress Disorder

Criterion A: stressor

The person was exposed to: death, threatened death, actual or threatened serious injury, or actual or threatened sexual violence, as follows: **(one required)**

1. Direct exposure.
2. Witnessing, in person.
3. Indirectly, by learning that a close relative or close friend was exposed to trauma. If the event involved actual or threatened death, it must have been violent or accidental.
4. Repeated or extreme indirect exposure to aversive details of the event(s), usually in the course of professional duties (e.g., first responders, collecting body parts; professionals repeatedly exposed to details of child abuse). This does not include indirect non-professional exposure through electronic media, television, movies, or pictures.

Criterion B: intrusion symptoms

The traumatic event is persistently re-experienced in the following way(s): **(one required)**

1. Recurrent, involuntary, and intrusive memories. Note: Children older than six may express this symptom in repetitive play.
2. Traumatic nightmares. Note: Children may have frightening dreams without content related to the trauma(s).
3. Dissociative reactions (e.g., flashbacks) which may occur on a continuum from brief episodes to complete loss of consciousness. Note: Children may reenact the event in play.

274

4. Intense or prolonged distress after exposure to traumatic reminders.
5. Marked physiologic reactivity after exposure to trauma-related stimuli.

Criterion C: avoidance

Persistent effortful avoidance of distressing trauma-related stimuli after the event: **(one required)**

1. Trauma-related thoughts or feelings.
2. Trauma-related external reminders (e.g., people, places, conversations, activities, objects, or situations).

Criterion D: negative alterations in cognitions and mood

Negative alterations in cognitions and mood that began or worsened after the traumatic event: **(two required)**

1. Inability to recall key features of the traumatic event (usually dissociative amnesia; not due to head injury, alcohol, or drugs).
2. Persistent (and often distorted) negative beliefs and expectations about oneself or the world (e.g., "I am bad," "The world is completely dangerous").
3. Persistent distorted blame of self or others for causing the traumatic event or for resulting consequences.
4. Persistent negative trauma-related emotions (e.g., fear, horror, anger, guilt, or shame).
5. Markedly diminished interest in (pre-traumatic) significant activities.
6. Feeling alienated from others (e.g., detachment or estrangement).
7. Constricted affect: persistent inability to experience positive emotions.

Criterion E: alterations in arousal and reactivity

Trauma-related alterations in arousal and reactivity that began or worsened after the traumatic event: **(two required)**

1. Irritable or aggressive behavior
2. Self-destructive or reckless behavior

3. Hypervigilance
4. Exaggerated startle response
5. Problems in concentration
6. Sleep disturbance

Criterion F: duration

Persistence of symptoms (in Criteria B, C, D, and E) for more than one month.

Criterion G: functional significance

Significant symptom-related distress or functional impairment (e.g., social, occupational).

Criterion H: exclusion

Disturbance is not due to medication, substance use, or other illness.

Specify if: **With dissociative symptoms.**

In addition to meeting criteria for diagnosis, an individual experiences high levels of either of the following in reaction to trauma-related stimuli:

1. **Depersonalization**: experience of being an outside observer of or detached from oneself (e.g., feeling as if "this is not happening to me" or one were in a dream).
2. **Derealization**: experience of unreality, distance, or distortion (e.g., "things are not real").

Specify if: **With delayed expression.**

Full diagnosis is not met until at least six months after the trauma(s), although onset of symptoms may occur immediately.

From: American Psychiatric Association. (2013) *Diagnostic and statistical manual of mental disorders*, (5th ed.). Washington, DC: Author.

References

Aamodt, M.G., & Werlick, N. (2001). Police officer suicide: frequency and officer profiles. In Shehan, D. (Ed.) *Law Enforcement and Suicide*. Quantico, VA: Federal Bureau of Investigation.

American Psychiatric Association. (1952). *Diagnostic and statistical manual of mental disorders*. Washington, DC: Author.

American Psychiatric Association. (1968). *Diagnostic and statistical manual of mental disorders* (2nd ed.). Washington, DC: Author.

American Psychiatric Association. (1980). *Diagnostic and statistical manual of mental disorders* (3rd ed.). Washington, DC: Author.

American Psychiatric Association. (1987). *Diagnostic and statistical manual of mental disorders* (3rd ed., revised). Washington, DC: Author.

American Psychiatric Association. (1994). *Diagnostic and statistical manual of mental disorders* (4th ed.). Washington, DC: Author.

American Psychiatric Association. (2000). *Diagnostic and statistical manual of mental disorders* (4th ed., text revision). Washington, DC: Author.

American Psychiatric Association. (2013). *Diagnostic and statistical manual of mental disorders* (5th ed.). Washington, DC: Author.

American Psychological Association. (n.d., para.,3). *Psychologists in public service*. Retrieved from http://search.apa.org/search?query=sections

Anton, E., Marti, J., Kwatra, M. M., Bohner, H., Schneider, F., Inouye, S. K. (2006). Delirium in older persons. *New England Journal of Medicine*, 354: 2509-2511.

Artwohl, A. & Christensen, L. W. (1997). *Deadly force encounters: what cops need to know to mentally and physically prepare for and survive a gunfight.* Boulder: Paladin Press.

Avram, M. M. (December 2004). Cellulite: a review of its physiology and treatment. *Journal of Cosmetic Laser Therapy, 6* (4), 181-185.

Beck, A.T., Rush, A.J., Shaw, B.F., Emery, G. (1979). *Cognitive Therapy of Depression.* The Guilford Press.

Calories in Protein, Fat and Carbohydrates. (n.d., para.,1). Retrieved from http://www.caloriesperhour.com/tutorial_gram.php

Cannon, W. B. (1915). *Bodily changes in pain, hunger, fear and rage: an account of recent researches into the function of emotional excitement.* New York: Appleton.

Cannon, W. B. (1932). *The wisdom of the body.* New York: W. W. Norton. Carr, K. F. (2003). *Critical incident stress debriefings for cross-cultural workers: harmful or helpful?* Retrieved from http://www.mmct.org/critical incident stress.php

Centers for disease control and prevention. (2009). *Body mass index.* Retrieved from http://www.cdc.gov/healthyweight/assessing/bmi/adult bmi/index. html

Cordingley, G. (2005) Walter Freeman's Lobotomies at Athens State Hospital. Retrieved from http://www.cordingleyneurology.com/lobotomies. html, August 3, 2014

Cosmopoulos, M. B. (ed.). (2007). *Experiencing war: trauma and society from ancient Greece to the Iraq war.* Chicago: Ares Publishers.

Da Costa, J. M. (January 1871). On irritable heart; a clinical study of a form of functional cardiac disorder and its consequences. *The American Journal of the Medical Sciences (61),* 18-52.

Digliani, J. A. (1992). *Guidelines for conducting a police critical incident debriefing.* Unpublished manuscript.

Dobbins, R. (2008). *Do what is right even when no one is looking*. Retrieved from http://www.af.mil/news/story.asp?id=123081361Environ International Corporation. (2002). *What America drinks*. National Health and Nutrition Examination Survey.

Freud, S. (1920). *Beyond the pleasure principle*. In J. Strachey (Ed. & Trans.), Standard edition of the complete psychological works of Sigmund Freud (Vol.18, p. 27). London: Hogarth Press.

Freudenberger, H. J. (1974). Staff burnout. *Journal of Social Issues, 30*(1), 159-165.

Freudenberger, H. J. & Richelson, G. (1980). *Burn out: the high cost of high achievement*. New York: Bantam Books.

Geldmacher, D. S. (2003). *Contemporary diagnosis and management of Alzheimer's dementia*. (2nd ed). Charlottesville: Handbooks in Healthcare.

Goodwin, J. (1987). The etiology of combat-related post-traumatic stress disorders. In T. Williams (Ed.), *Post-traumatic stress disorders: a handbook for clinicians*. (pp. 1-18). Cincinnati: Disabled American Veterans.

Gottman, J., & Silver, N. (1999). *The Seven Principles for Making Marriage Work*. Three Rivers, Random House.

Griffin, S. E. (31 October 2006). Fats & Cholesterol: out with the bad, in with the good. *Harvard School of Public Health Newsletter*. Retrieved from http:// www. hsph.harvard.edu/nutritionsource/what-should-you-eat/fats-full-story/ index.html

Halliday, D., Resnick, R., & Krane, K. S. (2001). *Physics*. New York: John Wiley & Sons.

Harrington, P., et al (2001). Equality denied, *The Status of Women in Policing: 2000. Retrieved from http://www.womenandpolicing.org/PDF/2000%20Status%20Report.pdf*

Hersh, K. & Borum, R. (1998). Command hallucinations, compliance, and risk assessment. *Journal of the American Academy of Psychiatry and the Law*, (26), 353-359.

Honig, A. L. (September/October 2007). Facts refute long-standing myths about law enforcement officers. *National Psychologist*, 16(5).

Honig, A.L., & Sultan, S.E. (December 2004). Under fire—reactions and resilience: what an officer can expect. *The police chief*. International association of chiefs of police.

Horne, P. (September 2006). Policewomen: their first century and the new era. *The police chief*. International association of chiefs of police, 73, 9.

International Association of Chiefs of Police (2010). *Model policy on standards of conduct*. Retrieved from http://www.theiacp.org/ zoomSearch/search. asp?zoom_query=conduct &zoom cat=0

Keller, M. B., McCullough, J. P., Klein, D. N., Arnoe, B., Dunner, D. L., Gelenberg, A. J., Markowitz, J. C., Nemeroff, C. B., Russell, J. M., Thase, M. E., Trivedi, M. H., Zajecka, J. (18 May 2000). A comparison of nefazodone, the cognitive behavioral-analysis system of psychotherapy, and their combination for the treatment of chronic depression. *New England Journal of Medicine*, *342*, 1462-1470.

Kirsch, I. (2009). *The Emperor's New Drugs: Exploding the Antidepressant Myth*. London: The Bodley Head.

Lebow, J. (2005). *Handbook of clinical family therapy*. Hoboken, NJ: John Wiley and Sons.

Lefkowitz, M. R. & Fant, M. B. (n.d., para., 1). *Women's life in Greece and Rome*. Retrieved from http://www.stoa.org/diotima/anthology/wlgr/ wlgr-romanlegal120.shtml

Lewin, K. (1935) *A dynamic theory of personality: Selected papers*. New York: McGraw-Hill.

Lieberman, S. & Bruning, N. (1990). *The Real Vitamin & Mineral Book*. New York:Avery Group.

Maffetone, P. (2000). *The Maffetone method*. Camden, ME: Ragged Mountain Press.

Malcom, A. (1972). *The Pursuit of Intoxication*. New York: Washington Square Press.

McCoy, S. & Aamodt, M. (2009). *Police officers divorce rates not as high as many think*. Retrieved from http://www.runet.edu/NewsPub/December09/1217divorce.html

McNiel, D. E., Eisner, J. P., & Binder, R. L. (October 2000). The relationship between command hallucination and violence. *Psychiatric Services*, 51:1288-1292.

Meichenbaum, D. (1993). Stress inoculation training: A twenty year update. In R. L. Woolfolk and P. M. Lehrer (Eds.), *Principles and practices of stress management*. New York: Guilford Press.

Mitchell, J. T. (2004). *Crisis Intervention and Critical Incident Stress Management: A defense of the field*. Retrieved from http://www.icisf.org/articles/Acrobat Documents/CISM Defense of Field.pdf

Mitchell, J.T. (1983). When disaster strikes . . . the critical incident stress debriefing process. *Journal of Emergency Medical Services*, 8(1): 36-39.

Mitchell, J. T. & Everly, G. S. (1995). *Critical incident stress debriefing: An operations manual for the prevention of trauma among emergency service and disaster workers*. (2nd ed.). Baltimore: Chevron.

Moberg, J. L. & Aamodt, M. G. (2007). *The use and effectiveness of the insanity plea by serial killers*. Retrieved from http://maamodt.asp.radford. edu/Research Forensic/SPCP 2007Moberg&Aamodt-NGRI.pdf

Mohandie, K., Meloy, J. R., & Collins, P. I. (2009). Suicide by cop among officer-involved shooting cases. *Journal of Forensic Sciences*, 54 (2): 456-462.

National Center for PTSD (2003). *Types of debriefing following disasters*. Retrieved from http://www.ptsd.va.gov/professional/pages/debriefing-after-disasters.asp

National Institute of Mental Health. (2010). *Suicide in the U.S.* Retrieved from http://www.nimh.nih.gov/health/publications/suicide-in-the-us-statistics-and-prevention index.shtml#factors

National Institute of Mental Health. (2010). *What medications are used to treat depression?* Retrieved from http://www.nimh.nih.gov/health/ publications/ mental-health-medications/what-medications-are-used-to- treat-depression National Institute on Alcohol Abuse and Alcoholism. (October, 1989). No. 6, PH 277.

NPR, (2005). *A lobotomy timeline*. Retrieved from http://www.npr.org/ templates/story/story. php?storyId=50145 76& ps=rs

Null, Gary (2006). Obsessive-compulsive disorder. *Get Healthy Now*. Seven Stories Press.

O'Hara, A. F. & Violanti, J. M. (2013). *Police suicide: a comprehensive study*. Retrieved from http://www.policesuicidestudy.com/

Pavlov, I. P. (1927). *Conditioned reflexes: an investigation of the physiological activity of the cerebral cortex*. Translated and edited by *G. V. Anrep*. London: Oxford University Press.

Povenmire, H. (1995). The Sylacauga, Alabama meteorite: the impact locations, atmosphere trajectory, strewn field and radiant. *Abstracts of the Lunar and Planetary Science Conference*,(26), p.1133.

Reiser, M. (1982). *Police psychology: collected papers*. Los Angeles: LEHI Publishing.

Restak, Richard (2000). Fixing the Brain. *Mysteries of the Mind*. Washington, D.C.: National Geographic Society.

Rosen, G.M., Spitzer, R.I., & McHugh, P.R. (2008). Problems with the PTSD diagnosis and its future in DSM 5. *British Journal of Psychiatry, 192*, 3-4.

Ross, C A. (2006).The sham ECT literature: implications for consent to ECT. *Ethical Human Psychiatry and Psychology, 8* (1): 17-28.

Schultz, E. A. & Lavenda, R. H. (2006). *Core concepts in cultural anthropology*. New York: McGraw-Hill.

Selye, H. (1974). *Stress without stress*. New York: Signet.

Slawinski, T. T. & Blythe, B. T. (2004) *When doing the right thing might be wrong: research questions the value of critical incident stress debriefings*. Retrieved from http://www.cmiatl.com/news article55.html

Smith, S. (2003). *Treating schizophrenia: medication versus therapy*. Retrieved from http://sophia.smith.edu/~kmackenz/schizopaper.html

Smith, D. (2012) *Anxiety; it's still the 'age of anxiety.' Or Is It?* The New York Times, January 15, 2012.

Staton, T. (2010). *FAA OKs four antidepressants for pilot use*. Retrieved from http://www.fiercepharma.com/story/faa-oks-four-antidepressants-pilot-use/2010-04-05

Stratton, J. G. (1984). *Police passages*. Manhatten Beach, CA: Glennon Publishing.

Taylor, G. J. (March 2001). Relicts from the Birth of the Solar System. *PSR Discoveries*.

True, W.R., Rice, J., Eisen, S.A., Heath, A.C., Goldberg J., Lyons, M.J., & Nowak, J. (1993). A twin study of genetic and environmental contributions to liability for posttraumatic stress symptoms. *Archives of General Psychiatry, 50* (4), 257-264.

U.S. Census Bureau (2012). *An overview of the U. S. population*. Retrieved from http://www.infoplease.com/ipa/A0004925.html

Van Zandt, C. (1993). Suicide by cop. *The police chief*, 7, 24-30.

Violanti, J.M., O'Hara, A.F, & Tate, T.T. (2011). *On the Edge: recent perspectives on police suicide*. Springfield, IL: Charles C. Thomas.

Vukicevic, M. & Fitzmaurice, K. (2008). Butterflies and black lacy patterns: the prevalence and characteristics of Charles Bonnet hallucinations in an Australian population. *Clinical and Experimental Ophthalmology, (36)*, 659-65.

Werder, P. & Rothlin, P. (March 2007). *Diagnosis Boreout—How a lack of challenge at work can make you ill*. Germany: Redline Wirtschaft.

Willett, W. C. & Skerrett, P. J. (2005) *Eat, drink, and be healthy: the Harvard Medical School guide to healthy eating*. New York: Free Press.

Williams, D. (2006). *Manic depression*. Retrieved from http://www.peaceandhealing.com/depression/manic.asp

Wolpe, J. (1969). *The practice of behavior therapy*. New York: Pergamon Press.

Worden, J. M. (1982). *Grief counseling and grief therapy: a handbook for the mental health practitioner*. New York: Springer.

Zimbardo, P., Sword, R.M., & Sword, R.K.M. (2012). *The time cure*. San Francisco, CA: John Wiley and Sons, Inc.

Zisook, S., Byrd, D., Kuck, J., & Jeste, D. V. (October 1995). Command hallucinations in outpatients with schizophrenia. *Journal of Clinical Psychiatry*,56(10),462-465.

Index

O

occupational imperative, 62, 270
one-shot learning, 80-81

P

passive suicidality, 211
patrol training officer (PTO), 25
Pavlov, Ivan, 80
peer support, 108-11
  history, 108
  interactions, 109
peer support team (PST), 112, 114, 118
  confidentiality, 105
  considerations, 124, 177, 181
  history, 103, 266-67
  policy, 114
  structure, 113
Pergament, Moshe, 220
Perseveration, 194
pocket response, 88
police officers, 14-15, 50, 62, 70, 85, 89,
    188-89, 222, 257
  gay, lesbian, bisexual, and transgender
    (GLBT), 263
  women, 262
Police Psychologist, 13
policing, 14, 50, 161
  challenges of. See application of
    authority; geography; report
    writing
  life after, 233
  risks in, 15
  three Ts of. See tactics; technology;
    training
Popeye philosophy, 159-60
posttraumatic stress (PTS), 74

posttraumatic stress disorder (PTSD),
    69-70
  diagnosis of, 69
  mental disorders associated with, 78
Proactive Annual Check-in (PAC), 65
projection, 161
Prozac, 201
psychoactive medication, 260-61
Psychologist and Training/Recruit Officer
    Liaison (PATROL) program, 27
  basic principles of, 27
  features of, 29
  pitfalls of, 30
psychology
  general, 13
  police, 13
psychopharmacology, 201
psychosurgery, 203
psychotherapy, 109, 202
psychotic disorders, 189-90
punishment, 243

R

rationalization, 161, 167
reciprocal inhibition, 244
recovery, 73
reinforcement
  negative, 243
    See also punishment
  positive, 33
  repetitive, 33
relaxation breathing, 40-41
reputation, officer, 20
resistance, 46
return-to-duty protocol (RTD), 93-94
reverse bias, 31
"Richard Cory" (Robinson), 217
Riverhouse Incident, 107

W

walk and talk, 82-83
weight, 54. *See also* mass
Werder, Peter, 63
Within Phase Emphasis Period (WPEP), 42
Within Phase Observational Period
(WPOP), 41

Z

Zimbardo, 101, 284
Zoloft, 75

Printed in the United States
By Bookmasters